How Hard Can it Be?

Nick Wharton

Thanks for everything
you have done
All my love
Nick x

First Edition published in 2021 by Nick Wharton, Kendal, Cumbria
Copyright © Nick Wharton 2021

www.nickwharton.co.uk

The events in this book have been recalled and recorded to the best of the author's ability, while at the same time, exerting his right to ensure that the truth did not get in the way of a good story.
All uncredited photos were taken by the author or the identity of the photographer has been lost in the mists of time – sorry if I've missed out your name.

Design and layout by Peter Sterling

Printed by Latitude Press Limited, Windermere www.latitudepress.co.uk

Distributed through Cordee Limited www.cordee.co.uk

ISBN 978-1-8384281-0-5

Contents

Delightful delicate climbing on *Glass Slipper*, Black Crag, Wrynose 📷 David Simmonite

"You shouldn't let other people get your kicks for you"
Bob Dylan

Foreword

Often when meeting somebody for the first time – a random encounter on a plane, or perhaps the partner or parent of a friend – to save explaining things I might not need to, I'll simply ask: "Do you speak climbing?"

This is, of course, mainly a reference to the plethora of specialist terminology we use to describe what we do, but also to a shared knowledge of certain geographical locations, geological formations, historical milestones and renowned characters as well as an acceptance of a certain life philosophy and comprehension of risk.

Sleeping in a dirty cave or cold church porch, hitchhiking around and hanging out in uncomfortable, exposed, often hazardous situations is not many people's idea of a holiday. If you say 'the Nose is such a proud line' to a non-climber, they would probably think you were referring to somebody's pronounced facial feature. Understandably, most people have no idea what a 'Grigri' is nor understand the meaning of 'runout', who 'Brown and Whillans' were or what we mean by 'blew the on-sight, sent it first red point'.

Climbing is, in fact, a far more widely spoken language than you might imagine. A recent estimate from the International Federation of Sport Climbing put the figure at an astonishing 35 million people worldwide, or approximately 35 times more than speak Welsh.

Without doubt, the vast majority of that huge figure would identify themselves as gym climbers and most of them exclusively indoor boulderers. But climbing is a very broad church – from indoor gyms to high-altitude mountaineering, bouldering to Big Wall, with much in between and subtle variants of each – and there are myriad dialects.

Nick's primary focus throughout his 40 years in the game has been at the opposite end of the rock spectrum to most – the more ancient, yet increasingly rare, on-sight, UK Trad climbing. That dialect is so thick that these days most fluent climbers would barely understand it.

This is very much the sect I come from – no doubt why I have been given the honour of writing these words. Having spent my entire adult life and most of my childhood caught up in this, in my opinion, the greatest of climbing disciplines, it's fair to say it is my native tongue.

This is unashamedly a book for climbers. But even if you don't speak climbing and much of the detail goes over your head, the pure adventure and joy that leaps out of these anecdotes will keep you reading.

It brought a tingle to my spine to read about Nick's initiations and adventures on the exact same routes – describing the precise same holds and particular gear placements I know only too well – on which a couple of decades later I would experience my own inductions, albeit often with much more struggle and certainly more gear! I felt a great sense of community and continuity reading his descriptions of the big runout on Stage Fright, that crucial smear on Footless Crow or the unique trepidation of climbing past the bolt on The Cad, details and nuances I too have savoured, remembered and which made me who I am, as a climber and as a man.

I first became aware of Nick soon after discovering the wonderful world of rock climbing as a schoolboy in the early 90s. I grew up in the Eden Valley just outside the Lake District and was soon adopted into the subculture by local elders. There's a lot of hard climbing in the Lakes. It's quite a unique style of climbing, never straightforward, often quite devious and route grades are always stern.

The names that illuminate climbing history tend to be those of the prolific new routers. But as part of another illustrious gang, the serial tickers of others' test pieces, Nick's name was frequently mentioned. "Wharton on-sighted that in Fires (an early development of the rock boot) in '86" someone would say as I flailed pathetically to top-rope a seemingly impossible E5. "And he only put two runners in," another would add as I searched desperately for all possible protection.

I left the Lakes in 1996 returning in 2009 and to my surprise Nick was still one of the most active climbers operating at a high standard, still ticking away not necessarily the very hardest routes, but always in the best style.

What set him apart from most, especially in those intervening 14 years, was his commitment to climbing from the ground up – that is, without prior inspection of the climb. It's hard to stress quite how much more challenging it is to succeed on a climb towards your limit without prior knowledge. Pre-inspection has always been around but through the 90s and into the 21st Century it has become far more commonplace and accepted. It's fair to say that, at the moment, none of the very hardest routes anywhere have been climbed ground up. To climb an E5 on-sight is far more difficult than to head point an E7 or even E8 with prior inspection.

I strongly share Nick's opinion that, in the same way that a bolt removes a level of spiritual depth from a climb, pre-inspection removes another, and though both have their places and everyone is free to climb as they please, I greatly respect Nick's steadfast commitment to getting the deepest, most meaningful experience from his climbs. There is something so pure and finite about that one and only chance to do it first go.

A great story our mutual friend Stuart 'Woody' Wood tells is of Nick's ascent of Twighlight Zone, a scary E6 6a next to the aptly named Risk Business on the fearsome crag of Tunnel Wall in Glencoe. This wall has an unusual mix of high-grade, bolted sport routes alongside difficult, bold Trad routes – Nick had opted to do one of the latter, one of four hard routes that day. True to reputation he was climbing in his characteristic, sparsely-protected fashion. No doubt the presence of Woody had meant the beers had flowed heavily the night before and Nick wasn't moving quite as fluidly as usual. Bystanders at the crag were becoming increasingly concerned by the struggle he was putting in at such serious distance above his last gear when the well-known Scottish climber and Glaswegian GP Mark Garthwaite arrived at the crag. "Don't worry boys, things are looking up. There's a doctor at the crag!" Nick calmly yelled down with a maniacal grin before continuing to complete his on-sight of the climb.

Nick's commitment and what some might call *underly* cautious attitude towards climbing may seem in stark opposition to his professional career as a Health and Safety consultant. But, as you will read, the opposite is true – they are very much two sides of the same coin. Laying out the clear distinctions between danger, hazard, risk and uncertainty, he explains here the powerful insights he has gained into safety through assessing risk and its management in both his professional and his climbing lives – hard-won lessons from which we can all learn, whatever language we speak.

Leo Houlding

Nick flashes *Cave Route Righthand*, Gordale Scar 📷 John Wilson

Preface

When I set out to write this book, my aim was simply to recount the many tales and anecdotes I'd accumulated from four decades of climbing and other assorted adventures. As it developed, first in my mind and subsequently on the page, I realised that perhaps I had something more to say. Writing could give me an opportunity, in addition to the storytelling, to share what I've learned and perhaps prompt some discussion – particularly on the topics of risk and the range of climbing styles on offer in the UK.

I was determined that this would not be a book about me and my life but about the adventures and the people with whom I have been lucky enough to share them. I can't help being the central character and the book necessarily follows my own development through school, university and my time in the army but I was keen to include the memories of others, told in their own voices. These are now scattered through the text and I'm grateful to a great cast of characters for their contributions.

Another group of voices recorded here are those of early readers of these pages who posed the questions that appear at the end of some of the chapters. Rather than just incorporate my responses into the text, I thought it would give their enquiries a little more force to reproduce them in full as they came to me.

I expect that this book will resonate most closely with other climbers and outdoor enthusiasts – there are tales of derring-do underground, on skis, on the water and on the fells – but I hope other readers will also enjoy this collection of my, at times challenging, nearly always enjoyable and sometimes frankly ridiculous, exploits. Any specialist activity has a language of its own however, so for readers not familiar with any of these terms I have included a simple glossary. You shouldn't need to refer to it to follow the stories but it's there in case you're interested to find out more.

Whatever activities we pursue, we do them to the level that suits us. In climbing it doesn't matter what grade we climb – if we're operating at our personal limit, the feeling is the same. My hope is that this book might encourage its readers to push that limit just a little. Don't let self-doubt hold you back. Just ask yourself: how hard can it be?

Nick

1 - Creation
E5 6A RAVEN CRAG, THIRLMERE
How it all started

My name is Nick and I have a problem. Yes, finally, I'm prepared to admit it. In fact, I've had a real problem for many years now, one that's shaped me and my relationships with friends and family profoundly. It's had an impact on my work and every aspect of my life. I realise, now I think of it, that it's come to define who I am. It's also put me at great risk, even made me selfishly push others into potential danger. It's a cruel master – all-absorbing, irresistible and insatiable.

It all started a long time ago, when I was at school. I'd just gone into Sixth Form and was adjusting to my new-found independence and freedom. For the first time in my life I could make my own choices – not all of them good, but at least they were mine. I'd been given an academic leg-up, an opportunity to go to a really good school – the Royal Grammar School, Lancaster. From the austere, classical exterior, it was clear it was a respectable establishment with a proud history – endowed in 1472 and given its regal title by Queen Victoria in 1851. Yet underneath the polished, high-achieving, Oxbridge-orientated surface was a murky undercurrent.

I was drawn into it by a number of friends: Rick Cooper, John Wilson, David Catlow – all from respectable families. I didn't put up much resistance. I was attracted by the sense of adventure and possibility. Of course, at that stage it was just a bit of fun, purely recreational. I had no idea how serious it was going to become. Others, including Neil Foster and Andy Wiggans, were already onto the harder stuff, even then. The warning signs were there, if only I'd seen them.

Then came the crucial piece of the jigsaw – the teachers. We knew some were involved but there was one in particular – 'Bandy' Barratt, the pottery teacher – who really encouraged us and indeed started to get us our weekly fix. And there was no shortage of supply in the area. I think the school was aware that something was going on and I believe they felt they could control it. As I was a boarder, my House Master, Dougie Cameron, tried to restrict my habit but he couldn't do it. If they'd known the scale of the problem, they would have taken much stronger action. My mother – a hard-working single parent, was also worried about what I was getting into. She didn't understand, probably hoped it was just a passing phase, and was just as powerless as Mr Cameron to stop me.

It was too late. I'd become a climber.

I found out that a few friends had been climbing for about a year and it sounded like fun so I just gave it a go. It turned out I was quite good at it. There was a lot of easily accessible cragging not far from Lancaster, around the Carnforth and Silverdale area at the top end of Morecambe Bay – in particular, Trowbarrow Quarry and Warton Crag. And we were only a stone's throw from the Lake District and had a couple of trips to the easier venues there. Little did I know then that I would make my home there one day and spend much of my adult life clambering all over those wonderful crags and running over the fells!

'Bandy' Barratt was a major influence. On Wednesday afternoons during the summer term, he would take a group of us out of school for the Games period – a welcome alternative to athletics or cricket. There wasn't any instruction as such – more supervision while we figured out for ourselves what to do. Equipment was scarce so we made do with a waist belay and we shared a pair of EBs – the rather basic rock climbing shoes of the day – the leader throwing them back down the crag for his second to use. And we really were 'leading' those climbs (making our own way up), not simply top-roping (climbing with a rope above us).

My first ever lead was on one of those Wednesday afternoons at Trowbarrow – a disused limestone quarry that has since become a nature reserve managed

Trowbarrow Main Wall. Tim Whiteley (left) on *Cracked Actor* and other climber on *Jean Jeanie*

by the local authority. Back then it was still owned and managed by the quarry company and we would often be chased off by their agent. I led *Jean Jeanie*, graded a mighty VS (not bad for a first lead), wearing John Wilson's old rock shoes, which I think he'd inherited from his dad, Eric. *Jean Jeanie* takes a line up the central crack, which wanders up the steep 25m Main Wall in the quarry. This wall is a unique feature. It's just off-vertical and made up of a wide expanse of fossils. The wall is seamed with cracks, created by blasting undertaken by the previous owners – ironically to try and stop climbing, all of which give fabulous climbs of differing grades. For years climbers were concerned that the cracks were getting wider and stories regularly went round that large sections had fallen down. A few large lumps have calved off the right-hand side but most of the stories were just that, stories.

John was to become, and remain for decades, one of my main climbing partners and closest friends – not to mention being best man at my wedding, as I was at his. Over the years, we often met up from opposite ends of the country for climbing and skiing trips. He and his dad were also the first people to take me skiing. We had a day up at Glenshee in Perthshire where I terrified one of the lift-operators by flying headlong down the slope towards his little shed, only to crash in a snowy heap moments before impact. John was an excellent skier however, and went on to represent Great Britain in speed skiing (the barking-mad discipline of pointing your very long skis downhill and going as fast as you can in a straight line wearing nothing but a very thin Lycra skin suit and an aerodynamic helmet).

The following week my second climbing lead was *Touch of Class* – an even more impressive HVS – the next crack to the right of *Jean Jeanie* on the Main Wall. It soon became obvious – to me at least! – that I was quite good at this climbing lark, as most of my friends weren't getting up these grades after a year's head-start. All the same I used the excuse that I was behind and needed the extra practice to persuade my mates to let me lead more often. I was eager, competitive and hungry to learn. I was soon well and truly hooked.

Let me explain how I came to be a boarder at this school in Lancaster when we lived 50 miles away in Burnley. My parents separated when I was four – my father was in the army, a senior NCO (Non-Commissioned Officer) in the Royal Electrical and Mechanical Engineers and later a teacher in the Army Education Corps. I remember him getting into our green Triumph Herald as he left our home in Colchester and saying, "I'll come and see you some time."

He never did. My mother was left with me and my eight-year-old big sister, Kate. The following year we moved back to Burnley in Lancashire where my grandparents and the rest of our extended family lived. Kate won an academic scholarship several years later, to Overstone girls' public school in Northamptonshire. The following year, my mother took a job as the school matron there and I needed to be schooled somewhere, so I was packed off to a village a few miles away across the rolling Northamptonshire countryside to board at Spratton Hall prep school. The school had small class sizes and large grounds and many of the pupils were weekly boarders, going home to their families every weekend and leaving only a handful of us behind. The duty teachers would take us out for walks or visits, and I often went home with one of my friends for the weekend. Going to my mother was never really an option in term time, as she was working and living in a bedsit within the school.

After the initial upset of finding myself spending the night in a dormitory full of strangers far away from home aged nine, I was happy at Spratton and soon took to my new surroundings. Come the school holidays, I had the run of the grounds at Overstone – a large country park and the biggest back garden I could have hoped for, complete with woods, a lake and even an outdoor swimming pool.

When I later got a .22 air rifle, I'd roam around the grounds of this former stately home in search of targets, happily lost in a world of my own. The main building was home to an over-abundance of pigeons. I used them as target practice and had, I thought, little success until one day the groundsman approached me.

"Have you been shooting the pigeons?" he asked.

"Er, I've tried,' I replied. 'But I'm not very good at it."

"Are you kidding? The roof's littered with them. Keep it up, you're doing a great job!"

When my sister left Overstone in 1976, my mother decided to move us back to Burnley. I was by then thirteen and my mother didn't fancy sending me to the local comprehensive. It didn't have a great reputation and I'd displayed some academic ability at Spratton. When I passed my 11-plus, she had to fight Lancashire Education Authority for a grant to cover the cost of me boarding at Lancaster – but she got it and so off I went.

The grammar school buildings were quite austere, and the old School House had a definite feel of Colditz Castle, the prisoner-of-war camp made famous by the film and 1970s TV series, but by then I was an old hand at living away from home. Once again, I soon settled in and made a new set of friends and acquaintances. This isn't a public school, just a regular grammar where most of the pupils were day boys drawn from all walks of life. We'd all earned the right to be there through merit, passing both the 11-Plus and the school entrance exam. Boarders were drawn, mainly, from across the North West and many were from the Burnley area, including my good friend of the time David 'Freddie' Catlow, one of my climbing companions. Freddie lived with his family in Blacko, a small Lancashire village beyond Nelson close to Pendle Hill. Like many families with boys at Lancaster, the Catlows were reasonably well-off – his dad an accountant and his mum a PE teacher. I loved going round to Freddie's house, which felt luxurious, and he had a gorgeous sister, Gillian, who was only a year a so younger than us.

Freddie took me on one of my first climbing experiences, to Witches' Quarry, nestling beneath the back side of Pendle Hill (infamous for its witches trials in the 17th Century). There I belayed him on a route called *Thrutch*, a VS. I knew nothing of climbing terminology at this stage, so the name gave me no clues. In climbing terms 'thrutch' means to climb awkwardly, often without positive holds, and it's generally an unpleasant experience. Freddie led up the route, getting almost to the top, but the last section, the top quarter of the route, consists of an awkward, off-width crack with very few features to help you up. The crack eventually disappears into the steep, grassy top of the crag. He tried to work his way up this unpleasant feature but eventually had to admit defeat and I lowered him back to the ground.

"I suppose I'll have to set up an abseil to get the gear back," he called out.

"Can I have a go first?" I asked. He agreed, so I set off up the route with the rope still through all the runners – effectively 'top-roping' – and got to his high point without much difficulty, finding myself at the bottom of the finishing crack that had defeated my more experienced companion.

"I might as well see if I can do this," I called down, before starting to thrutch my way up the awkward crack.

I was now effectively leading the climb, as I was beyond Freddie's last piece of protection, which he'd placed at the bottom of the crack, and I didn't have any other gear with me – mind you, even if I had, I wouldn't have known what to do with it. I battled my way up the wide crack until I was right at the top, where the only holds left were handfuls of grass, which I vaguely remember trying to grip in my teeth as well as both hands. But all to no avail, my failure was inevitable and, when it came, it did so with quite some style. I fell right from my grassy highpoint and kept on falling for most of the length of the crag – at least 30ft – coming to a rest just above Freddie's head. 'Well, that was exciting!' I thought to myself, but back at Freddie's house his mum for some reason couldn't see the funny side of our gleefully recounted tale. (Freddie went on to become President of the British Veterinary Association. I used to hear him sometimes on Radio 4's *Farming Today* programme if I had a particularly early start.)

Our boarding house was ruled strictly by Senior House Master Dougie Cameron. I have an image of him as ancient, but he can only have been in his forties. His speech impediment made for easy impersonations, but nonetheless he was an imposing figure that everyone respected. Any serious misdemeanours were dealt with by a cane to the backside.

I seemed always to be in his study, being told off for something. It was at these times that his stutter always came to the fore. "T-t-t-touch your toes, I'm going to have to t-t-tan you."

On one memorable occasion, the school had a large-scale school fair to raise funds. As part of that, I'd won a prize in the raffle – a large stilton and a bottle of port – and shared my winnings with lots of my friends but 'Dougie' found out. He called me to his study, demanding I bring the unopened port for safekeeping until the end of term. I guiltily entered the room with a near-empty bottle but, because there had been so many of us, we got away with fairly trivial punishments. Looking back now, I should have been a bit sharper, topped the bottle up with water and claimed to have had only the tiniest of sips. He was probably tipped off by one of the Prefects – an untrustworthy, self-important bunch of sixth formers. Needless to say, I was never to be promoted to such heights.

A much more amenable House Master, Tony Halliwell, ran the cross-country team, of which I was a member. I reported to Mr Halliwell once, after returning from a half-term holiday with a bit of asthma (I was allergic to my mother's three cats) and told him I was having a little difficulty breathing. I was worried it might affect my performance in an upcoming race. In a response perhaps reminiscent of recent cycling scandals, Mr Halliwell procured Ventolin tablets and instructed me to take them – all without medical consultation or prescription, of course – "for the sake of the team".

Boarding school undoubtedly nurtured my spirit of independence and gave me the ability to step into a new situation and just get on with people. It probably also taught me a healthy disregard for rules I didn't see the point of, and a suspicion of the enforcers. (Little did I know that I would one day become an Environmental Health Officer.)

I soon found my appetite for climbing would never be satisfied by a few hours on a Wednesday afternoon but, being a boarder, it would have taken an organised trip with a member of staff to get out climbing at the weekend. We were allowed, however, to book outings with friends who lived locally. So each Friday I queued outside Mr Cameron's office for permission to "go out for tea", usually with Rick Cooper who lived in Hest Bank, just north of Lancaster. His mother was very welcoming, despite an already full house – an older sister and two younger, twin sisters. Rick had passed his test and had use of his mum's white Toyota Corolla so just after Sunday breakfast my old rucksack would get thrown over the wall and I would follow, climbing into the waiting car to be whisked off to Silverdale for a day's climbing. Rick and I had many escapades in that Corolla. I often stayed at Hest Bank in the holidays and met many of the Hest Bank crowd of friends that way.

Covert climbing weekends continued generally with great success, but on one occasion our youthful exuberance – combined with inexperience and naivety – almost got the better of us. I'd already got up *Touch of Class* when some guys at school suggested I try *Plastic Iceberg* in Warton Main Quarry, at the time also graded HVS and with a reputation for being 'special'. The route follows the most striking line in the quarry – a deep groove with a smooth slab forming its right side, clearly visible from the M6 motorway and surrounding areas. I'd already climbed HVS so I wasn't too concerned.

At Warton Main some of the routes are less than solid and this was only my fourth lead. I hadn't had a lot of practice in placing gear, but before long I was well up the route, having left the relative security of the groove for the more delicate and precarious slab. Then, I don't know whether a hold broke or my foot slipped, but the next thing I knew I was rattling down the groove with poorly-placed runners popping out as I went. I must have fallen a total of 30ft before being stopped by John who was belaying me at the time. Phew!

Dazed but not too traumatised, we packed up and went back to Rick's for well-earned afternoon tea. Perhaps I should have been more shaken up by such a significant fall. Maybe it should have been a shot across my bows, but in fact it taught me that you can push yourself, you can fall off and you needn't come to any harm. (*Plastic Iceberg* is now graded E1 5b, by the way, and well deserved at that.)

Warton Main Quarry, although a bit scrappy and loose, was appealing because it was so much bigger than any of the other local crags. I remember once, after a day's climbing during the holidays, I went back to Lancaster to stay with a (non-climbing) schoolfriend called Gavin Graveson. His was another welcoming family who owned a waste company, based in Carnforth, with the unforgettable strapline 'We specialise in talking rubbish'. None of them were climbers but they always showed a real interest. The conversation with Gavin's dad on that day went like this:

"Where were you climbing today?"

"Warton Main – the big place you can see from Carnforth."

"Oh? What's it like?"

"Exciting. It can be a bit dodgy – I fell off once – but it's fine."

"Are you allowed to climb there – does the owner not mind?"

"No, as far as I know they're fine with it."

"Do you know who owns it?"

"No, actually, I don't."

"I do… I own it!"

Ah! Embarrassing. They'd bought the place, presumably with a view to using it as a tip or a transfer station for their waste business, but thankfully they never did.

Back home in Burnley, I could only climb as far afield as I could cycle, which gave me two options in opposite directions – the gritstone outcrop at Widdop over the moors towards the Dark Side (Yorkshire) or Witches' Quarry to the north, on the far side of Pendle Hill. I also had to climb alone so I was pushed towards soloing some of the easier, bigger routes at quite an early stage. Widdop had boulders that also provided some easily accessible, roadside sport. Bouldering is all about climbing just a few moves on relatively small lumps of rock, staying close to the ground. These days it's become safer and more comfortable with the advent of large, cushioned mats that are taken to the crag for a softer landing.

Local outcrop climbing gave all of us a great start but we were keen to explore bigger, better options further afield. In the Middle Sixth, when a Biology field trip to near Betws-y-Coed in North Wales was scheduled for the last week before half-term, a plan emerged. By then I had my copy of Ken Wilson's iconic

Nick climbing at Warton Main (*Crunchy Kibble* F7a) many years later 📷 David Simmonite

1978 book *Classic Rock* and would pore over the descriptions and photos of those great routes, imagining what it must be like to tackle them. North Wales – especially the Llanberis Pass – was an irresistible magnet. So the plan was to hitch round to Llanberis after the field trip and meet Rick, having been dropped off by his parents as they made their way to Mid-Wales for a short break. They were then going to pick us up on their way back at the end of their holiday.

As the time drew near, we planned the routes we'd do and assembled the gear we thought we'd need – including a large and heavy Vango Force 10 tent, a Trangia stove and cooking utensils, plus all the food we thought we'd need for the week. We packed far too much of everything. But one thing we didn't have was any pegs! Now, we'd never used a single peg (or piton) in all of our short climbing careers. We had, however, acquired a guidebook from somewhere (probably the library) and there they were in many of the route descriptions – many references to pegs: "Climb the crack/wall/groove to a ledge with peg belays". But we didn't have any pegs. What were we to do for a belay? We asked around but none of our friends had any experience of these real climbing areas. We did eventually acquire a set of assorted pegs and a hammer. I have no idea where we got them from, maybe John's dad, Eric, had some from years back. At no point did anyone suggest that we might not really need them – and we still had absolutely no idea how to place a peg into rock. You can perhaps imagine my surprise when arriving at the first belay ledge on one of our first 'big' routes, where the guidebook had said it was a peg belay: "Richard," I shouted down. "Someone has left the pegs in on this ledge!" It was only later that we discovered nobody carried pegs – they were always left in place.

Once our field trip was finished, I hitched round to the head of the Pass and waited for Rick and his parents at the Pen-y-Gwryd Hotel, close to the foot of Snowdon. I was awestruck – the place was so full of history. This, after all, was Sir Edmund Hillary's training base before his 1953 ascent of Everest – real climbing territory. When we eventually made it down into the heart of the Pass, we were even more inspired. We'd seen nothing like it, even on our couple of trips to the Lakes. We were surrounded, on both sides of the valley, by towering hills with imposing crags littering their flanks. We'd planned to pitch the tent by the side of the road below the Cromlech but soon discovered a welcome alternative – the fairly dry, relatively comfortable caves formed by the boulders in the area. We ditched the tent and made these our base camp that week and on many future occasions.

This first exploratory trip turned out to be typical of many subsequent visits to Llanberis – it rained a lot. In between, we began to tick off many of the *Classic*

Rock routes and others besides. We'd been warned to lower our expectations and climb at an easier grade as "these are proper routes". As a result, we found the climbing easy, if a bit more exposed and committing. The biggest challenge was finding our way around the crags and negotiating the descents.

It nearly all went horribly wrong one evening on Dinas Mot, on the south side of the Llanberis Pass. We had climbed the *Classic Rock* route *The Cracks*, but it was getting a bit late and the light was starting to fade. The description told us to scramble down the east gully but in the gathering gloom that was not as obvious or as easy as we'd expected.

"Let's abseil – it'll be safer," I suggested to Rick.

So we set up a simple belay in the gully – one runner, which we could always retrieve the next day – and down I went. Before Rick followed, I checked that the rope would pull through so that we could retrieve it, but it wouldn't budge.

"Move the belay closer to the edge," I called out.

Rick fixed a new anchor – largely by feel, it was really quite dark by now – and I tried the rope again. It felt secure and ran smoothly when I pulled one side, but as soon as Rick attached his Figure 8 and leaned back to descend, the nut ripped and he was suddenly heading straight for me. It wasn't that far – maybe fifteen feet – and, miraculously, he wasn't badly hurt. He got away with a badly-sprained ankle and we got the runner back!

We made it back to the caves with me carrying the kit and Rick hobbling over the rough terrain in the dark. We hadn't got head torches at that point - we'd never even come across them. After a quick supper it was clear that what we really needed was a restorative visit to the pub. So after a slow, painful limp down the road to the Vaynol Arms in Nant Peris we found our reward: warmth, comfort, beer… and analgesics.

"Two pints of Robinsons please… oh, and have you got any painkillers for my friend?" I asked as we leaned our tired elbows on the bar. The helpful barmaid pulled the pints and produced some strong tablets – codeine or something.

"He shouldn't really be drinking if he's taking these."

"Ah, ok, but I've just bought two pints."

"Fine, but he isn't planning on having any more is he?"

Rick and I looked at each other. "Er, maybe a couple?"

"Hmm, I suppose it can't do him any harm," she smiled.

What an understanding soul!

It turned out to be a great evening. Our story soon went round the pub, resulting in several pints being bought for us by the sympathetic locals. At closing time it was clear to everyone that my poor, wounded climbing companion and I could do with a lift back up to base camp in the Pass, and word went round the bar for a volunteer driver. Eventually someone offered their services. Not only was our chauffeur well lubricated, but someone had just told him a story which he found hilarious. All the way up the Pass, as he weaved from one side of the road to the other, our new-found friend repeated the punchline that had caused his hilarity – "The boulder fell on him… the boulder fell on him" – through tears of laughter. We had no idea what the story was about!

I would return to Llanberis on many occasions over the coming years, but my second trip was the following summer, after we'd finished our A-Levels and finally left school. On that visit, with my long-time climbing partner, John Wilson, I led my first extreme graded climb – *Cenotaph Corner,* perhaps the most classic and most striking line in the Pass, taking the plumb-vertical, open-book, corner crack between two large, smooth walls. I remember clearly how, after a celebratory pint back in the Vaynol, John and I crammed into the phone box outside the pub to call Rick, back in Lancashire, to tell him all about our accomplishment. Nowadays we'd be posting something on social media to tell the world, I guess.

Back at school, other challenges faced us in our final year. Aside from exams to prepare for, careers to think about and university applications to be made, I'd hatched a far more interesting challenge in the form of a new route. The grammar school in Lancaster, on the city's East Road, is a hotch-potch of buildings on both sides, up and down the hill. The oldest part, School House, requires a bit of detailed description at this point. It's the rather imposing, stone building on the left as you're going uphill, and was at the time the main boarding house, with dormitories and studies for all 'inmates'. Its main entrance is a large, wooden, double door, deeply set within an arch, above which is a statue, set into a slender recess. Above that are the large, deeply mullioned windows of one of the dormitories. The front of the School House roof comprises numerous other dormer-style windows, with what look like battlements between them. Finally, at the left end stands a tall tower, and inside the tower is a spiral staircase leading to a trapdoor, for access to the flagpole on top.

This trapdoor was never locked – presumably no one had ever thought it might need securing – and the flagpole proved to be an ideal belay point from which a certain budding climber could abseil late at night. I did it on a few occasions without a hitch, but one memorable time I must not have left it late enough.

I was halfway down my descent when my chemistry teacher walked right underneath me. Luckily he had no reason to look up, and passed by none the wiser, but the sight of him below set my heart racing more than the challenge of the abseil itself.

The ultimate challenge however was an ascent of *School House Direct* – up the arch of the doorway, past the recess with a sling round the statue, on up to the windows above, pinch-gripping the mullions and so on, to breach the battlements and reach a secure belay. On the chosen night, I pre-placed a sling round the heating pipes of the dormitory and out through the window. I didn't want to be accused of being reckless!

I'd borrowed a climbing rope from John. He smuggled it into school in a sports bag and, as he handed it over to me during a lesson, our teacher – one of those who'd occasionally taken us out climbing – spied it. He looked at me as if to say: "Why would Wharton be taking possession of such a piece of kit?". We bluffed our way out of it (I'm sure he knew we were up to no good) and I'm pleased to say the first and (to the best of my knowledge) only ascent of *School*

Lancaster Royal Grammar School and *School House Direct*

House Direct went smoothly, belayed and followed by Richard (Andy) Capp. HVS? Who knows? It's often the case that the grade of a route gets confirmed or changed after subsequent ascents. Not that I'm encouraging other schoolboys to repeat it – perish the thought! It was the middle of the night and, although there was a lot of light from streetlights to see by, we were, by the same token, in plain view of the main road. Looking back all these years later, I can see that it was quite a bold undertaking. It wasn't just the risk of getting caught and all that might entail but the climbing itself was no pushover and success was definitely not a foregone conclusion.

Nick arrived at LRGS a year after me and I got an early insight that fearlessness was not in short supply when he turned up for a trial to join the rugby squad. Nick had played full back at his previous school, and it was suggested he be tested out. The biggest, fastest member of the first fifteen, Tim Robson, was briefed to start on the halfway line, get up a full head of steam and run straight through Nick who'd been dispatched to the 25-yard line. Rhino-like Tim was widely recognised as the one person you didn't want charging at you when you're the last line of defence and I winced at the moment of impact. In the crunch and with little fuss the rhino was downed by a textbook tackle that was met with nods of approval all round and a shake of the hand from Tim, still lying on the ground. Nick had established his credentials amongst his peers and impressed me no end. "Brave lad, I wouldn't have done that," I thought.

Some years later we'd both started climbing. He was a member of the Cadet Force and had a talent for cross-country running, but the opportunity to break out from the Colditz-like establishment of the boarding house, albeit temporarily, was behind all these activities. Finding ways to entertain yourself as a boarder must have been challenging at times and he had a growing tally of escapades to regale me with after each weekend. Nick has always had a keen eye on getting value for money as many of his friends would know. The best-value antics were those stacked high with mischief, daring and bravery.

That bravery and mischief was brought to bear with his ascent of *School House Direct*. With my Dad's limited collection of climbing gear

– a very old rope, a few old slings and some other bits and bobs – I'd become Nick's supplier. He brought me into the plan he'd hatched for a covert night of high adventure with maximum pay-out. We scoped out the route from the railings outside the main entrance to School House trying not to look too furtive. The line and (limited) gear options were assessed. After the initial layback it looked like a sling could be threaded behind the statue in the recess to protect the first half of the route. Pre-placing a sling on the radiator pipes inside the building so that it could be dangled out of the window higher up would protect the crux move overcoming the little ledge above the statue. One rope, two slings and the cover of darkness – how hard could it be?

We had to work out how to smuggle the goods into school in broad daylight. Getting caught handing over a rope and some climbing equipment to a boarder under the noses of the guards was never going to end well. My Adidas shoulder bag was just big enough to hold the stash. We agreed the drop – biology lessons, as the classrooms were tucked away from the busy main buildings and the teachers were an adventurous bunch. They might be more prepared to overlook the exchange if we were spotted doing the deal and needed to spin a yarn. The main problem was that biology lessons were in the afternoon which meant lugging the kit around all day without attracting attention. But the planning paid off and the successful handover of the gear meant that the ascent was on. All that was needed now was for Nick to not fall off, which was by no means a given.

At this point in his climbing career, Nick's success rate had room for improvement – he'd had a few tumbles along the way. That doesn't really matter when you're in the back of beyond on a crag with half-decent gear and the only witnesses are like-minded climbers. Lobbing off the front of School House, on a main road, at night was an entirely different matter. It would have been considered poor judgment at the very least by the climbing peer group and a scandalous catastrophe for the school that would have to be brushed under the carpet. The climb was going to take some time, with the obvious risk of a passer-by interrupting the fun. The possibility of a trip to meet Dougie Cameron's cane en route to the Headmaster's study and all the consequences that would follow added to the risk. The reward on the other hand was an exploit brimful of mischief, daring and bravery and the prize of making a first ascent.

I had the greatest faith in his success and, with Andy Capp's help, and in the dead of night, *School House Direct* came into being. The tale of daring was told with relish to the other climbers at school which secured another round of approving nods. Modestly given HVS at the time and almost certainly unrepeated, I suspect it'd be worth E2 5b now and would have been Nick's hardest lead to date. It was, without doubt, the most audacious.

John Wilson

That particular period of scholastic incarceration was nearly over, my sentence duly served, one final adventure remained before leaving for ever. Half a mile up the road from the school, Williamson Park overlooks the city of Lancaster, and the park's main feature is the Ashton Memorial. At around 150ft (50m) in height, this early-20th-Century folly dominates the skyline and is visible for miles around. Its large, domed roof can't be missed as you drive past Lancaster on the motorway. I'd been in the park one day with friends, loitering with no particular intent. Sitting at the foot of the Ashton Memorial I noticed one of the grilles at ground level was loose and easily removed, possibly leading into a basement space of some sort. This clearly needed further investigation under cover of darkness so, some time later, a small group of us absconded from our sleeping quarters and sneaked up the hill to the park. We removed the grille and discovered that it did indeed give access to an underfloor space. The question was, would it lead any further?

By torchlight we identified stairs up to the ground floor, and further stairs upwards and outside onto a balcony, but then… a disappointing dead-end. Not to be defeated, we found a route to climb up the outside to a second, higher balcony, where we came up against a locked door. Through the window in that door we could see a way – if only we could get through – into the higher reaches of the Memorial's copper and stone structure. After much pondering we suddenly realised the window was unglazed, simply an open space just big enough to squeeze through, and minutes later we were on the summit of the Ashton Memorial. At the apex of the roof is a small glass structure about the shape and size of an old telephone box, a perfect place into which our small band could proudly cram ourselves and enjoy the splendid view over the nightscape of Lancaster, Morecambe and beyond.

Nick on descent of Sa Calobra, Mallorca

QUESTIONS

Q *You suggest climbing is an addictive behaviour. Is it?*

A I think that, as for most things, there's a spectrum of 'addiction', maybe something like this:

Addicted – cannot stop, even if you want to
Obsessed – your life revolves around it
Committed – prepared to put in the maximum effort
Passionate – love it, can't get enough
Enthusiastic – you climb regularly, alongside other activities
Keen – like it, but it's not your first choice

(I put myself in the committed category – but friends and family might place me higher!)

Q *Why climbing? Could you have been drawn into any another activity?*

A It could have been something else if circumstances had been different. Climbing captured my interest because I found, by chance, that I had a kind of natural talent for it, but I'm sure I would have embraced another activity with similar enthusiasm and commitment, trying my utmost to reach a standard I could be satisfied with.

Q *When you nearly landed on Freddie's head in that first fall at Witches' Quarry, what did it feel like, and do you think it might all have been different if you'd landed badly or caused significant injury to either or both of you?*

A It was all quite funny at the time. I didn't really know what was happening and the actual falling was over so quickly. I think this is usually the case: it isn't the falling that's frightening as such, but the realisation that you're about to fall. But overall I saw the incident as part of an exciting new adventure and I probably didn't think through the potential consequences. I was only young and we're all invincible then, aren't we? Even if I had hurt myself I'd probably just have seen it as a minor setback. I was keen and competitive and had really enjoyed what we'd achieved on the climb. I fell off, yes, but I still got further up than Freddie!

2 - Boy Racer

E4 6A RAVEN CRAG, THRESHTHWAITE COVE

Cycling and other challenges

I'm knackered! I feel like I've been slogging up this hill for ages. No wait, hang on, I *have* been slogging up this hill for ages. It's hot, I've got beyond sweaty and am now in that dangerous stage of dry overheating – and I've run out of water. There's enough sweat encrusted on my shirt to keep a chip shop going for a week. The Alpine sun is beating down. There may be beautiful scenery all around me – glistening glaciers and pointy peaks above, flowery meadows below – but I'm in no fit state to take them in. I'm just grinding it out, my feet slowly rotating in a monotonous, steady rhythm. That's right, I'm sitting on a bike trying to get to the top of the next col and it's still a long way to go. We set off at 0500 this morning – before daybreak – and it's now the middle of a very hot afternoon. I think I'm still in Italy, but to be certain would mean having the mental capacity to do more than just follow the ribbon of tarmac stretching out in front of me. I'm pretty sure I left Switzerland around midday. At some point I'll be back in France, which I left this morning.

I'm cycling the Tour du Mont Blanc cyclosportive. It's been declared the world's hardest one-day cycling event and I can believe it. An astonishing 330km route starting and finishing at Les Saisies, a ski resort in the French Alps, it circumnavigates Western Europe's highest mountain through France, Switzerland and Italy before returning to France. It's quite hilly round there, 8000m of hilly. The very fastest riders will get round in something over twelve hours. It's going to take me a few hours more. Finishing is as much about grit, resilience and bloody-minded determination as it is about fitness and strong legs. Nobody said it would be easy – it's definitely 'type-2 fun' (enjoyable when it's over) and I'm hoping at some point I'll be able to look back on this day fondly. But I'm not feeling fond just now. To make things worse, I'm in desperate need of nipping behind a bush or a boulder to 'do a Paula Radcliffe'. The obvious challenge is finding somewhere appropriate. I don't want to offend anyone with my toilet antics and the road has been constantly busy with cyclists, cars and spectators.

Only on reaching the summit of the col do I find long-awaited relief and then I kick myself for having carried so much excess weight up the 1400m climb. People obsess about the weight of their bikes and spend a fortune upgrading components to shave the grams off. I could have saved myself a lot of effort without even spending a penny, as it were...

The year was 2015 and I hadn't done any climbing for nearly three years. Instead, I'd put all my time and energy into cycling. If I'm going to do something, I do it to the max – there's no point doing things by halves – so when Bradley Wiggins won the Tour de France in 2012, Team GB stole the show in the velodrome at the London Olympics and the MAMIL (Middle-Aged Man In Lycra) became a phenomenon, I threw myself into it. I started by going out with like-minded mates and then moved on to organised events – sportives (officially non-competitive affairs... but we all know different). Events became longer and more challenging and my first overseas race was the Mallorca 312. In those days it was a 312km circumnavigation of the whole island. It was an amazing 12 hours, with great camaraderie among participants and enthusiastic support from local residents all the way round. (Sadly the route now skips the south and east of the island.)

My ultimate cycling challenge was the Tour du Mont Blanc. This spectacular route drops down past Megève to Passy before climbing back up through Les Houches and the Chamonix valley, then over the Col de la Forclaz before descending to Martigny in Switzerland. Then comes the toughest climb of the day, from Les Valettes to Champex-Lac, before dropping once again to Orsières and the start of the longest climb – the Grand St Bernard pass. From this high point, the subsequent 1800m descent down to the Aosta Valley is magnificent. After that, having endured the ferocious 40°C heat of the valley, it's a pleasure to climb back up to higher altitude, over the Petit St Bernard and back down into France, and Bourg St Maurice. From Bourg it is up and over the Cormet de Roselend to Beaufort before the final climb back to the finish line at Les Saisies.

I'd been talked into this gruelling endeavour by a great friend and fellow adventurer, Pete Robinson. We'd agreed from the start that there was no point in trying to stick together. Over that distance we were bound to have differences in pace, and there were plenty of others to ride with. My wife Karen drove round the route during the day, meeting us at various locations, and she came across Pete at the top of one of the cols late in the event, with the finish within reach. He was very despondent, having spent too much time with another competitor – a Dutchman – who'd been very negative, talking constantly of missing cut-off times and giving up at the next checkpoint. When Pete told Karen he was ready to throw in the towel she gave him exactly the tongue-lashing he needed to get him back on his bike and finish – with time to spare. He was extremely grateful afterwards for her unsympathetic abuse!

The final climb was a killer. We'd done it as a final warm-up the day before when it felt easy. Now, with all those miles in the legs, it was desperate. I was driven on by the ecstatic crowds lining those last few kilometres. They made the effort so much easier to bear, even after seventeen hours of pain, and made the finish emotional. All in all it was a great event and eminently achievable with the right preparation – and, more importantly, the right mindset. After all, half of it is downhill!

Nick reckons it was my idea... maybe it was. I've suggested worse ventures... or have I? It's supposedly the hardest day on a bike – the longest ride with the most ascents and most countries visited in a day. Any other superlatives? We certainly endured the biggest thunderstorm ever when the tour went into Switzerland, up to Lac Champex, with cobbles the size of house bricks washing down the road. Do bikes conduct electricity? Do road-bike tyres insulate you from savage mountain lightning storms? I think that was the last time I saw Nick that day until after the race – at the feed station before the ascent of Les Valettes.

"All good?" he asked. "Right, we'd better crack on then."

Team Wharton (Karen) was fabulous. She gave me a good talking to at the top of one of later summits, after that Dutch bloke had ground me down and said we were going to miss the next cut-off. Karen pronounced him 'ridiculous' and so, suitably chastised/encouraged, I carried on into the next storm and gathering darkness, making it back to Les Saisies 23 minutes before cut-off. Karen, Nick and Hamish – another cyclist from our campsite – were all still there waiting for me, and I was so glad to see them.

Pete Robinson

Shortly after the Tour du Mont Blanc I changed my focus to much shorter, more explosive time trials. I was attracted by the idea of trying to go as fast as you can over a relatively short distance. It meant getting another new bike but they do say that the number of bikes that any cyclist should have is 'n+1', where 'n' equals the number of bikes they currently have. My local club, Kent Valley RC (Road Club), organised a 10-mile race every week during the season – April through to the end of August – with the occasional extra, often longer, event at the weekend. I did as many of these races as I could, although midweek work commitments forced me to miss many, much to my frustration.

For me, each 10-mile race was over in around 24 minutes – it took me longer to warm up and squeeze myself into the skin suit than to ride – but the background training mushroomed into a daily programme. Most of that training was indoors on the turbo-trainer or the rollers (a set of rollers that you sit your bike on so that you can cycle on the spot, not easy) with my eyes fixed on the power readout. I really missed that kit when working away from home and having to make do with cheap exercise bikes in hotel gyms around the country or abroad.

When you're riding a time trial (TT), every second counts, and cyclists go to great lengths to find improvements in all aspects of preparation and execution.

These are the 'marginal gains' pursued so effectively by British Cycling coach Dave Brailsford and Team Sky. The biggest advantage comes from improving aerodynamics. Time trial bikes are 'aero' in design with tapered tubing for the frame, brakes that are tucked away, and handlebars that allow the body to hold the most aerodynamic tuck position. At the very least, wheels have deep rims to slice through the air and often the rear wheel is a solid carbon disc. Clothing is vitally important – nothing loose or flapping, as eighty per cent of the aerodynamic drag that a rider has to overcome will be created by the rider themselves. So most competitors wear a 'skin suit', an ultra-tight, one-piece suit made from thin, stretchy Lycra. Tests by the magazine *Cycling Weekly* demonstrated a 28-second difference over a 25-mile TT between wearing a normal cycling jersey and a skin suit. And who wouldn't want an excuse to wear something so sleek and slinky? In the 80s and 90s, it was *de rigueur* for climbers to perform in colourful Lycra tights, especially on sports routes, a fashion that's sadly given way to much more drab, baggy pants, more akin to snowboarder style. There was a time

On the TT bike, Lyth Valley   📷 Tim Whiteley

a few years ago when I tried to encourage a return to Lycra – my 'Lycrevival', as I termed it – but, funnily enough, not many were keen to join the movement.

Time trialling turns out to be very similar to climbing in some respects. It's really a solo activity. Sure, you're interested in others' times but the real competition is with yourself. It's all about you and the route, nobody else. It requires total concentration – allow your mind to wander off the task for a second and you're off the pace – and no one else is there to help you stay focused. I was delighted to see my times getting ever quicker. I loved the competitiveness, even if that competition was with myself.

It hasn't all been plain-sailing on the bike. During an event in February 2016, I was flying down the small back road to the east of Coniston, on a great time and with no intention of letting up until the finish line. It was a beautiful, clear, yet frosty morning and we'd been warned of the possibility of ice on this stretch of road. When I saw a large patch of water-ice ahead of me – where water had

Lycrevival – boys on tour in South of France. L-R: Greg Foster, Tim Whiteley, Neil Cooper, Graham Iles, Nick 📷 George Gilmore

drained off the fell and onto the road – I slowed right down to go around it, which I managed easily, but at that point I was on the wrong side of the road and a car was approaching. It was still some distance away, but beyond the patch of thick water-ice the road was slick with invisible black ice and, as I turned sharply to get back on the right side of the road, the bike went from under me and I landed with a thump on the tarmac. If I'd been going faster I'd no doubt have skidded down the road, ripping my shorts and giving myself a gravel-rash.

My first thought was for my bike. When that seemed okay I tried to get up off the ground and back on the saddle, as I was losing valuable time. But when I put any weight on my right foot, I had the peculiar sensation that it was sliding around on the ice – without moving. I sat on the verge to rest it for a minute or two. Eventually, after fellow competitors had whizzed past looking concerned and an event first aider had come to my aid, I was taken to hospital where my main priority was to prevent the well-meaning nurse in A&E from cutting off my best Castelli racing shorts. The first indication I'd done anything significant came with an audible gasp from the radiographer looking at my X-ray. I had a complete break through the neck of the femur. The foot-sliding-around sensation had been the movement of the two halves of the broken bone. Bugger.

I rang Karen who offered to drive over with everything I'd need. (My top priority was my laptop, of course, so I could upload my data to check I'd been on pace up to the point of impact.) Meanwhile, our fabulous health service leapt into action and provided me with a new titanium hip the next day. (The consultant said he didn't trust me not to break a ceramic one.)

Recovery became another personal competition. So I made the most of the physiotherapy on offer and drove myself to complete all the exercises I was given to do which meant that three weeks later I was back on the turbo-trainer. Only six weeks post-op I was out on the road again, the main issue being that I couldn't twist my right foot out of the cleats securing me to the pedal. The following year I surpassed my previous best times on the time trial bike and I beat the hour mark for a 25-mile event.

In 2018, two years on from my crash and hip replacement, we had a marvellous holiday in Provence. We were camping in a lovely village called Villes-sur-Auzon, nestling in the shadow of the mighty Mont Ventoux and eight miles from the small town of Bedoin, the usual starting point for a ride up the 'Giant of Provence'. In cycling terms, Ventoux has iconic status. It has been the scene of many ferocious battles on stages of the Tour de France and sadly the setting, on one of those stages, for the untimely demise of British cyclist Tom Simpson in July 1967.

An incredibly successful professional cyclist and Britain's first world road race champion, he was also the first British rider to wear the yellow jersey in the Tour. He collapsed off his bike in the final moments of the stage and died from heat exhaustion – a combination of the merciless heat along with a cocktail of amphetamines and alcohol. This is just part of the history that has earned this particular mountain such a fierce reputation.

The highlight of the trip for me was a ride up Ventoux. It wasn't the first time I'd ridden up this mountain. A few years earlier, a group of us had a sporty-spring climbing trip to Malaucene for a week of bolt clipping. Mid-trip me, Tim Whiteley and Tim's mate Alex chose to have a 'rest day', hire some road bikes and cycle up Ventoux. We'd planned this ahead so had our cycling kit with us. April in Provence was bound to be warm, so I'd taken shorts and a short-sleeve jersey and fingerless cycling gloves. The last few kilometres had deep snow at the side of the road, indeed we had to get off and walk the last few hundred metres as the summit was still snowed-in. Thanks to the effort, riding up was fine, but the descent was freezing.

On this return trip I was planning something different. I would ride up again, not once but three times in one day. There are three main roads that lead to the summit and so three starting points: Malaucene to the northwest, Bedoin to the south and Sault to the east. The routes from Bedoin and Sault join at Chalet Reynard for the final, searing section surrounded by an almost lunar landscape of white rock that reflects any sun that has missed you on its first pass. There is no shade and no escape from the elements.

As the name suggests (*venteux* means windy in French), the winds on the mountain can, at times, be strong. The day I had programmed for my ascents was one of those times. My route took me up from Bedoin to start with, generally considered the toughest route and the one used in all but one of the occasions it's been part of the Tour. The clag had descended and the Mistral wind had appeared to make it even harder. When I arrived at the summit, I was in the clouds and I had the place to myself – it was only 7.30am. I descended to Malaucene and immediately turned round for my second climb. The wind was still strong but had at least started to blow some of the cloud away. After reaching the summit the second time, I could enjoy the descent to Sault. This is a lovely town and the centre for the region's famous lavender harvest. In July the air is full of the beautiful fragrance and the fields look like they have been painted different shades of purple, row after row.

The final ascent of the day was the most enjoyable. The gradient from this side is a little gentler and I knew I was on the final stretch. But the wind hadn't let up and as I approached the top for the last time I caught up with and passed another rider. We exchanged grunted greetings as best we could as we fought our own personal battles with the gradient and the wind. Moments later I felt a particularly strong gust, followed immediately by a clattering and groans of pain. I looked back to see my fellow cyclist sprawled across the rocks on the side of the road – he had been blown off his bike by the wind. I went back to check he was okay and put him back on his bike, for which he was most grateful.

So that was 141 km, 4420m of ascent and just under 8 hours. I met Karen back in Bedoin for a well-deserved coffee and ice cream. She made her own ascent of the *Giant* a couple of days later.

I've had a strong competitive streak ever since school – I've always felt the need to push myself, never content to mooch along in my comfort zone – and this has been a huge driving force in my climbing. At school I wanted to get up harder routes, preferably harder than my friends' routes, and many times since I've thrown myself – unashamedly and blindly – onto climbing routes, with complete confidence of success, purely because someone else has done it before. If they can do it, I know I can do it.

The equivalent to watching your time trial stats improve in cycling is when you see your grades creeping upwards. One of climbing's great thrills must be to operate at your limit, pushing yourself around the edges of the unknown, and one of the great things about climbing is that everyone can experience that feeling, whatever grade they're climbing. They just need to keep pushing at the boundaries, whether 'Severe' or 'Extreme'.

I've entered many climbing competitions, both bouldering and leading, most of which have been local affairs, but in 1991–92 – with the words "How hard can it be?" ringing in my head – I entered the National Indoor Climbing Championships. The first event was at the National Indoor Arena in Birmingham, a grand stage on which to perform. I knew I had absolutely no chance of getting anywhere close to winning but that wasn't the point. It was a very uneven playing field. Many competitors were dedicated professional climbers who trained full-time and I was far too realistic to think I had any chance of winning. I came somewhere in the middle of the field. I can't remember where exactly but it was great just to be there having a go. For me it was about being able to compete and feel the rush of adrenaline, with the added impetus that comes from pitting myself against others.

My competitive mindset goes beyond sport. In my working life, particularly in the consultancy where I worked from 2005 to 2019, I was determined to get the best sales figures, get the best feedback from clients or come up with the best new ideas and models for getting messages across. At one point I invited my fellow Mont Blanc cyclist Pete Robinson to help us improve the teamwork and co-operation within our Leadership Team. As part of that exercise, Pete got all six of us to complete a Myers-Briggs Type Indicator test – the psychological self-assessment that allocates people 'types': introvert or extrovert; sensing or intuitive; thinking or feeling, and judging or perceiving. As we sat round the table awaiting Pete's announcement of the results, I had an idea.

"Hang on," I said. "Why don't we all try and guess each other's types, and the person who gets most right is the winner?"

Pete looked over at me with a wry smile. "Only *you* could turn Myers-Briggs into a competition!"

The several times I've done this test, it's scored me the same, identifying me

Karen at the summit of Ventoux

Relaxing in Bedoin after the triple
Karen Wharton

as an introvert rather than an extrovert. Introverts are commonly understood to be shy, reticent and withdrawn, and I'm definitely not any of these. However, the definition of introvert in the Myers-Briggs sense is about being focused on internal, rather external, sources of stimulation, and this internal focus is so true of me. Most of my motivation comes from within, even if I'm naturally influenced by those around me. As a result, I'm very self-driven and very competitive – as is my wife, Karen, as a matter of fact. If there's someone up ahead on a bike ride, Karen has to catch them, whatever it takes.

In 2018, 40 years on from those childhood climbs and antics and six years on from, temporarily, swapping the crags for the cyclosportives, I suddenly found myself asking a truly life-changing question: 'Why should I keep working full-time?'

Some might think 55 a bit young to be giving up full-time work but Karen and I had just returned from a meeting with Stuart, our long-time financial adviser. We'd been studying the projections he'd calculated in light of Karen's impending retirement from working full-time in the NHS. She'd been a district nurse team leader in Newcastle since 1990 and then at Grange-over-Sands after we'd moved to the Lake District. We'd been married for twenty-seven years, and our only child, Flora, had graduated from Glasgow University and was at the time working as a rowing coach in New Zealand. She'd thrown herself fully into rowing at Glasgow, becoming Scottish Indoor Champion as a Lightweight and winning many gold medals representing Scotland. Perhaps unsurprisingly, she too, is very driven, with a strong competitive spirit.

Karen and I had put a large part of our earnings into savings and pensions and paid off the mortgage on our comfortable-but-modest house in Kendal. Stuart had charted all our estimated outgoings and incomings well into our 90s – based on Karen retiring at sixty then returning to work at a lower grade for fewer days and me doing something similar in five years' time. It was immediately apparent that, if we were careful, at the rate we were going, we'd have enough to see us through.

"As a matter of interest," I asked, "what would happen if Karen and I finished full-time work at the same time?" After a few simple adjustments we had a viable proposition and the matter was decided. I had better things to do with my life than carry on working. Emboldened by Stuart's new financial projections, we also allowed ourselves a most uncharacteristic extravagance. We finally decided to splash out on a campervan. It seemed we were the last ones in our circle of friends still relying on a tent for our holidays away.

At the time, I thought the main benefit of giving up work would be more time to ride my bike, do all the time trials I wanted to, and get back into climbing. As it turned out, as soon as I started climbing again it was obvious how much I'd missed it. That was where my true passion lay. And if I was going to be climbing, I was going to be doing it full-time. The very next day, after finishing my full-time job, I went back to Kendal Climbing Wall. I've barely been on my bike since.

Another gold for Scotland in the Lightweight Pair (Home International Regatta, July 2016) – Flora (R) with crew member Laura McDonald

QUESTIONS

Q *After all that time climbing, how come you gave it up for a few years?*

A I've let climbing take a back seat on a number of occasions over the years, partly through a desire to try new activities I saw others enjoying, but also as a result of getting fed up of the same routine. I've always preferred Trad climbing out on the crags, which requires dry conditions that we often don't get. Spending time on the climbing wall is fun, but a poor substitute. There's also the frustration of not always being able to find a partner to climb with, whereas I was always happy to go out for a solo bike ride. It can also feel pretty relentless always pushing, always aiming for better and harder. I don't get the same satisfaction from just kicking back a bit and doing easier routes – for me, it's better not to do any at all!

Q *Did you learn anything from cycling that you could apply to climbing?*

A The most significant element here is the training. Although the nature of the training regime is different, the principle is identical. In order to put in the best effort for a 10-mile time trial I'd put myself through three, four or even five one-hour sessions of directed training. Each of these would be different, working on power, endurance, sprints, intervals. The result was rapid improvement in my times. Sure, I was never going to break any records – I'd started way too late in life – but the personal satisfaction was immense. Learning to take that mindset and discipline into climbing would get me back to the higher grades I aspired to.

Q *What's the equivalent in climbing terms to the thrill of cycling at full tilt? Is it height? Difficulty?*

A On the bike, the real pleasure for me comes from covering a large distance quickly. On a day when it's all going well there's a kind of flow and the miles just fly past. There's something similar in climbing: it isn't necessarily on a very hard route – more often than not, on a route that's just below my upper limit – but the holds keep coming and there's a fluidity to the upward movement. Then there are the moments of great exposure, again perhaps on ground that's physically comfortable, maybe high up on an exposed edge with hundreds of feet of air beneath – that's thrilling. It's like making a fast descent on the bike, on an empty road with a good surface of smooth, clean tarmac and sweeping bends and no cars to get in the way of the perfect racing line and breaking the 80kph barrier. Now that is a thrill.

3 - Fine Time
E5 6B RAVEN CRAG, LANGDALE
A year off before university

It was the summer of 1981. I had completed my A-Levels, had a university place lined up all being well and then a career in the army to follow. It was time to enjoy the freedom that comes when you finally shake off the shackles of school and get access to a car and before adult responsibilities start to pile up.

I was going to York University to study Biology and after that the Royal Military Academy Sandhurst. I'd gone through the army selection process by that time and been offered a bursary – a bit of extra funding on top of my full university grant (what a quaint concept that sounds now!) – in exchange for signing up to a three-year Short Service Commission. For the time being however, I was free to do as I pleased. I'd deferred university until the following autumn with no real plan as to how to spend that year off, but something was bound to turn up.

One of the non-climbing highlights of that summer of '81 was seeing Bob Dylan in concert at Earl's Court in London. I went with my music 'guru' from West Cumbria, Jon Dixon, a boarder in the year above me at school who was an excellent musician – playing piano, organ and guitar – and looked like a 70s rock star – tall and rangy with long (by school standards) straggly hair. He was always practising guitar chord sequences with his left fingers on the back of his right hand. At school Jon was often roped in to play piano or organ to accompany the hymns at Sunday evening service. All the boys and the duty master would be sat in the main school hall waiting for the Headmaster to appear in order to officiate. While we were waiting, Jon would be playing some incidental music to pass the time. I certainly recall large sections of *Dark Side of the Moon* and, particularly poignantly, on the weekend that John Lennon was shot he gave us a beautiful rendition of *Imagine*. Even the Head was visibly moved.

Jon was hugely influential in the development of my musical tastes and introduced me to all sorts over those few years. He had an amazing collection of vinyl and tapes which he would happily lend out or copy. One such introduction was Pink Floyd. They'd released *The Wall* at the end of 1979 and performed it live at Earl's Court in August 1980 and again in June 1981. Jon had gone to one of the 1980 shows and I was desperate to go when they put it on again the following year. I tried to get permission to go from school, but the request was flatly denied, the only reason being that I had a Physics A-Level the following day. These people just couldn't get their priorities right! At least Jon furnished me with a bootleg recording of the 1980 concert – copied onto two TDK C90 cassettes. So, getting to see Dylan after my exams were over was particularly sweet. I saw the great man again in 1984 at St James' Park, Newcastle, supported by Santana on that occasion – what a fabulous concert! And I finally got to see *The Wall* performed by Roger Waters in Manchester many, many years later – well worth the wait. Once again, shortly after that evening, my old mate Jon Dixon was able to present me with a recording of that specific concert, on a CD this time. Oh, the march of technology!

At school, many of us had record players – it was nearly all vinyl in those days – in our studies, and would often use headphones to avoid having to compete with the selection from our neighbours. I'd borrowed *Wish You Were Here* by Pink Floyd one evening and was sat listening to it for the very first time, through the headphones. I had no idea what was coming, so when the music suddenly stops to the sound of closing elevator doors I was horrified – I thought my record player had destroyed Jon's disc. Jon went from Lancaster to Oxford and from there into a long career with the BBC.

I spent a lot of time that summer in the Lancaster area rather than at home. That's where my mates were and I could hitch there from Burnley in no time. More often than not I was camped out at the ever-welcoming Cooper household, although not wanting to overstay my welcome I did spend some nights in a rough and ready bivouac among the scrub of Warton Crag. It was an amazing time. We could climb every day and spend the evenings in the Hest Bank Hotel bar or, for a special night out, at the German-style drinking den, the Bierkeller in Morecambe. These drunken nights would end up in a stagger back along the prom to whoever's house was parent-free at the time. We obtained a very fancy video player – quite a breakthrough in home entertainment – to use over the summer. It was 'bought' from a shop in Lancaster, who assured us that we were welcome to return it within 28 days, free of charge if we weren't entirely satisfied with it. And so it transpired. It didn't quite cut the mustard and it went back after 28 days of excellent service.

That summer, we climbed on the familiar crags around Silverdale and Carnforth but also ventured further into Yorkshire, making our first exploratory trips to the fabulous limestone of Malham, Kilnsey, Gordale and the smaller Attermire. When I was back at home, I'd borrow my mother's car, if available, and head over to Witches' Quarry. It was also during this period that John Wilson and I returned to Llanberis, upping our game and ultimately making that ascent of *Cenotaph Corner*. Following this breakthrough to leading extreme, I started to keep a record in a little red notebook: "Extreme-grade routes I have led to-date". Each entry was simply: route name, grade, crag, initials of my climbing partner and a couple of lines on what I thought of the route. I also allocated between one and three stars for the more deserving routes. Keeping this record was one of the best things I ever did. I kept it going, across several volumes, for the next 20 years until 2001.

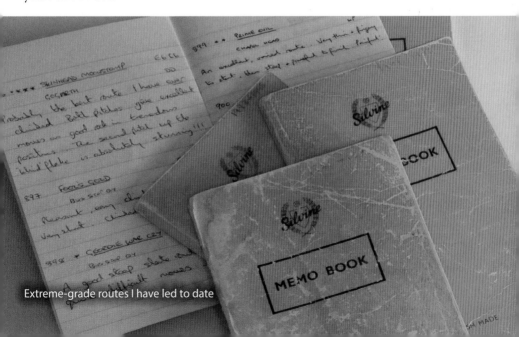

Extreme-grade routes I have led to date

It's great to look back at what I did, when and with whom. Some of the comments are quite enlightening. This record also enables me to recall exactly what I achieved in those early days. Most routes – and these are only the ones I led of course – I did with John Wilson, with a couple of early trips to Yorkshire with Neil Foster. What's interesting to note, at that early stage, is that of the first 15 entries, five were climbed solo – and many more would follow. All the routes I did that summer fell into the E1 to E2 category, except for one outlier, a route at Witches' Quarry called *Devil Worshipper*, graded E4 6a. The notes in my first little red notebook, where it's recorded as Route No 10, go as follows: "Strenuous, technical, delicate, no gear – a fantastic route. Doubtful grade". There is no record of who I did it with, just a question mark. I must have found a random passer-by to hold my ropes.

Someone else I met at that time was another local climber of my age, Mark Jackson. Having a climbing partner in the Burnley area was a major step forward. I eventually lost contact with him, but we were able to climb together for the next year or so and it was through him that I was to embark on my next adventure. Mark had been down to Cornwall, on a course with Rowland Edwards at his Compass West base in Sennen. He'd stayed on afterwards to help Rowland who, at that time, was renovating the large granite property where he lived with wife Betty and sons Mark and Carl. On his return north, Mark suggested I might do the same. Without further ado, I wrote to Rowland who, clearly recognising free labour when he saw it, invited me down. At the time I was working behind the bar at the Cat's Whiskers nightclub in Burnley – and, yes, it was as bad as it sounds, if not worse! I handed in my notice, packed a rucksack and was off. I had no transport of my own and clearly wasn't going to pay for a train. What I did have was time on my hands, a sense of adventure and a thumb that I could stick out at the side of the road. I made that journey several times, back and forth, over the coming months, nearly always taking a consistent 12 hours from door to door.

Down in Cornwall at the Edwards' household, I was treated like a member of the family. I slept in an old caravan in the back garden and, in exchange for Betty's lovely meals, I did a range of labouring jobs for taskmaster Rowland. It was fun and easy work, even if Rowland was working hard at perfecting his grumpy-old-man persona. Mark and I were good friends and he put his graphic design skills to good use, creating a large, cardboard fist and thumb into which I could slot cards with name places written in large letters to help me with my hitchhiking. What didn't happen, however, was much climbing, which had been my main reason for going there in the first place.

Come Christmas I decided I needed a change, so I headed home for the last time. Plans were made with the Hest Bank crowd to spend New Year in Glencoe. We cobbled together a rag-tag assortment of ice-axes, crampons and other random winter kit and headed up to Scotland with a serious freeze forecast. I had a vague idea that it would be good to spend the winter in Scotland – but doing what? I had no idea. Luck was on my side. On our first night, having got ourselves settled into the chalet that we'd booked for the week, we wandered the short distance down the road to the Clachaig Inn. This is a well-known watering hole in the climbing community, with a long history and a busy place all year round. At the time it was run by Mike Gardner, originally from the Borders, and his wife and son, some years older than me. On that first night I approached Mike and rather sheepishly enquired: "Do you have any jobs going? Do you need anyone to work in the bar?" He looked me up and down and, to my surprise, rather than dismissing me as a "cheeky wee Sassenach" said "Hmm … Come and see me at the end of the week, laddie." And that was it. At the end of that week, I was taken on as barman with board, lodgings and a meagre wage on which I could start to accumulate new kit.

That winter, the first three months of 1982, turned out to be amazing. Lots of snow and sustained low temperatures meant that many classic winter lines formed and remained in condition for some time. Many new routes were also established and often the first ascensionists' first port of call after their success would be the bar of the Clachaig, where we'd get all the details of their heroic endeavours that day. As it happened, despite a few trips out climbing – including with the great, late Mal Duff – I spent most of my time off at the other end of the valley, skiing at the White Corries. The skiing infrastructure was notoriously basic, to say the least, but that was part of the attraction. A small chair-lift took you up the first hill from the valley before a trudge across the plateau led to a rudimentary building. This housed a simple café and provided oft-needed shelter from the terrible weather. From there, a couple of lifts – a single-chair and T-bar – took you to the top of the mountain and a range of options for descending. The conditions were often bad, but when they were good, they were amazing – still some of the best days' skiing I've ever had. I managed to buy a pair of skis and boots for £15 and of course I had to pay for use of the lifts. I bought a punch card pass but thanks to a mutual agreement with the lift staff, including complimentary drinks in the Clachaig afterwards, that punch card somehow lasted all season.

The work at the Clachaig was great. The weekdays were generally quiet, with a few locals keeping us going, often until quite late, sat in the snug. When the weekends came round, the place would fill up, particularly when there was a good forecast. The chalets and bunkhouse were filled with visiting climbers, walkers and skiers. Occasionally we'd get groups coming in off the hill midweek. One time, a military group descended on us after completing the Aonach Eagach ridge (the Clachaig being perfectly placed at the foot of the descent path, down the side of Clachaig Gully). It was a hot day and they were gagging for refreshment. First up, some burly corporal asked me for a pint of lemonade to quench his thirst, which I duly poured out. Without hesitation he went to down it in one – only to spit the lot out with a look of utter disgust on his face. Oops! I'd given him a pint of peppermint cordial. One of the squaddies in this same group was looking thoroughly despondent, despite having had a great day out on the hill.

"I dropped my duvet jacket into the gully on our way down – I'm in for it when I get back to camp," he explained.

My ears pricked up. A month or so later with the onset of spring, at the first opportunity, I climbed Clachaig Gully – a rather wet and greasy experience, more gill-scrambling than rock-climbing. But it was well worth it, for there it was, still in its stuff sack at the base of one of the pitches: an army-issue, down-filled duvet jacket. What a coup!

I was sorry to leave Glencoe after Easter, but I'd been invited to join my intended future regiment on a month-long trip to Canada on their major live-firing, training exercises. This was too good an opportunity to miss. I'd be back again the following New Year once again, helping out behind the bar, much to the advantage of John and the other friends I was there with.

After a month of playing at soldiers in northern Alberta, including some welcome but rather tame adventure training in the Jasper area, I was back home in time for a full summer before heading off to uni. I hooked up with my local climbing partner, Mark, for trips into Yorkshire and a fantastic trip to High Tor in Derbyshire. But then I joined an old schoolfriend and rising star of the climbing scene, Neil Foster. Neil had great plans for new routes in Yorkshire, particularly at Malham. Also in on the fun was Lancaster-based Leo Hermacinksi. Neil led the charge with a number of excellent first ascents: *Wild West Hero*, *Grandfather Clock* (because it's halfway up *Terrace Staircase*), *Swift Attack* (both a rapid ascent but also something to do with the birds buzzing around at the time), *Stat-*

ic Contrasts and others. I added my own contribution with *Ripsnorter* but would be the first to admit that it comes nowhere near the quality of the others.

At one stage Neil and I chose to camp out at Malham. I'd acquired a really old, heavy tent from an uncle but it was just a single layer of white canvas, wooden pegs and no groundsheet so in the end we rejected it in favour of a small cave at the top of the cove, just left of the centre, hence the route name *The Stone Tent*. It could, with great care, be reached by scrambling down and across from the access to the Terrace. We used the tent as a sheet to block up the entrance to the cave and provide additional shelter in our exposed position. A few days later we were visited by a National Park warden who nearly killed himself getting to us to ask us to remove the tent which could apparently be seen from many miles away.

I had many other adventures at Malham over this period, nearly all on the Right Wing. On one occasion I was sat at home in Burnley, feeling a bit bored and frustrated, so I borrowed my mum's car and drove out to Malham. I didn't have any plans and had nobody to climb with, but just wanted to be outside doing something. As was the norm in those days, I parked the car in the layby on the road up the hill out of the village, level with the Right Wing of the Cove. I walked across the fields and dropped down the short scramble by the wall to approach the crag from the right. As I walked underneath the crag in my jeans and trainers, with rucksack on my back, I could see a couple of other climbers sat on the large flat rock that sits on the hillside below the Wombat area of the crag.

I gave them a passing acknowledgement from the base of the crag then, without changing my shoes or removing my pack, I soloed up *Kirkby Wall*, a route I'd done several times before. It was only a VS (it was given HVS in the next guide) but even in those days it was quite polished and involved a delicate traverse, which in trainers was somewhat precarious. I pulled over the top and sat in the sun for a while, savouring the view down the valley but still feeling a bit frustrated at not having anyone to climb with. I wasn't going to do anything else there so headed back to the car and drove back home. That afternoon I called Neil Foster on the phone and, after arranging a future trip, I described my briefest of visits to Malham. That evening, by pure coincidence, he was at a party somewhere in Yorkshire and told me later that he'd been chatting with Pete Gomersall and Bonny Masson. They recounted a strange incident they'd witnessed earlier that day:

"It was the weirdest thing. We were sat beneath the Right Wing today and this lad turned up, walked along the bottom of the crag, soloed up *Kirkby Wall* then just disappeared. It was bizarre!"

Neil was in stitches, knowing exactly who the mystery climber was.

On another occasion, my mum offered to drive me out to Malham and accompanied me across to the Right Wing. This time I put on my climbing shoes and soloed *Carnage Left Hand*, the two-pitch HVS variation to the brilliant Barley brothers' route that avoided the aid point over the roof by climbing a tree and heading up and left. Once again, I'd done this route a few times before. It wasn't even the first time I'd soloed it. But it was only years later that I reflected on this and realised that my mum must have been terrified watching me climb up there unprotected. "Shouldn't you have a rope when doing something like that?" she said when I got back down. I told her it was quite easy and a rope wasn't necessary but, on reflection, I was just a typical, selfish and rather thoughtless teenager who couldn't see how my actions might affect someone who cared for me.

My most audacious solo at Malham was a few years later. Once again, I was there on my own and found myself up on the Terrace at the very top of the Cove. In its centre, the Terrace presents a wide and comfortable area with some great short routes on beautiful limestone. This grassy ledge tapers rightwards until it eventually peters out beneath a clean, vertical wall with several hundred feet of exposure to the beck below. This is where *Sundance Wall* starts. I'd led it previously, but on this occasion I teetered out along the ledge alone and launched myself up the steep wall with all that space beneath my feet. There was absolutely no margin for error but clearly, as I'm recounting this tale, I made it to the top successfully. And at the time I felt fine. I had confidence in my ability and I had no doubts. Again, it's only years later that I can look back on this and reflect that it was probably beyond the bounds of sensible behaviour and into the realm of recklessness – a hold could have snapped, a bird could have flown off a ledge and I would certainly have fallen hundreds of feet. There were too many factors outside my control that I hadn't considered. Thinking of it now gives me the creeps.

John Wilson had gone straight from school into a job with an insurance broker. At that time, he lived near Perth in central Scotland from where he could readily access the fabulous range of crags at Dunkeld. He already had a car of his own at that stage, but I recall one day we'd been climbing with Eric, his dad, a terrific bloke who became a lifelong friend. He was a bit of a wheeler-dealer, always involved in some scheme or other and keen to be at the cutting edge. He loved his cars and didn't hold back when driving them. This was the first time I'd ever encountered a 'mobile phone'. He had the latest model installed in his car of the time. It was huge: a normal telephone handset and a battery the size of a shoebox. To use it meant going through a relay station, but at the time it was still amazing. We'd only seen such things in Bond movies.

With John working, we had to wait until his allocated summer holidays to revisit North Wales. We made the most of that week, climbing mainly in the Llanberis Pass but also fitting in a visit to Tremadog. One very memorable evening, we went up to Cyrn Las, the largest and most impressive of the crags on the south side of the Pass. We would climb many routes on this forbidding crag in future years, but on this first visit we were keen to tick off the *Classic Rock* route *Main Wall*. By now this brilliant route was well within our capabilities, so we decided to go truly traditional and do it in big boots. What a great adventure that was as we made our way up this massive lump of rock, swapping leads and relishing the exposure. John even spied a guidebook on a heathery ledge off to one side that some previous party must have dropped. I gave him a top-rope so that he could make his way carefully over and retrieve the booty.

Our accommodation of choice was still the cave beneath the Cromlech Boulders, but it was on one of these trips that we had the great fortune one evening, to meet Iwan Jones in the Vaynol Arms. A strong-looking redheaded Welshman, Iwan was a teacher from mid-Wales who was also visiting the Pass to climb during his long summer holiday. It turned out that he didn't have anywhere to stay so we magnanimously invited him to join us in our luxury accommodation – in the cave. Iwan was to become a great friend and regular climbing partner. Not long after this, he moved up to Llanberis to teach at a nearby school and for many years provided us with a (more comfortable) base to stay whenever we were in the area. A really warm-hearted and generous soul and a true character, Iwan became very much a part of the Llanberis scene, ultimately getting involved in writing the guidebooks. He was the fount of

Young guns – Nick and John Wilson below Tremadog in 1982

all knowledge regarding routes in North Wales. He hadn't necessarily led them all but he'd certainly been on them, following many leaders up all the desperate test-pieces. But his vast, internal database wasn't always entirely reliable.

I was on a trip to North Wales with Stuart Wood, one of my regular Lakes climbing partners in 1993. We were staying with Iwan and one day the three of us went up to the immaculate Rainbow Slab, a fabulous clean sweep of perfect slate in the Dinorwig quarries above Llanberis. The routes on here aren't endowed with the biggest of holds at the best of times. More often than not you have to rely on edges that are literally the size of a matchstick and the lines aren't always very distinct. My record shows that on that day I led both *Splitstream* and *Cystitis By Proxy*, both of which have very delicate, balancy moves with the grade of E5 6b – hard enough. However, rather than reading the route descriptions in the guide we relied on Iwan, the human guidebook, to point us in the right direction. When it came to the second of our two routes that day our helpful guide identified the start point. Woody went first as it was his go, following Iwan's directions. He got a long way up but it looked desperate – much harder than expected and he was getting a long way above his last gear. Eventually it all went horribly wrong and he cartwheeled a long way down the slab.

My turn to have a go – no pressure then! Up I went, once again following Iwan's helpful guidance. It was truly desperate climbing – really sustained sequences of hard, technical moves and way above the meagre protection. It was as hard as anything I'd climbed and much harder than I'd expected. Nevertheless, I battled on and finally made it to the top, just! I commented afterwards that if there had been a bolt or some other good protection, I would undoubtedly have fallen off. On return to ground level, after I'd brought Woody up, Iwan admitted rather guiltily, "I'm sorry boys, I think I just sent you up the crux of *Raped By Affection*". No wonder it felt hard. This John Redhead test-piece is graded E7 6c.

The guidebook of the time has the following introduction to the route: "Still just about the neckiest undertaking on the slab; an on-sight lead would be just about the most impressive tick in this guide." It should be pointed out that the guidebook author was one Iwan Arfon Jones! What was frustrating for me was that, although I'd climbed the crux section and upper-half of *Raped*, I hadn't done the start, which by all accounts isn't quite so hard, if less well protected, than the rest. If only I'd started up it, as Iwan's intro in the guide suggests, that would've been one hell of an achievement.

Back to 1982 and later that summer I was to return to North Wales, this time with Neil and Leo. By now the new routes at Malham had dried up, with Neil having established *New Dawn Fades*, much to his dismay, having to resort

Nick on *Poetry Pink*, Rainbow Slab. *Raped By Affection* climbs the wall to the right

Iwan Jones

to a point of aid – just one reason for the name (also his initials and the title of a track by Joy Division). The aid point was subsequently dispatched by another Lancaster hot-shot, Alan Clarke. On this return trip to Wales, we ticked another long list of routes at Tremadog and in the Pass. We were also fortunate enough to spend a day at Craig y Forwyn, a tremendous limestone crag on the North Wales coast. Sadly, climbing was later banned here for many years, preventing others from sampling its delights. *Great Wall* (E3 5c) was the highlight of that day for me. Back at Tremadog, the stand-out route of the year was *Silly Arete*. Also coming in at E3 5c, the notes in my notebook from the time say it all: "A brilliant route ranking with the very best. Very delicate climbing with negligble protection in a brilliant position," and three stars! One other route at Tremadog that just had to be climbed on that trip was *Tensor* at Craig y Castell. Like many others, I'd been inspired by watching Ron Fawcett solo this, played in slow motion during the opening credits of the *Rock Athlete* series by Sid Perou, on TV the year before. On that first occasion I led it but I was to solo it myself the following year.

At this early stage in my climbing career, I was slowly building my collection of equipment. I'd moved on from sharing boots and throwing them back down the crag. I had my own second-hand pair of EBs, a Whillans sit harness and a small but growing selection of runners and karabiners. All of us were the same, often on the lookout for new or second-hand bargains – or even better, kit left behind on routes by previous ascensionists.

Each trip to North Wales, we'd eagerly visit the Clog factory at Deiniolen to purchase reject karabiners (or krabs). I remember being shown into a side room with boxes of the krabs stamped as 'seconds', told to sort through them and select what we wanted and then return to reception where we'd pay for them. Pockets stuffed, we'd walk out innocently and present a couple of the bits of kit that were to be paid for, hoping all the extras weren't clinking in their hiding places.

Around that time, I'd loosely hooked up with the Craven Mountaineering Club in the search for additional partners when at home. Tragically, one of their members had recently died while climbing at Witches' Quarry. It wasn't a climbing accident as such but he was climbing when he died, probably from a heart attack. His family wanted to dispose of his accumulated kit, so an auction was arranged at a pub in Skipton, with proceeds to charity. I didn't have much money but I did manage to pick up a few items to boost my collection, including the rock

Nick on *Silly Arete* at Tremadog

boots he'd been wearing at the time he died, which nobody else seemed keen on. They were a reasonable fit and in great condition – just one bad scuff mark!

And so, that first summer drew to a close. With a host of adventures and routes under my belt I prepared myself for the next big step, going to university. I didn't really know what to expect but was absolutely sure that I was going to make the most of it. I just hoped that there'd be a good supply of climbing partners to get out with. And, as it turned out, there was.

QUESTION

Q *What led you to solo those relatively hard routes with limited experience?*

A Perhaps the lack of experience or naivety had something to do with it. I felt confident in my ability and, as a young adult, I was probably over-confident, feeling indestructible. Having said that, I wouldn't have soloed just any route – I knew, or thought I knew, what I could get away with. That nearly all went horribly wrong sometime later – as you'll read about.

4 - Run Wild, Run Free
E5 6A St Bees
Wild times as an undergrad

And so, to university. What a place. Such a lot of new things to do, new people to meet and your own life to organise. I had a head start on the last bit – used to being away from home and looking after myself – but I was thrilled by the prospect of meeting new people and trying out new activities. I was really looking forward to studying Biology, a subject I loved, and despite the heavy workload of lectures, tutorials and practical sessions in the lab, there was going to be more than enough free time for everything else.

Like most First Years I went to the Freshers' Fair, full of enthusiasm and with an open mind. First stop was the Karate Club where I joined up to continue a sport that I'd already been doing for several years. I went on to become the captain of the university karate team but ultimately the training became too time consuming. To progress any further, I would have had to give up something else and so, despite valuing the strength and discipline I gained from karate, I gave it up to focus on my climbing. I signed up to give hang-gliding a try with the prospect of an initial trip out to the Dales in a few weekends' time. But it wasn't long before I found myself at the climbing club stand. The guys I met were interested to hear of my previous experience and were delighted they wouldn't have to teach me from scratch. They invited me to an initial get-together at Derwent College later that week, with the promise of free beer. So it was, a few nights later, I made my way along, hoping to meet some climbers to team up with. Beer was indeed flowing freely – we were helping ourselves from the barrel! – and there was a big crowd of members, old and new. As we swapped stories of past climbs and crags, it soon became apparent that most of the folk I met were content to plod along at a steady grade without pushing themselves but, thankfully, not everyone. By the end of the evening, three of us were standing round the barrel – myself, Duncan Holdsworth and Phil Baines – drawn by some unseen force (other than beer?) perhaps. It was immediately clear that we were kindred spirits and we went on to form the core of the university climbing club for the next three years.

At 24, Duncan seemed ancient. He had previously worked as a lab technician at a Bradford hospital before coming to York to do the same Biology course as me. He had fair hair and slight build and tastes that suggested that he'd have been more at home in the 60s. For all that, he was a true Yorkshireman from Haworth, famous for the Bronte family, the Keighley & Worth Valley Railway and the Fleece Inn on the cobbled Main Street. I'm not sure about his interest in the Bronte sisters, but he liked his trains and certainly had a taste for the Timothy Taylor's at the Fleece. Dunc had been living at home with his mum, Jean and his brother Stuart, a couple of years younger. Stuart, along with a wide circle of climbing and caving mates, was to become as much part of the scene as any of us. Dunc's mum put me in my place the first time I met her. She was a lovely lady, warm-hearted and always very welcoming and interested in all the people that Dunc would bring round. "Where are you from, sonny?" she asked in her kindly tones. "Burnley" I explained with enthusiasm. "My, that's a droll spot," she shot back. "Still, someone has to live there, I suppose."

Phil, on the other hand was from the North East – a proud Mackem from Sunderland. He was also a couple of years older than me and very much a man of the times with his Duran Duran haircut and his jumper tucked into his trousers. He liked to look his best. He worked out at the gym and had the muscles to show for it. You'd see him out and about in his red Ford Capri or walking with a bit of a swagger down the street – 'more edge than a Gilette G2', as we used to say! He was a great person to have as a friend with a quick-witted, *Viz*-inspired sense of humour, always the first to come up with a good nickname for someone. But he had a fiery temperament – not someone you'd want to get on the wrong side of. Whereas Dunc's climbing relied on technique and finesse, Phil's was more about strength and power. We made a great team.

The room was filled with a lot of fresh faces including a large group of the 'chequered shirt' brigade from the Freshers' Fair. I was a bit unsure about this lot. As they quizzed me on my experience, it was soon apparent that they all operated in the VS or below category. Nice people, just not my scene.

They pointed me toward a beer barrel and left me to get on with it. One thing I'd gleaned was that they'd signed up a couple of other lads that climbed at Extreme and I was keen to meet them. Somehow I felt that if I hung around the barrel long enough, eventually the two fellas I needed to meet were sure to show up.

Natural selection played its part and, sure enough, after about an hour three of us were stood around the barrel, lashing it down, ignoring the rest of the room, and we've been good mates ever since.

Nick and Dunc arrived as a pair. They seemed to know each other and I thought they were from the same area (Yorkshire) initially. It turned out Nick was Lancastrian (oops) but they both studied Biology. We got on like a house on fire.

I liked Nick straight away – his cheeky face and mischievous manner were a world apart from the more staid core group. More to the point, he'd done a lot of climbing, pushed his grade and was really keen to get on the climbing wall and push harder. We were definitely on the same page. He was a little younger but seemed fiercely independent and confident in where he was heading and how he planned to go about it.

Dunc was right up my street. He'd already done loads, climbed in America, the Alps and all over the UK. He seemed a fair bit older and I was a 'mature student' at 21 (so how old was he?). His winning smile never failed to brighten my day. When he was around we always had a bloody good laugh. And, boy did he like a drink!

It turned out Dunc also had his own transport – an Escort van – and we quickly hatched a plan to ditch the club and go climbing on our own if things didn't work out. We needn't have worried. Within a few months we had gained a full grip on the club and infiltrated the management of it. I became Treasurer and eventually Chairman, Nick became President and our mate Tony became Secretary. A total coup d'état! We controlled the budgets, organised the transport, set the meet locations and arranged any talks, films or meetings. We got one of the largest grants from the university and we used it to great effect to subsidise our weekend trips. It couldn't have worked out better.

Phil Baines

Duncan Holdsworth climbing at Crookrise

Having an army bursary meant that I didn't have to get a job during the long summer holidays. It also gave me a guarantee of a job at the end of my degree, not something to be taken lightly in the early 1980s. There was no requirement for me to be involved with the army while I was at uni but there was an implied expectation that I would join the local OTC (Officer Training Corps). Dutifully, I made my way down to Leeds (our nearest unit) to attend one of the initial open days.

I showed some interest and had a very encouraging interview with the CO (Commanding Officer) who said he was delighted to have me there. "Always good to have bursary students… great to see someone with your experience… I'm sure you'll be a great asset… blah, blah, blah." At one point we were all gathered together by one of the senior NCOs (Non-Commissioned Officers) who went on to explain that it was essential that everyone attend a first weapon-training session, 'Introduction to the rifle', the following weekend. When he'd finished his briefing, I approached him to explain, rather apologetically, that I wasn't available as I'd already booked and paid to go hang-gliding. He reiterated the importance of this first session. I tried again, explaining that I was very familiar with this weapon already, having spent a month using it on live-firing exercises in Canada just a few months earlier. He stood his ground: "You either come next weekend or you don't come at all!". That made the decision much easier – I never went back. I did, shortly afterwards, get a grovelling letter from the CO explaining that the sergeant hadn't realised I was on a bursary but it was too late. I never really wanted to go in the first place.

Back in those days, university clubs and societies were allocated a budget each year based on the number of paid-up members that they had and the travel and equipment that they estimated they would need. Fortunately, at the beginning of each academic year, lots of keen, impressionable newcomers would eagerly sign up for rock climbing. As a club, we tried to be as welcoming and encouraging as possible, but the vast majority never made it past the first Freshers' Meet – usually a coach trip to Stanage or Froggat in the Peak. This meant that we attracted a huge budget for kit and transport at the weekends for the handful of members who stayed to use it.

Most weekends we'd hire a minibus, or even just a car, to take us off to the

Dales, the Peak or the Lakes. The university would pay for the hire and for the fuel, provided you had a receipt of course. We did discover one garage, just outside York, that also sold food and drink and would happily put it all down on the receipt under "fuel". In the winter months, just because the crags were wet and climbing wasn't an option, we saw no reason to stay in York. More often than not, we'd head to the Dales and go caving or just get out for a bit of a walk. The main attraction was a night in the pub.

A normal weekend might go something like this: Saturday morning head off to the Dales, meet up with some of Dunc's mates from Keighley (Moose, Charlie, Lofty, Stuart) and go climbing or, if wet, play around underground in the Ingleton area. Evening would be spent in the Marton Arms, Thornton-in-Lonsdale, just outside Ingleton. At one point they used to hold a disco in the back bar, which meant additional entertainment as well as extended drinking hours. At the end of one night, one of our number, Tom ('Bombadil') Gray was stood at the bar as the premises emptied. With his head resting on a hand and elbow on the bar, he looked much the worse for wear. We watched in great amusement as his elbow slipped sideways on the beer-soaked bar-top and he took a couple of steps sideways to stay upright and repeat the routine, slipping and staggering the full length of the bar, accelerating as he went, until abruptly dropping off the end and landing in a crumpled heap on the floor – time to leave.

Tom was a tall, big-boned, rangy chap with a very quiet manner and was a bit of an enigma. We never saw him around campus but he never missed a climbing meet. He always turned up, said very little and got hammered afterwards in the pub. He was also a pretty useful climber during the days at the crag. He was a really nice guy but after three years at university none of us knew a thing about him and none of us have seen or heard from him since.

When we were finally thrown out of the pub at closing time on those Saturday nights it was a simple stagger across the road to the church opposite. Its spacious porch was a great place to bed down for the night. Next day, after breakfast in Ingleton, we'd once again find something to do, dependant on the weather and often still suffering from the night before. Once the day's activities were over, we would be back into the minibus or car for a rather circuitous trip back to York. First stop would be my mum's in Burnley, not exactly en route but she was always pleased to see us and would knock up a large batch of scones for afternoon tea. Next up would be a drive "ovver t'erders" ("over the moors past the Herder's Inn near Laneshaw Bridge") to Yorkshire for an evening session in the Fleece, Haworth. Once all but the allocated driver had downed a skinful of Timothy Taylor's it was back to York, via a stop-off in Bradford for a curry. Those curry houses must be some of the best in the world – the fact that they're always full of Yorkshire-Asian customers is testament to that. Our most regular haunts were the Kashmir and the Kismet, both definitely of the no-frills variety. The Kashmir was a plain, basement room, accessed by a set of dingy steps and lit by strip lights with bare, Formica-topped tables. Each curry arrived in a bowl without cutlery, just three chapatis to eat it with, and it always tasted superb. We'd arrive back at uni very late on the Sunday night ready for another week before starting all over again.

Not all our club activities went according to plan. A small group of us took a trip to Langdale in the Lake District for a weekend during the winter of my second year. I can't remember everyone that was there but the group definitely included me and Dunc, both confident that we knew what we were doing, familiar with the area and reasonably well equipped; young Mairi, equipped with a pair of trendy Kicker boots; and Tony Stirland, a Sociology student from Preston, part of our wider circle of friends, definitely not a climber or even much of a walker, although he became Secretary of the climbing club, wearing his usual donkey jacket.

We planned a simple walk up Mickleden towards Rossett Gill at the head of the valley, to then cut directly up the hillside to Bowfell Buttress and up the wide, snow-filled gully to its left. This would put us on the summit of Bowfell from where we could simply follow the path down the Band and back to the Old Dungeon Ghyll bar. All went well to start with. It was a good day out and much fun was had in the considerable accumulations of snow, particularly in the gully. We reached the top in reasonable time but were shrouded in thick mist by now with visibility severely restricted. No problem, it was an easy descent and Dunc and I both agreed we were heading in the right direction. Sometime later, after much descending, a huge, majestic crag loomed out of the murk. "Heck, what's that?" we asked each other. It shouldn't have been there. "Oh no! It's East Buttress on Scafell!" Impressive as it always is to see this fabulous climbing venue, seeing it at that point was definitely not good news. It dawned on us that we'd taken the wrong direction off Bowfell and were now in the upper reaches of Eskdale. "Err, sorry guys, but we aren't quite where we should be".

The rest of the team didn't appear too despondent, apart from Tony who had already walked more that day than he had in the previous month, because they had no idea of the implications. The return slog involved a trudge through the snow down Mosedale to Cockley Beck then up one side of Wrynose Pass and down the other to Little Langdale before having to get from there over into Great Langdale. Added to the distance, we had a significant amount of snow, which was completely obliterating the tarmac on Wrynose. By the time we got to Little Langdale, we were facing a serious mutiny so the very welcome decision was made to head to the Three Shires pub in the village in the hope of finding a lift. We all made it back unscathed, but it was a long, weary walk in shocking conditions.

On another winter weekend a similar group, this time including Nick Velissarides (nicknamed 'Scoop' by Phil, for his student journalism) went on a trip to Glencoe. I'd arranged with John Wilson that he'd drive over from Perth and meet us at the Clachaig. He and I were keen to ski a couple of the gullies on Stob Coire Nan Lochan. We walked up from the valley on a glorious day with a good snowpack. We were mostly well equipped and suitably clothed for the mountain environment, all except Nick who was wearing wellington boots and a gabardine mac, carrying his provisions for the day, not in a rucksack like most, but in a Sainsbury's carrier bag. I remember it was a Sainsbury's bag because we thought that quite posh at the time – but then Nick was from the south country.

We made our way up Broad Gully, a wide, snowy slope of very easy gradient. At the top, John and I changed into ski boots and clipped into our ski bindings for the descent. Easy as it was, it's always a thrill to be skiing in such a place, with the gully walls and proper mountain terrain that makes the gradient feel much steeper than it really is. On our way down we passed a couple who were ascending, roped up. Our ski descent past them might have made them think twice about the need for so much security, but that was very soon overshadowed when Nick came hurtling down sat on his plastic carrier bag with mac flapping behind him, whooping with delight.

When the better weather arrived, we'd make the most of it with more trips, often to the Lakes or to North Wales. First thing in the Easter holidays, Dunc, Phil and I headed down to Pembroke for the week. It was my first visit and it was Heaven – so many routes, all within easy access and we had good weather, too. I can't remember how we got there but it must have been in Dunc's Escort van as it certainly wouldn't have been Phil's Capri (too precious for a climbing trip). The climbing was brilliant, we got loads done, but what stands out most in my memory of that trip was the three of us, all sharing a single tent and each one of

John Wilson (L) and Nick ready for a descent of Broad Gully, Stob Coire nan Lochan, Glencoe

us trying to out-do the others in refusing to wash. Eventually Dunc broke and stormed off for a shower in disgust. Loser!

That was the first week, to be followed almost immediately by a return trip with Neil Foster and a couple of other Sheffield hot shots. Neil was a student in Sheffield by then. He was climbing really well by now and between us we amassed a big tick-list. For me, it was great to lead my own routes, up to E3, but also to get the chance to second up some harder routes that I wouldn't otherwise have had the chance to be on at that point. Being on harder terrain and climbing with people who are much better than you is a great way to raise your own standard. On this second trip we had initially planned to camp. On arrival, on our first night, I suggested we replicate our habit of kipping in the church porch as had proved so successful through the winter in the Dales. There is a very pleasant, small church at Bosherston. Lo and behold! A gift from above, the church door was open so we proceeded to make very comfortable 'beds' on the beautifully embroidered kneelers between the pews. Being sure to be up early with our beds tidied away, we were out on the crags again, repeating the same procedure every night that week. The climbing highlight for me that week was *Pleasure Dome*, an E3 on Stennis Head. What an amazing route – three stars in the little notebook.

That was two weeks' climbing already and I was on a roll. After a couple of trips to Malham with Neil, it was down to Llanberis with Richard Cooper and Sarah Clarke, sister of the super-talented climber Alan Clarke who died tragically young. The classic climbs kept falling that week: *Left Wall* and *Memory Lane* on the Cromlech and *Stroll On* down the Pass at the Grochan. The latter was a very tough route and it should have taught me a valuable lesson. At E3 6a it is well protected but pretty strenuous all the way. There is one particularly hard move which I managed without too much difficulty. Having done the crux I ignored the remaining runner placements, choosing instead to head for the top as fast as I could. But it kept going all the way, including after the 'hard moves', as I discovered as my fingers uncurled from the finishing holds and I plummeted down to below the crux. Despite moments like this one, that charge for the top became quite characteristic for me and although it paid-off 99 per cent of the time, saving time and energy placing gear, just occasionally it would bite me on the backside. Next time up – a few moments later – I added a couple of extra wires and, knowing what was coming, made it to the top without further drama.

Back to York and the summer term. My trusty notebook reminds me that we had weekend trips through the summer term to Curbar and Froggatt, Ilkley, several trips to Malham, Hodge Close and Pavey Ark in the Lakes, along with a trip to Llanberis and Gogarth in North Wales. It was a time of great exploration for me, visiting many of these tremendous crags for the first time. I could also feel myself getting stronger, comfortably climbing any E3 and the occasional E4 and also soloing a lot of routes up to E2.

A big change for me at that time came when I bought my first motorbike, an old Honda 125cc but good enough to get me out to local crags for an evening bouldering or soloing. At that point, I was building up my strength and fitness just by climbing as often as I could. Climbing walls were very rudimentary and most of us, outside the Sheffield elite, had no real concept of 'training' for climbing. We did have a wall at York and we used it as best we could. It was typical of the time – an end wall of the sports hall with a few bricks missing and some extra lumps of rock cemented into place.

This was 1983 and the greatly anticipated *Extreme Rock* was in preparation. My old school mate, Neil Foster, was keen to be in on the action. He'd arranged with Bernard Newman, the compiler of the book, that we'd have a trip to Scafell to climb *Shere Khan* so that Bernard could get the photos for 'the book'.

The trip didn't get off to the best start. The plan was that I would drive up from Burnley to Neil's parents' house in Caton, outside Lancaster, on my trusty motorbike. Not so trusty as it turned out. Something was wrong and I carefully and slowly nursed it along until I got as far as Hellifield on the A65 where it finally packed in. There was no option but to abandon the bike in a layby and hitch the rest of the way. Hitching, with a motorbike helmet, I soon discovered, can result in some very exciting lifts. Cars weren't stopping but the next bike to come past did. It was a huge, powerful Moto Guzzi, driven by someone who clearly enjoyed the power, knew how to handle it and was keen to share that enjoyment with his temporary passenger. We flew up that road and, in what seemed like moments, I was dropped off just outside Kirkby Lonsdale, only for the same experience to be repeated for the ride down the Lune Valley on the back of another big beast. Despite the fast lifts, I was still running late, and Neil was rightly none too pleased and had no sympathy for my poor bike abandoned in Yorkshire. From his parents' place we drove up to meet Bernard at a pub in Eskdale before heading over to Wasdale to stay at the Fell & Rock hut at Brackenclose. In order to get the light on our route, which lies at the right-hand end of the East Buttress, we had a crack-of-dawn start and were on the route early in the morning. Neil did a great job of leading it, Bernard got his photos and I followed. It was still only mid-morning and a beautiful day at one of the finest crags in England –

Nick on the fabulous top pitch of *Dry Gasp*, Upper Falcon, Borrowdale. Note the selection of equipment on the harness 📷 John Wilson

what next?

Climbing preferences were very different in those days. Everyone was climbing Trad. Sports routes were only just starting to appear on the limestone in Yorkshire and the Peak. It'd been a great forecast for the weekend and so Scafell was mobbed. Everyone was there. All the strong Lakes teams were out plus Fawcett, Berzins, Livesey and a host of others. It was a *Who's Who* of 80s climbing and many big lines were being ascended, in some cases by multiple teams.

Neil was in his element. At that time he did have a bad habit of wanting to talk to all the current stars of the climbing scene, getting the low-down on the routes they'd done – how they found them, the crux sequences and any top tips. And he'd just made a good ascent of a fairly tough route himself. He was justified in having a breather. I, on the other hand, just wanted to climb. "Neil, can we do another route please?" "Yes, yes. Let me just watch Ron do this route first." This went on for most of the day until, eventually I dragged him round to the Main Crag so that I could lead *Saxon*, as the evening light finally reached that part of the crag.

The rest of the summer followed a familiar pattern of time spent between home, Lancaster, the Lakes, Wales and Yorkshire. The stand-out route of that summer for me was *Capital Punishment*, an E4 on Suicide Wall, Idwal, on a very productive trip to North Wales with a friend of Dunc's from Keighley, John Whittock. It was fingery, just about vertical and quite runout – perfect!

The second year at university followed a similar pattern. There were new additions to the climbing club including the irrepressible 'Big' John Austin. John was no lightweight and he'd a personality and a mouth to match the size of his frame. His wasn't the ideal physique for a climber, maybe, but his phenomenal strength was more than enough to make up for it. Most remarkable was his partner 'Little' Judy Harris. It's hard to imagine a more mis-matched climbing team. John was large and noisy – everyone knew when he was around – but the diminutive Judy seemed quiet as a mouse. I was always worried that if John were to take a significant leader-fall, Judy would be pulled through her belay device, Tom & Jerry style. Thankfully that never happened and Judy later moved to the Lakes as an ecologist for the Lake District National Park and married Paul Clavey with whom I have climbed many routes over the years. She also became godmother to our daughter Flora.

The following Easter break, Dunc and I returned to Pembroke for another route-fest all along the coast. In the area at the same time was a strong team from the Lakes that we kept bumping into. Among them was Bill Birkett. I didn't know Bill personally at the time, but of course knew the books he'd written, and I'd read his monthly Lakes reports in the climbing press. I was impressed: "He writes in the magazines, he must be really good". The reputation of the others in the team also preceded them. I was interested in what they were doing and how they were getting on – after all, we should grab any opportunities we can to watch and learn from others (though maybe not to the extent of Neil). As the week went on and we watched this illustrious team in action, I couldn't help becoming slightly disillusioned – they were doing similar routes to ours.

The bubble finally burst as I watched Bill climb *Pleasure Dome*, excited at the prospect of an impressive performance. I'd done this superb route myself the year before and, quite frankly, I'd cruised up it, barely stopping to place all the good gear that's available. As I watched this Lakeland legend battle his way up slowly, much more slowly than I had, I was somewhat confused. But he did get up and I got some photos of him in the process.

That experience was to have a profound effect on me and helped me make my next major breakthrough a couple of months later. We were back at uni for the summer term and, as usual, one weekend we had a trip to the Lakes planned. We'd recently been to North Wales and I was climbing well, having had no problem on *Resurrection* on the Cromlech or *Vulture* and *Cream* at Tremodog – all good, well-known E4 routes. So I was feeling strong and looking for a challenge. On the Friday night when we arrived, we went to the Golden Rule in Ambleside – the best place to plan the weekend – and bumped into Bill Birkett there. I went over to talk to him and to let him know about the photos I had from his ascent of *Pleasure Dome*.

In the course of the evening, he explained that he'd recently done *Footless Crow* on Goat Crag, Borrowdale. This is a big route. At the time of its first ascent by Pete Livesey in 1974 it was a significant breakthrough and thought to be one of the hardest routes in the Lakes. Ten years later it hadn't got any easier. Bill went on to talk me through the crux sequence in remarkable detail with particular mention of an essential, small foothold down on the left. "Oh, and by the way, it is much better if you do the whole route in one big pitch" added Bill. This is where I have to be honest and own up to my youthful arrogance. Having watched Bill climb *Pleasure Dome* all I could think was "if he can get up Footless Crow, then so can I!"

I now know that Bill was one of the strongest climbers out there and could hang around for ever and of course he'd a long history of impressive first ascents

Bill Birkett climbing *Pleasure Dome*, Stennis Head, Pembroke

behind him. However, the decision was made, I now had a plan. *How hard could it be?* The next day, full of enthusiasm and self-belief, as well as the essential beta (see Glossary for the distinctive meaning of this word to climbers), Phil and I made our way up to the crag and I launched myself onto it. It went like clockwork. The crucial, small foothold down on the left was exactly as Bill had described and it did the job, getting me over the crux like a dream.

Just to add to the adventure of our ascent, after I'd got through the crux sequence, Phil shouted up from the ground: "Er, I don't want to worry you, but you haven't got much rope left". We'd taken Bill's advice and done the route in one long rope-length, only it turned out that our rope wasn't quite long enough to reach the top! "You'll have to start climbing then," I shouted back down. I was on the hardest lead of my life and now I was no longer being belayed. Phil was climbing the hard, 6a first pitch of *Athanor* and he wasn't being belayed either – what could possibly go wrong? As it was, I got up the easier ground above without any problem and was able to tie myself onto a tree and start to belay a now somewhat-concerned second.

I sat at the top elated with what I'd achieved. As I rested there, belaying Phil, someone came over. I think they'd just finished *Bitter Oasis* and had been watching me climb. "So, what do you reckon?" he asked. "Is it 6b?" "I don't know," I replied. "I've never done 6b before." "Oh… right… but it is E5 isn't it?" he went on. "I couldn't tell you for sure, I've never done one of those before either!" "Bloody hell, it's not a bad one to start on, mate". I was delighted – what a massive breakthrough.

Later that day we went across the valley to Black Crag and I did *Grand Alliance* but not without some drama. I was battling my way up the thin upper section above the roof when, feeling a bit fatigued from the morning's exertion, I parted company with the rock, landing back at the lip of the overhang. "I think I can see where I went wrong," I shouted to Phil and quickly jumped back on to find success on the second attempt.

We followed this up the next day with *Nagasaki Grooves* on Great End Crag. The comments in my notebook for this superb Livesey route say it all:

"*Nagasaki Grooves*, E4 6b, Great End Crag, Phil Baines (***) – This route is the technically hardest and most sustained route I have ever done. It is probably also the best."

What a weekend!

We'd had another tough session in the Golden Rule, followed by a rough 'doss' in the park shelter at Ambleside before an early start. Nick had been blabbering to some old fella all night, judging by the hand and foot gestures it was obviously all about climbing. I remember a few hazy comments from Nick about doing *Footless Crow* before I passed out. Something about "If that old bloke can do it, I can."

So here we were at the bottom of the *Athanor* groove on Goat Crag. I'd been here before a few years earlier, pushing my grade on *Praying Mantis* (E1) just over to the left. We were pushing the grade today all right. No one I knew had done this or even attempted it. It was top of the graded list in the Borrowdale guidebook, possibly the hardest route in the Lakes and one of the hardest in Britain. Strangely, none of this really mattered at the time. I was nursing a bit of a hangover, sweating from the rapid walk in and very focused on the fact that our ropes might not be quite long enough!

"Are you sure about these ropes?" I asked. Nick was totally fired and clearly not really listening. "It'll be fine, you can start climbing if they do run out, just don't fall off."

"OK, it's not brilliant but I'm alright with that if you are. I'll belay as high as I can in the groove and tie on to the other end now. All ready to go?"

Clearly, he wasn't fazed. We were doing this regardless. This was typical Nick, focussed on the objective, competitive as hell!

"Right let's get on with it then. There's a crucial tiny foothold way out to the left at the flakes. Bill told me about it in the pub last night."

So that's what the conversation in the pub last night was all about.

In no time at all he'd got up to the steep section and, barely pausing to draw breath, he'd made the crux moves through the steepest section and onto the upper wall. Then the rope ran out.

"That's it!... the rope's gone, are you close?"

He shouted down something about me starting to climb. I'm stone cold sober now! My eyes are on stalks and I can't mess up in this groove. "OK, I'm setting off now, take it easy, let me know when you hit the belay." Gulp... Why do I let him get me into these situations?

In comparison to the sombre and serious Goat, Black Crag across the valley was like a holiday camp. Bright sunshine, big open buttresses, warm, bone-dry rock. There was a party atmosphere in the air, the crag was littered with groups of climbers all lapping up the good weather.

The stance under the roof was a pain in the ass. I couldn't see what was going on. The kid from Manchester on a route to my left had a good view though.

"Your mate's starting to blow a bit, you might..."

Wham! the rope pulls tight... A shout, then a large cloud of chalk billows over the lip of the roof as Nick impacts with the wall above and blows out his chalk bag.

Nick shouts down "Got that sequence wrong." I can tell he's laughing about it from the tone in his voice, but I can't see him.

"He's fine, took a bit of a winger but he's OK," the kid from Manchester reports.

"Weren't you fellas over at Goat this morning? Get anything done?" he asks.

"Footless" I tell him.

The kid is well impressed, slightly taken aback. I can see he has a million questions.

He gapes up at Nick. "And now he's here trying this? He must be knackered."

"OK, I'm back on, watch us Phil." Business as usual. As soon as the tank's refilled Nick is off like a rocket, a couple of grunts and it's all over. I can barely pay the rope out fast enough.

I'm now above the roof, asking for a tiny bit of slack so I can get the runner out before the crux sequence. Its welded into the slot from the earlier fall. A shout of advice from above – he can sense my unease – "Start with your right hand then you'll finish in the correct position for the big pull up."

I look at the tiny chalked undercut holds leading left and glance down at the black scuffs used for footholds. I start to laugh out loud as I catch sight of the big white smack of chalk on the wall below my feet. Madness, brilliant madness!

Phil Baines

By the time the long summer holiday arrived I was on fire. I spent the whole summer with Iwan in Llanberis, albeit I had to take a couple of days every fortnight to head back to Burnley to sign on. These were halcyon days for students and climbers when you could turn up at the job centre, look at the limited jobs available, recognise that none were suitable and get a dole cheque sent through. It wasn't so good for those that either wanted or needed a job.

The summer was fantastic. Buoyed up by my ascent of *Footless Crow*, I did *Right Wall* on the Cromlech – much easier but still a big tick. I've always said to people subsequently, the hardest thing about *Right Wall* is its name. Technically it's very straightforward and well-enough protected, but it's still intimidating. During those months I climbed a lot with Iwan and some of his local mates, Fred Hall of iconic climbing kit company DMM, and, mostly, Tom Thomas. I got the distinct impression that they were delighted to have an ever-keen, young gun they could fire up routes and be happy to get a rope on. Pretty much every day we headed up to the Pass, round to Tremadog, out to Gogarth or, occasionally, to more esoteric venues such as Castell Cidwm or Crafnant. One of the routes that stands out now, though at the time I saw it as just another good, on-sight lead, was the technical and, for some, puzzling groove of *Zukator* at Tremadog, graded E4 6b. Many years later I heard a presentation at the Kendal Mountain Festival by Jerry Moffatt around the time his book *Revelations* came out. He told a fantastic story of how he and Andy Pollitt had kept trying and failing to get up *Zukator* and how Pete Livesey had completely sand-bagged them one day with totally inaccurate beta on how to do the crux – resulting in yet another failure. All that I could think was: "What were they playing at?"

At some point, around this time, I had a very close call. I'd borrowed my mother's car and driven from home in Burnley over to Earl Crag, just inside Yorkshire. It was a lovely day and my aim was to do some bouldering and solo a few routes on this quiet gritstone edge, looking north towards Airedale and Skipton. I made my way along the edge, finding good-looking lines to climb and boulder problems to try, just myself for company, equipped with boots, chalk bag and a beer towel as a launch pad, in the days before padded bouldering mats. Eventually I arrived beneath the classic line of *Early Riser*, E5 6a. At the time I wasn't aware of its reputation, it just looked fabulous – a narrow, steepening ramp heads rightwards up an otherwise vertical wall providing a very delicate and precarious set of moves. It was begging to be climbed and how hard could it be? I had to give it a go!

I got onto the ramp and balanced my way up using the marginal smears on the outer edge of the ramp with finger and thumb pinching a tiny pebble on the vertical wall to the left. I was at the crux of the route, one move from the security of the top when a foot slipped. It all happened so quickly – I fell onto the heathery ledge below, landing on my feet but was unable to prevent myself from being carried over the edge, head-first, to the slope beneath. I landed with quite a thump, grazing my forehead and winding myself. It was only when I'd got my breath back and was able to stand up that I could see the couple of boulders I'd somehow slalomed around. That could have ended very badly. Time to go home. If I hadn't fallen, that would have been quite an early on-sight ascent.

To bring home just how fortunate I'd been, it was around this time that my old schoolfriend, Neil Foster, sustained a serious injury. At the time he was climbing incredibly well and seemed unstoppable. He was right up there with the best. Building on his immense natural talent and innate strength, he'd created numerous, very hard new routes on the grit in Derbyshire including, ironically, *Ulysses or Bust*. At the time of the accident he was trying to on-sight Jerry Moffatt's test-piece *Ulysses' Bow*. He fell from the crux moves at the top resulting in terrible injuries to his ankle. If it hadn't been for that injury, we can only speculate at just how far his climbing might have gone.

I've said that we sometimes hired a car, rather than a minibus, for our trips away and so we did one weekend towards the end of my time at York. There were four of us: Me, Dunc, Nick Velissarides and Mairi Macleod. When I turned up to collect the car, it was a brand-new Ford Orion, the recently released, saloon version of the Escort. Our plan was to drive down to Manchester University for a party, stopping at Haworth on the way to pick up Dunc's brother Stuart and his mate Tim 'Lofty' Lofthouse, another regular climbing companion, who lived just down the road from Dunc's mum. I drove to Haworth where the other two crammed in and Dunc took over the driving to get us down to Manchester.

The party turned out to be one of those rather disappointing affairs and late in the evening we were looking for something better to do. "I know," said Stuart. "Moose and Charlie are camping at Ribblehead this weekend. Let's go there". It was the only suggestion anyone had so off we headed, this time with Stuart at the wheel. After weaving our way across Lancashire and into Yorkshire on tiny roads we finally made our way up past Horton-in-Ribblesdale to arrive at Ribblehead in the middle of the night. There, as expected, were the two one-man tents of our acquaintances. Not entirely delighted to see us at that time, they still made us a brew. It wasn't long after we'd arrived that someone asked the obvious question: "Where are we going to stay?" We had sleeping bags but no tents as we were supposed to be crashing out on someone's floor in Manchester. It was a cold, frosty night. There was no way that six of us would squeeze into two small and fully occupied tents and a night in the car was equally unappealing. "I've got it!" someone chipped in. "We could drive to Ambleside and sleep in the park shelter." This was a familiar refuge from previous trips to the Lakes and we all thought it a great suggestion. "I'll drive," said the other Nick.

It should be made clear at this point that as over-enthusiastic young lads, our driving couldn't be described as sedate, especially given the chance to test a smart new car. One advantage we did have was prior knowledge: I knew the roads from York to Haworth very well, Dunc knew the route from Haworth to Manchester and Stuart... well, he could give any Formula One champion a run for their money wherever he drove. There was a clear pattern.

Nick, or 'Scoop', on the other hand, was a refugee from the south country and still unable even to place Yorkshire on a map of Britain. He had no idea. He didn't know the roads at all but sadly the pace of driving had already been set by the time he got behind the wheel and we all piled back in. Mairi was sat in the passenger seat alongside Nick and Stuart, Lofty and Duncan were squeezed in the back, with me wedged on Dunc's lap. The road from Ribblehead towards Ingleton is almost dead straight but there's a sharp right-hand bend about half a mile short of the village. Nick didn't know this. He was going too fast. We didn't make it! We left the road, hit the dry-stone wall and the car flipped over onto its roof. When the car landed back on the road, upside-down, Dunc and I were both fine having been pretty well wedged but Lofty's and Stuart's heads went through the shattered rear window and hit the tarmac.

We crawled out of the wreckage and dragged the other two out of the back window. Nick and Mairi were able to squeeze out of their own side windows, a bit battered and bruised but miraculously nothing worse. Stuart was a bit dazed and had a lot of blood coming out of a head-wound while Lofty, despite also bleeding profusely, appeared fine. In fact it was Lofty who dashed off to the village to get help – in the wrong direction! Thankfully, another car came down the valley, stopping to pick him up by White Scar Caves. The local policeman (remember those?) was called out and we eventually got taken by ambulance down to Airedale General Hospital near Keighley for a check-over and patch-up for those that needed it. I saw Lofty many years later after he'd moved to the Lakes. He told me then that he still would occasionally find tiny pieces of glass or gravel embedded in his scalp.

The car was due back on Monday morning. I went into the car hire office rather sheepishly and explained that I didn't have it. "Where is it?" he asked, reasonably enough. "It's at Ingleton, beyond Settle, near the Lancashire border," I explained. "But it'll take me ages to get it back from there," he sighed. "It'll take longer than you think, I'm afraid. It's a complete write-off!" I told him with just a hint of a smirk. "Bugger, that's the third this morning!" he said with some resignation.

And so, three excellent years of student life was drawing to a close. I'd done a lot of climbing, had a lot of fun and many adventures – and got my degree in the process. I would continue to climb with Duncan, Phil and Lofty over the coming years. In the meantime, the party was over and things were about to get quite a bit more serious.

QUESTION

Q *What impact did the fall at Earl Crag have on your climbing?*

A Certainly at the time it shook me up. I realised how lucky I'd been. The outcome could have been really serious, particularly as there was nobody else at the crag when I fell. Neil's accident brought that home as well. But long-term I'm not so sure that it really changed my behaviour. In the same way I was more wary on my bike after I'd broken my hip, to start with anyway. A year later I came off again on very wet, greasy roads in Mallorca and landed on exactly the same part of my leg – the new gravel rash was in exactly the same spot as the previous one.

5 - Wargames
7B CHAPEL HEAD SCAR
Time at Sandhurst

"And now for something completely different!" to quote Monty Python. I wondered how different it might be – going from the laid-back, liberal-minded university life to the rigid, authoritarian regime of military training. I wasn't completely new to the army's way of thinking. After all, I'd spent five years in the cadet force at school, even ending up as Senior Cadet and winning a Speech Day prize for it. The visiting speaker that year was LRGS old-boy Cecil Parkinson, a member of Margaret Thatcher's Conservative government. He was later forced to resign due to an affair with his secretary, which caused quite a storm at the time. The prize was a book of my choice and the book I chose was the current *Yorkshire Limestone* guide published by the Yorkshire Mountaineering Club. Through those cadet years, I'd been away on many field days, camps, training courses and visits to military units. I could lead a section attack and I knew my way round several weapon systems. And at that moment, the end of the summer of 1985, I was as fit as I'd ever been and doing a lot of running, in addition to my usual climbing and karate, to prepare for the coming ordeal.

Before starting at Sandhurst, I was given the opportunity to go for one last visit to my future regiment. At the time, they were doing a valiant job, based in West Germany as part of the BAOR (British Army of the Rhine), holding back the Russian hordes. We were still in the throes of the Cold War and the Red Menace was expected at any moment! They never did come, of course, and many years later when I was working in Russia, I had a laugh about it with a factory safety officer who'd been in the Russian Army. I told him how I'd spent several years in West Germany waiting for him and his comrades to come storming over the border. "I spent my time in East Germany," he explained. "We were told you might invade any day!"

I didn't have to go on this final familiarisation trip, along with a handful of other, younger POs (Potential Officers), but I couldn't see a reason not to. It was free and what could possibly go wrong? Soon after our arrival at the Battalion's base in Paderborn we were told to change into sports kit. We were going out for a run and fitness session led by the subaltern who was overseeing our visit and organising our activities for this week. It was very apparent from the start that this young officer, only fairly recently qualified himself, had an over-inflated ego. His sole aim during that initial bout of exercise was to lord it over us all and astound us with his level of fitness.

It didn't all go according to plan. I was able to keep up with him comfortably, even if the younger lads were struggling. As we approached the entrance to the camp he allowed everyone to regroup before challenging us all to a final race to the Officers' Mess at the far end of the camp, some 500m away. But I beat him back there, which wasn't in the script.

Sadly, this idiot's misjudgement was to have a much more serious effect later in the week. On the last night, I and the other lads went out on the town and enjoyed a few too many beers, little knowing that the next day there was to be something of a grand finale to our visit. At daybreak the next morning, hungover and dehydrated, we were dragged out of our beds with much shouting and hollering. Blokes in balaclavas put empty sandbags over our heads before bundling us into the back of a truck and then driving off to a remote part of the nearby military training area. There the ruse was uncovered – we hadn't really been kidnapped by terrorists. Well, fancy that! I guess it provided some amusement for our jumped-up chaperone and the NCOs he'd enrolled in his game.

Next up was some orienteering to test our map-reading skills. It wasn't meant to be competitive, but I couldn't help myself running round the entire course and visiting all the checkpoints. It's worth highlighting that this was late summer on the North German plain. It was a scorcher. By way of refreshment, we were provided with a single mug of tea to share between two after the orienteering. That afternoon we had more tactical exercises – fire and manoeuvre, one person providing fire cover while the other dashes forward and throws themselves down behind cover to do the same for his partner. It was very hot and sweaty – still without additional fluids.

The culmination of the day was a stretcher-run. One of the sergeants (the largest!) had supposedly been shot and wounded during the previous activity so we had to carry him on a stretcher back to the transport as fast as possible. There were five of us rotating round the stretcher, with four carrying and one getting a chance to recover except I didn't take my turns to rest. I was far stronger than the others, had adopted a leadership role and recognised that their need for rest was greater. I just kept going – until I didn't. Next thing I knew I was waking up in hospital with no idea of how I'd got there.

It's hardly surprising when you think about it – lots of beer the night before, up at the crack of dawn with nothing to eat or drink, running round an orienteering course, running about in full uniform carrying a rifle and webbing in the midday sun and putting in maximum effort carrying some fat bloke on a stretcher – all with half a cup of tea to drink. Heat exhaustion. It doesn't take a lot of working out. A few days later I was out of hospital and, so I thought, back to normal. I left the hospital and travelled home. It was now time to head off to Sandhurst.

The Royal Military Academy Sandhurst – "A global centre of excellence for leadership", "A world-leading military training academy"… I think I must've gone to a different place. The one I went to put the main emphasis on mindless nonsense and endless hours of drill practice. All these years later, I'm still struggling to see the value of all that time spent in a weird form of line-dancing while sergeant majors and colour sergeants tried to humiliate you with pointless abuse about your ironing and boot-polishing skills, always remembering to call you 'Sir' in the most sarcastic tone possible. We all expected it to be hard work. Military training needs to be tough. You want your military personnel, especially the officers to be, not only physically fit but tough, resilient, able to rough it. But why all the rest of it?

Much of the nonsense persisted, to varying degrees, for the whole time we were at Sandhurst but it was served up in extra large doses in those first five weeks. There was no let-up and no free time. Every moment of every day was occupied with a mix of weapons training, drill, physical exercise, communications, more drill, first aid, map reading, even more drill… And once the lessons and exercises were over, it was back to our rooms in Victory College to spend hours ironing, polishing and preparing kit for the next day. Meals consisted of huge mounds of carbs and protein wolfed down at lightning speed. There was never time to savour it, which was a shame because it was actually very good. At any moment you could have your kit or room inspected so that the staff could delight in finding a solitary hair in a sink plughole or a speck of dust on the most inaccessible surface in an otherwise spotless room. If they did, all your kit, including all those carefully ironed shirts and uniforms, was liable to be hurled in a heap on the floor or even out of the window. Character building apparently!

Four weeks into the course was the day of the annual Academy cross-country race. This was an inter-college affair involving all students: those of us on the Graduate Course as well as the non-graduate officer cadets on the SMC (Standard Military Course, or Simple Minds Course as we called it). It was a very hot afternoon on what had turned into a glorious Indian Summer. Little did I know that my recent experience in Germany was about to come back and haunt me. I liked cross-country, I was good at it and I was going to give it my best shot.

From the start I raced out to the head of the pack and continued to lead the way. As we progressed round the tough, hilly course, over the sandy terrain of the training area within the grounds, it started to really hurt – of course it did, I

The Russians are far more impressive when it comes to marching –Tomb of the Unknown Soldier, Kremlin Wall, Moscow

How Hard Can It Be?

was trying hard and I was maintaining my lead. My legs and arms started to feel incredibly heavy – well that was normal, I was setting a cracking pace. I don't remember the lights going out. I don't remember carrying straight on at a bend in the track before collapsing in a crumpled heap. The next thing I did know was that I was lying in a hospital bed, on a special, water-cooled mattress intended to get my temperature down. The medical staff started to ask all sorts of surprisingly challenging questions, such as: "What were you doing at the time?" as I lay there in my shorts and running vest. "We were doing some weapons training out on the ranges" I confidently replied. "What day is it?" "No idea." "What year is it?" "Still no idea." "What is your home phone number?" "Sorry, I can't remember." I started to find my lack of recall quite amusing. I genuinely had no recollection of any of it and was unable to answer anything until: "What is your Army Number?" "521921." No problem. That's army training for you!

At some point over the following days, once I'd regained my senses, I was asked whether anything like this had ever happened before. When I explained about the previous incident in Germany six weeks earlier, the medical staff were horrified. "It takes months for your body to get back to the correct electrolyte levels. Why are you even on this course, let alone running a cross-country race?"

For me, this episode shows the army in its true colours. Remember, I was trying my utmost to do well in that cross-country race. I didn't have to but I wanted to do well, for myself and for the college. If I'd managed to cling on to the end and won, that would've been heralded as a great success. And of course that hidden, medical condition was entirely the result of the thoughtless incompetence of a serving officer, completely out of my control.

So that was it for my part in the autumn 1985 intake. I was to be 'back-termed' and start all over again with the next batch four months later. Of course, I couldn't leave. I joined a select band of the sick, lame and lazy that had similarly fallen by the wayside. There, the unseen nature of my temporary condition proved to be a problem for some. It was fine for colleagues who were sporting a plaster splint on a limb or hobbling around on crutches or those with visible stitches. Less than a week after the incident, in myself I felt absolutely fine. More importantly, to the outside world, I looked as fit and healthy as anyone else. Clearly, the college sergeant major couldn't see beyond this exterior or understand the underlying physiology. It was much easier to make assumptions based on his own prejudices. Never mind the fact that I'd pushed myself to the limits – beyond as it turned out – in an attempt to win that race for his college. If only I'd broken my leg, I would've been a hero. In his eyes I was a waste of space, a malingerer. Thank goodness it wasn't the First World War – he would've probably had me shot!

As it turned out, the delay in my training had no significant impact on my progress and indeed there were a number of clear benefits. The first was that I had time to be shipped off to the Army Education College at Beaconsfield in leafy Berkshire for an intensive German language course, which was to prove extremely valuable later that year. (While I was there, someone saw my name and asked me about my father who'd been based there a few years earlier – a rare 'encounter' with this elusive character.)

The next benefit was more subtle. When I returned to Sandhurst in January, I had a clear advantage over the rest of the intake. I knew the score and what to expect. I'd gone through the pain of most of the initial five-week period. This time round it was much easier. I would often be asleep in bed, getting much-needed rest many hours before others still slaving over the ironing board or trying to assimilate some new information for the following day.

A minor example of the five-week nonsense was something called a 'bed block'. Each person was issued with two sheets and three blankets with which to make up their bed each night. Every morning these items were to be folded in exactly the right formation and left neatly displayed in the centre of the bed. The blankets had three thin lines woven down their length and, naturally, these had to line up with pinpoint precision. All that careful folding was a real pain in the backside and added time to an already tight schedule. But I found a way to

Perfecting that essential military skill – shoe polishing

get round this ridiculous waste of time. Each student officer had their own study bedroom. They were very basic and functional with identical bed, desk and army-issue armchair. I discovered that the armchair had a cavity in the back – just big enough to hide a fleece sleeping bag liner. So I took great pleasure over those first five weeks, in carefully moving my pristine bed block off the bed each night and sleeping in my fleece liner. A triumph for independent thinking and a major psychological victory!

Another bonus of my restart soon came to light. Our rooms had been allocated along the corridor in alphabetical order. My next-door neighbour introduced himself as John Vlasto and, to my delight, he turned out to be a fellow climber. What were the chances? John was well-spoken – very 'south country' – but beneath that posh exterior was a subversive character. He also had a car, a sporty Mini Cooper S. Once we had a bit more freedom, we used to jump in it and escape to the Avon Gorge or Swanage for some climbing. We'd drive out of the grounds in our regulation blazer, grey flannels and college tie only to change at the first opportunity into Ron Hills leggings, T-shirts and Helly Hansen jackets. We did recognise the irony in how we couldn't get out of one uniform quickly enough, only to replace it with another uniform. John and I were similar in other aspects, too. Although we came from quite different backgrounds, I think both of us were fighting our own internal battles against being subsumed into the Sandhurst mindset. Over time I've come to think of John as possibly the most unmilitary person I have ever met.

It was a pleasant surprise to find my next-door neighbour at Sandhurst was a fellow rock climber. The army liked old-school mountaineers with their camps and teams and logistics and heavy boots. It wasn't so keen on 1980s rock climbers with their Lycra and individualism and aversion to authority. Thus, we formed an early bond, spending our weekends on climbing trips here and there.

One weekend, to balance our training in how best to kill people, we joined the New Age Travellers and their Peace Convoy at Stonehenge. As an army-sponsored student, I'd always enjoyed the incongruousness of celebrating the summer solstice with hippies and druids while surrounded by a ring of military police. So Nick and I went off to savour the experience one last time, before our military careers began in earnest.

On the way back, as we were crossing the parade ground, Nick mentioned having seen the northern lights in Canada. I'd never seen them, so asked what they were like. "Oh you know" he said, "imagine you've just taken some acid, how everything starts moving around in different colours". I did know. While the army might just about have tolerated Lycra and individualism, dropping acid was definitely a step too far. This comment cemented a friendship which lasts to this day. Though we are yet to drop acid together.

John Vlasto

As the time at Sandhurst progressed, we got more freedom, although it could never be taken for granted. It was not quite normality, but at least we had the opportunity to get out from time to time. As well as going climbing occasionally, I also made the most of being only a short train-ride from London. I'm no great fan of any city but when it comes to culture, London has a lot on offer. My cultural preferences include opera and ballet (I'm not sure what the sergeant major would've made of that!). At the time it was quite easy to get a 'standing at the back' ticket at the Royal Opera House and I made use of this on a number of occasions.

An even greater cultural highlight of that year and another benefit of being in the area, was going to see Queen perform live at the old Wembley Stadium with 72,000 other people. None of us were to know that we were watching Freddie Mercury's penultimate appearance with the rest of the band. It was phenomenal. An amazing spectacle and an unforgettable atmosphere. Having watched them steal the show at *Live Aid* on TV the previous year, to see them live in the same venue was something else. All through the preceding week at Sandhurst I was on tenterhooks, just praying that there wouldn't be some more mindless nonsense to stop us going.

A rather unmilitary-looking Lt Vlasto after our training, Calanques, South of France

Our course was split into two terms with a break in between, which for us fell around Easter. John and I were keen to get away for a climbing trip and Adrian Rose, who'd just finished his time at Sandhurst, was planning to join us. He'd been on my original intake. This was long before the appearance of the budget airlines and cheap flights were few and far between. The three of us went into the British Airways office on Regent Street in London. "Got any cheap last-minute flights to anywhere?" we asked the girl behind the counter. After a brief search through files and lists, she came back with the suggestion: "How about Yugo-slavia, tomorrow morning, £30 each?" It sounded like a bargain. "Do you think there'll be any climbing?" we asked each other. "Bound to be some limestone" was the general consensus. "Let's go for it!"

Next day, with rucksacks full of gear, we landed in Pula on the Istrian Pen-insula, now part of Croatia, with nothing but blind faith, self-belief and a sense of adventure to get us through. Having found a cheap hotel for the first night, we set out to discover whether there was indeed any climbing to be had. One minor problem – we didn't even know what the language was, let alone how to speak it, although my recently-acquired German turned out useful as the Germans had been holidaying in the area for some time.

It was soon apparent that we were in the wrong part of the country. We didn't know where the right part was, but it certainly wasn't where we were at the time. So we got a bus to Rijeka, the nearest large city, hoping to find someone to point us in the right direction. It seemed that every time we tried to ask about climb-ing, which generally involved some peculiar mime, we got the response "Ah! mountains – Sarajevo". But Sarajevo was miles away and we didn't want moun-tains. We wanted sun-kissed Mediterranean limestone – we just didn't know how to get that across. The Tourist Information Offices weren't much help either, but then I guess a visiting Croat going into the equivalent premises in Liverpool wouldn't be offered a lot of detail about climbing in North Wales. The language barrier continued to provide something of a challenge, but we persisted. In yet another likely-looking office, speaking slowly and carefully in a mix of English and German, we asked one more time: "Do you know where we might find some rock climbing? Not mountains, rock climbing". And finally, we hit the jackpot. "No problem," came the reply, in perfect English, "let me call my husband. He wrote the guidebook."

We were pointed in the direction of Paklenica National Park, further down the coast. Armed with photocopies of the guidebook, we were sorted. It proved to be a great few days of climbing on bolted limestone in a beautiful environ-ment. One day we ventured up to the imposing Anica Kuk for some Trad adventure climbing. We slept in what we assumed was a half-built hotel by the park entrance. The climbing was good, but the overall adventure of the trip was excellent. I'm not entirely sure that we should've even been visiting a Communist Bloc country, still under the influence of the Soviet Union, but I'm glad we did.

Back on the course, it was a matter of keeping your head down, getting on with what was required and trying not to stand out for the wrong reason. I have to say that, on reflection, I am disappointed at the lack of really good leadership or man-management training that was provided. I can't help but think that it could've been so much better. This is supposed to be Sandhurst's Unique Selling Point. I learnt considerably more in the few months after leaving the army, some years later, when I was working in a management training centre – just basic concepts that would've equipped us to fulfil our role so much better like understanding and looking out for the soldiers that we'd be responsible for. 'Leadership' at Sandhurst was all about taking control, giving orders, getting a job done, standing fast and setting an example for others to follow. There's nothing wrong with any of that, but what about listening to and understanding the soldiers for whom we'd be responsible? What about recognising when you don't know the best solution or have got something wrong and being prepared to ask others what they think? Many of the soldiers we were to manage would have had much more experience than us rookie officers. Surely it would be better all round to ask them for their opinion.

Many of the 'man-management' scenarios that were discussed in the few theory sessions we had were very outdated and even patriarchal. I remember one scenario that described how a young officer was walking past a group of soldiers who made some joke about his headgear. What would you do? My own view was something along the lines of have a laugh with them and come back at them with some equally witty remark. The correct answer of course was to stamp down on this disrespectful behaviour, which to me sounds like the sort of response to be expected from General Melchett and Captain Darling in *Blackadder Goes Forth*.

The hugely respected leadership guru John Adair had been an academic based at Sandhurst. One of the models he is best known for is the three overlapping circles that represent the Needs of the Team, the Task and the Individual. The principle being that if you fail to meet any one of these needs you'll detract from the others. If you don't hold the Team together, meet its requirements with good communication, common purpose, structure and cohesion, then the Individuals within that team will suffer, as will the Task – the job in hand. While if you fail to administer to the basic requisites of the Individual, provide them with skills and knowledge along with a sense of belonging, well-being, self-respect and so on, this will not only affect the Individual but also have an effect on the Team as a whole and the Task it is trying to achieve. The concepts are very simple but also very sound and practical. On one occasion we were gathered into a large lecture hall to hear a presentation on leadership from some visiting general. I don't know who it was but got the impression he was someone very senior. He launched into an explanation of how the Falklands conflict of a few years before had been won by great leadership, using John Adair's model – only he completely missed the point! It isn't just getting the individuals together, putting them into teams and then giving them a job to do, it's about addressing the needs of each element.

I found the overall approach to training in the army quite baffling, not just at Sandhurst but also subsequently. You'd be given a new task to perform with only the most basic brief. Because it was new, you'd invariably get it wrong, or at least not entirely correct, at which point you'd be criticised for failing and then shown what you should've done. Why not explain beforehand to give us a chance of getting it right? Maybe it's about the balance of power, but it can certainly be quite demoralising.

Some of the training was great fun and sometimes quite eye-opening. Our

Happy officer cadets digging a trench on exercise at RMAS

Platoon Colour Sergeant (the NCO responsible for most of our training) was a guy called Steve Greenwood. He was from my regiment, which could've gone either way (he might've had even greater expectations of me). Thankfully, I got on well with him. He was definitely one of the good guys. One time we were at Sennybridge in the Brecon Beacons and CSgt Greenwood was supervising John Vlasto and myself as we attacked an enemy foxhole. We were doing the fire and manoeuvre thing, making our way forward, under each other's covering fire, using blank ammunition. It was full action, there was lots of noise and shouting, the adrenaline was flowing and we were doing well. When I was still about 10m from the objective, I ran out of rounds in my rifle. "Out of ammo," I shouted over to John. "Me too," came the reply. "What do you think you should do now?" shouts CSgt. "Get the f**k out of here!" I suggested cheekily, having quickly weighed up the rather hopeless situation. "NO!!!" he shouted back in despair and started to kick me. "Fix your bayonet and charge!" "Really??"

In climbing terms, I see this period at Sandhurst as I imagine a Himalayan expedition to be – a long, arduous slog, to be endured rather than enjoyed. Yes, there'll be some interesting and satisfying highlights along the way and, after it's all over, a chance to look back with some satisfaction at getting through the whole ordeal. Ultimately, you've just got to put your head down and get on with it. The mountain, like the institution of the army, isn't going to give way. It's been that way for years and isn't going to be changed by one individual's fleeting presence.

I think what was so different about this experience was that, up until joining the army, everything I'd done had been as a result of my own choices – often without even much parental input – which had led to a strong sense of independence. I'd developed into the individual that I was through doing what I chose to do. In the army, and particularly at Sandhurst, we were denied choice. They didn't want individuals or independence. They didn't want the Me that I'd created. They wanted a re-creation of themselves, someone who'd do as he was told, follow the rules and fit the mould. Even as trainee leaders, the decisions you made were expected to fit the predictable norms. That is the point of all the drill – conditioning you to respond to commands without thinking, to do the same as everyone else around you, to fit in. Drill is so central to the army and army life in general is pretty similar – everyone doing the same thing as one single body, an amorphous mass, following instructions to the letter and not deviating. I understand the need for this – up to a point – but I can't help feeling this approach is a hangover from a style of warfare that involved 'going over the top' and unflinchingly running towards the enemy. I think we've moved on.

We got through to the end eventually, having lost a few comrades along the way. John was going to the Signals while I was off to the Infantry. The end of our time at this august establishment was marked by one last episode of marching up and down in straight lines, this time dressed in our finery, while the brass band played in the background. More importantly it was time for the Commissioning Ball – the end of term party. And they certainly knew how to throw a good party. It was great to be able to invite some of my old climbing mates: Dunc, Phil, Nick Velissarides and John Wilson with their respective partners, to share in the celebration and get a glimpse into a very different world.

Dressed to kill – Nick in Mess kit on the steps of Old College RMAS © John Vlasto

6 - Shot By Both Sides

E5 6B ST GOVAN'S HEAD, PEMBROKE

Serving with the Queen's Lancashire

A few weeks after leaving Sandhurst, I found myself at my new base at Paderborn, West Germany – Lieutenant Wharton, Platoon Commander with the Queen's Lancashire Regiment. It was a good place to be. I soon bought my first car – a second-hand Mk 1 Golf GTi. By now I spoke reasonable German and got out and about to make the most of it. Our unit's role at the time was as part of the mechanised force to counter the supposed Russian threat. That meant driving around the German countryside in armoured personnel carriers and digging defensive positions. Occasionally we'd do joint exercises with our NATO counterparts, including the Americans, during which we would beg, borrow and steal the better equipment they always seemed to be issued with.

Away from the work side of things, there were a number of crags within driving distance. To the south was a large volcanic outcrop called Bruchausen with a good range of Trad routes. To the east, a ridge line called the Ith separates the Weser and Leine rivers. It has a series of pocketed limestone crags set in beautiful beech woods. However, as I hadn't yet made any local contacts and there wasn't really anybody from the military community to climb with, these first few months at Paderborn turned out to be a rather fallow period.

Not long after I arrived in Germany, my unit's role changed. We started training for our deployment to Northern Ireland. We got busier and busier as we prepared for a six-month stint in West Belfast, learning new skills and trying to adapt to what would be a very different type of soldiering and an altogether novel and much more real threat. I tried to get my head around the centuries-old background to the conflict. It was essential to recognise that there were definitely two sides to the argument, and it wasn't our place to take sides. This was 1987 and the paramilitary activity, especially from the Republican side, was in full swing, partly due to recent disappointing election results for Sinn Fein.

Finally, our training was complete. We were ready to deploy. The whole battalion had a week's leave and many people were heading back to the UK. On the last day before that leave, Friday 6 March, everyone was gathered together in the sports hall for a briefing-cum-pep talk by the Brigadier. I don't remember what he said. I don't suppose many people were listening, but he did go on, and on. As soon as he'd finished there was a mass exodus. It was like the Wacky Races. Many of the soldiers were booked on cross-channel ferries that evening and now it'd be tight to make them on time. All the officers were staying behind as we had a regimental dinner arranged in the mess. These are grand affairs with everyone in 'mess dress' – scarlet tunics and gold-embroidered waistcoats. The regimental band would perform while the officers and their guests were waited on hand and foot through a fabulous dinner with all the mess silver on proud display. These are pretty special occasions.

The delay in many people leaving for the UK that afternoon turned out to be a blessing for most as the ferry that many were heading for that evening was the Townsend Thoresen boat from Zeebrugge to Dover, The Herald of Free Enterprise. Only a handful of soldiers from the battalion, some with their families, made the sailing on time. Moments after departure, as it was leaving the harbour, the boat capsized when the bow doors were not closed, killing 193 passengers and crew. News of the disaster came through to us later that evening as we were back in Paderborn enjoying our after-dinner drinks and it made for a very sombre end to the evening.

The following week we arrived in Northern Ireland. The battalion was spread over various locations around West Belfast. For me and the rest of 'A' Company, our home for the next six months was to be Fort Whiterock. If this sounds like something out of the Wild West, conjuring up images of cowboys and Indians, it wasn't far off! The only difference being that our walls were made of corrugated iron and not timber. Otherwise, it was just the same – high walls all around with a watchtower in each corner and one large, fortified gate. Inside, facilities were cramped and very limited but then all we did was work, rest, work, rest… repeat, so it didn't bother us much.

Work involved going out on patrol either on foot or in a vehicle around our own, local patch. Ours was made up of numerous housing estates and small local commercial areas, just like any other suburban part of the UK. Our primary role was to escort a police officer from the Royal Ulster Constabulary while he (it was almost exclusively 'he') went about his job pounding the beat, providing a presence on the ground and delivering summonses. In the morning, if I were on duty that day, I'd meet my RUC copper to find out where he wanted to go and which, if any, specific addresses he needed to visit. Having got this information, I'd then plan a route for us to follow.

Before heading out, I'd brief my platoon on what was required of each 'brick' (half-section of four soldiers). Half the platoon would be on foot with me and the other half would be mobile in armoured Land

Fort Whiterock, West Belfast – our home for six months

Rovers or waiting back at camp as a QRF (Quick Reaction Force). The foot patrol would be four bricks, including mine with the policeman. I would choreograph the remaining three to move so as to provide a protective cordon around us at the centre. The idea was to keep the unseen enemy guessing where everyone was. Some of the soldiers would be carrying complex electronic jamming equipment to prevent the detonation of remote-controlled IEDs (Improvised Explosive Devices). Also available and on-call to most patrols was a helicopter, flying high above our area of operation, that was armed with a very powerful optical sight, capable of seeing, in fine detail, any suspicious activity that might be hidden to us. In summary, we had 16 soldiers on foot, another eight in armoured vehicles and a further eight on hand and ready to move instantly, as well as a helicopter above – all this so that a policeman could knock on someone's door and hand-deliver a summons for not taxing their car or some other minor misdemeanour. Fair enough, that was the price of maintaining the rule of law there at that time.

An incident one day highlighted the bizarre, localised nature of the situation. I'd planned a route that took us to a particularly dodgy area in the south of our patch. Having shown a presence and allowed our policeman to do his thing, I took us across a patch of waste ground between the staunchly Republican estate that we had been patrolling to a much more relaxed, middle-class area of well-kept front gardens and manicured lawns. It was, at most, 250 metres from one to the other. The area we were heading to was, strictly speaking, outside our area but I thought it'd provide a nice change and it was always important to avoid being predictable. As we reached the far side of the waste ground and started down the leafy avenue of the adjacent area, I saw two policemen walking calmly up the street towards us. "What are they doing?" I asked my copper. "They're just out on their duties, same as us," came his relaxed response. "Who are they with? Where is their escort? Who is protecting them?" I enquired, somewhat puzzled as I couldn't see any military personnel. "Oh, to be sure, they don't need any of that kind of thing here. This is a lovely, calm area!" They were 250 metres from one of the toughest IRA strongholds in the province. A half-decent shot with a sniper rifle could've taken out either or both of them!

It certainly did get serious at times. The local hoodlums took to setting fire to buses on the Andersonstown Road, while the big boys would remind us of their presence by firing automatic weapons into the air in a defiant show of strength. The country had a general election during our spell, which meant that polling stations needed protecting for the several days leading up to the vote. Two soldiers from our battalion were killed by terrorist action during the time we were there. One was killed by a pipe bomb dropped from the balcony of a tower block onto the soldiers patrolling below. The other, in our own company, was shot as he was stood in the rear of an armoured vehicle, head and shoulders protruding through the roof, providing observation and cover with his rifle for the vehicle from the surrounding area.

One day when I was out on patrol, I had my own very hair-raising moment. At the time, my platoon and I were travelling back towards camp in our armoured vehicles, having finished our daily routine. A message came over the radio diverting us to a small cul-de-sac that backed on to the rear of our camp. A terrorist cell had fired a homemade mortar bomb into Fort Whiterock, and we were dispatched to seal off the firing point until the bomb disposal guys could clear the area and ensure it wasn't booby-trapped, as was often the case. Meanwhile, over the wall in camp, the unexploded, improvised mortar bomb had landed slap bang in the middle of the fuel store, surrounded by dozens and dozens of jerry cans filled with fuel. Great shot! If it had gone off it would've been truly spectacular and quite devastating. The fact that it didn't explode might be seen as a lucky escape for the camp – a faulty detonator or a botched job in the making of this improvised device being to blame. Or maybe it shows who was really fighting this conflict. It wasn't us, the foot soldiers out in the open, escorting PC Plod, but the undercover units acting on hard-won intelligence and carrying out incredibly high-risk operations to infiltrate and sabotage the terrorist units before they could wreak their havoc. What I've just described was almost certainly the result of another successful covert operation to tamper with the device and render it ineffective before it was deployed by the cell, so that it was never going to detonate.

At some point during these six-month tours of Northern Ireland, everyone

On patrol with the RUC

got a four or five-day furlough back at home – a chance to truly relax and see friends and family. Naturally enough, I spent mine in Llanberis. John Wilson drove down from Scotland and picked me up at Manchester Airport and we headed up from there for a few days with Iwan. It was quite a party. John had arranged for a few others to converge there too. Clearly, I was going to be quite out of shape for climbing but, no problem, Llanberis provided the perfect solution – slate! It's all about technique, balance and balls rather than brute strength. And so it worked out. I managed to amass quite a tally of routes before heading back to the mean streets of Belfast.

I also managed to wangle another, more local climbing break, this time just a couple of days during an off-duty period. I'd become friendly with one of the RUC officers based at the Andersonstown Road police station. He was a bit of a climber and part of a group that would often head up to Fairhead on the North Antrim coast. I got a weekend away and an introduction to the best crag that Northern Ireland has to offer. With a 9mm pistol in my rucksack (that was a first!) I spent a great couple of days with him climbing the amazing walls and cracks of this superb, dolerite bastion overlooking the North Channel of the Irish Sea. This trip also brought home to me something that none of us in the battalion had realised – only 20 minutes' drive away from our areas of operation, everything appeared to be quite normal. People were going about their daily lives, just the same as in any other part of the British Isles – and why not? It should've been obvious.

Armoured Land Rovers on the streets of West Belfast

There was one final incident that weekend which sticks in my mind and perhaps goes to show how deep-rooted some attitudes were at the time. My companion for the weekend, the police officer, was a really nice bloke. He was quietly spoken, generous, calm and very mild-mannered – not the standard-issue RUC policeman! He was driving me back to our camp in his car to drop me off. As we drove along the road, past Musgrove Park Hospital towards West Belfast, we passed underneath the M1 motorway and onto Kennedy Way. This point marks the divide between largely Loyalist, Protestant East Belfast and Republican, Catholic West Belfast. Just after we'd passed beneath the motorway bridge, a pedestrian stepped off the curb to cross the road causing my acquaintance to brake slightly. Suddenly the air was full of expletives about this hapless pedestrian's religion and parentage! It was so out of character. I feel sure that if the incident had occurred 200 metres earlier, on the other side of the motorway, the response would've been a calm and dignified "Careful, there my friend. Watch the road!"

Our time in Belfast drew to a close. The battalion was ready to return to Germany and I'd received notification of a new role back in the UK – a new chapter in my army career and, more importantly, an opportunity to reconnect properly with climbing.

It was something of a relief to finish our tour of Northern Ireland. Most soldiers at the time would've agreed that they wouldn't want to miss the experience. After all it's something more real than the imaginary invasion of Western Europe, which was the other main focus for our forces at the time. Operations in Northern Ireland were very different to the 'conventional' warfare being prepared for in the BAOR (British Army of the Rhine) theatre. It's one thing facing up to a known enemy wearing different uniforms, but in Belfast we were operating around the daily lives of the local inhabitants, just like the normal people of any other city in the United Kingdom. Except that some of those apparently 'normal' people were active terrorists whose objective was to maim and kill policemen, soldiers and other local residents who didn't agree with their views. Unlike a Russian or Argentinian soldier, they didn't wear a uniform or openly carry weapons. They weren't readily identifiable. Of course, we knew who most of the 'players' were, but the Rules of Engagement didn't allow us to engage with them. We had to wait until they tried to have go at us first.

There's been a very obvious change in the world of terrorism since these times. Members of the PIRA (Provisional Irish Republican Army) and INLA

(Irish National Liberation Army) and, of course, on the other side of the political divide organisations like the UVF (Ulster Volunteer Force) and UFF (Ulster Freedom Fighters), were hardened, committed fighters who absolutely believed in their cause. But they didn't actively want to die for it, unlike the suicide bombers of today.

Having left Northern Ireland, life quickly returned to some degree of normality. The rest of the world seemed oblivious to the shootings, bombs, hijackings and punishment beatings going on in the Province. The only visible sign of what we'd been up against, when we went back to Germany to pack our bags for a well-earned break, was that we still had to get down on hands and knees to search under our vehicles for explosive devices. The number plates gave us away as military. This, naturally, quite upset some of the locals – it wasn't their conflict, but car bombs are indiscriminate weapons and our presence put the local residents at just as much risk as us.

I packed up my room in Paderborn and loaded up the car for the trip home. I wouldn't be returning. I was moving to the North East of England, just outside Newcastle, to take up a new role, and I'd offered someone a lift back to the UK in my car. Off we set, down the autobahn towards the Ruhr Valley and so on to the channel ports. I was steadily motoring along, at average motorway speed with my passenger dozing in his seat next to me when suddenly – BANG! – there was an almighty crash and everything in front of me went black.

The bonnet had come undone and flown up to smash into the windscreen. It took me by surprise, but at least I could see what had happened. My passenger on the other hand was rudely wrenched out of half-sleep with no idea what was going on. Remember, we'd just returned from a highly fraught six months during which every loud, unexpected noise represented a potential life-threatening danger. He didn't sleep again all trip! The windscreen was badly cracked and the bonnet somewhat crumpled, but once it was tied down, we were able to get on our way. In truth, the bonnet and windscreen stayed like that for a few months until I eventually got round to getting them replaced. I finally found a scrap yard in Newcastle that could provide me with a replacement one that did the job perfectly, except it was red while the rest of the car was black. In the corner, the scrap yard had painted, very neatly, the name GOLF in yellow paint – I called it my designer logo. I never did get it repainted. Why would I? It was quite unique.

QUESTIONS

Q. *You sound quite disparaging about many aspects of army life. What was your overall impression.*

A. Most aspects of the work that I did during my time in the army were enjoyable, challenging and interesting. It also presented many opportunities to do things and see places that would otherwise have been difficult. What I struggled with was the life in the background: living in the Officers' Mess, the attitudes of some of the people I was forced to live and work with. There was, sadly, a narrow-mindedness along with a sense of superiority and privilege that I could never embrace. So many of the traditions and cultural norms meant nothing to me, mainly because I didn't see what value they added. Some people clearly needed those norms to cling to. I didn't.

Q. *What did it feel like, taking your platoon out on the streets of Belfast for the first time?*

A. You might imagine it'd be a bit intimidating, a bit scary, particularly at first. However, we'd done a lot of good quality, realistic training before going there. In fact, the reality was far more mundane and routine than the training. In addition, when we first got there, we had a short handover period with the lads that we were taking over from, so for the first few times out on patrol they took the lead. For a climbing analogy, I would say it wasn't entirely on-sight – we'd practised the moves and knew what to expect – more of a head point!

7 - The Northumbrian
E6 6B ESK BUTTRESS
Out and about in the North East

Back in the UK, I had several weeks of holiday to enjoy before reporting for my new job. My little red notebook recalls that it was quite a frantic tour. First up was a visit to John Wilson, now resident in his own flat in Perth. We drove over to Glencoe to do the classic Hard Rock route *Carnivore* on the side of Buchaille Etive Mor. This is an impressive crag that I returned to many years later for a very memorable weekend. From there we headed back to Perth for several days climbing at Dunkeld. On one of these days, we were climbing at Upper Cave Crag – one of those rare examples where Trad and Sport climbing co-exist side-by-side in a beautiful setting. Having done *Rat Catcher* (E3) the day before, I recognised that it was time to step up and try *Lady Charlotte*, an E5 next to it. I was well established on the route, which is quite steep but with good holds. John was belaying, perched on a small grassy ledge a few feet off the ground. Keen to see the action at one point, he stepped back to get a better view, fell off his perch and plucked me from my tenuous position, high on the route – not what I was expecting as I navigated the crux!

John had to go back to work, so I drove myself the length of the country, first to Devon to visit my sister Kate in Appledore, then on to Looe in Cornwall to catch up with old university friend Mairi McLeod who was living and working at the Monkey Sanctuary. I also managed to fit in a brief visit to the crags at Sennen for some sunny, seaside soloing. Then it was back north to the Lakes. John's parents, Ruth and Eric, were moving into a new house in Grange-over-Sands and I'd offered to lend a hand with some decorating while also meeting up with Duncan Holdsworth, also living up there by then. That weekend, John drove down to visit his parents. One afternoon, a couple of Ruth's friends from the Women's Institute called round for tea and cakes. While we were having a break from moving furniture and painting the house, one of them, an accomplished artist, was sketching simple portraits of me and John. Eric – an early adopter of the carphone – suggested we make a copy of the two drawings using his newly-installed fax machine. "A fax machine? What's that?" enquired the elderly lady. "It's a machine for sending documents down the telephone," explained Eric. With a puzzled look on her face, she imitated holding a telephone receiver in her hand, then looking between the imaginary earpiece and mouthpiece she asked: "But, where does it come out?" Modern technology! What will they think of next?

The long holiday was over and it was time to start a new chapter. I moved into the Officers' Mess at Albemarle Barracks, a large training facility on the site of an old airfield, RAF Ouston, to the west of Newcastle. (I was asked to park my multi-coloured car – with its 'designer logo' – round the back as it "didn't give the right impression"!)

Built during the Second World War as a base for fighter aircraft to defend the shipyards and industry of the North East from enemy bombers, RAF Ouston's current use was as a base for training Junior Leaders and Junior Soldiers, 16- and 17-year olds, for Infantry Regiments in the King's Division – drawn from all the regiments across the North of England, and the Scottish Division – made up of all the Scottish infantry regiments. As well as basic military training, the lads also got further academic education and other extra-curricular activities. I was responsible for overseeing the military training of my platoon of recruits, along with a team of NCOs. Being very aware of my own experience of training within the army, I tried to introduce a more progressive approach, helped by an equally open-minded platoon sergeant. We made the training enjoyable, interesting and, while still getting across the ethos of discipline and obedience, we allowed plenty of time for fun.

Life at Ouston was fantastic. The job was fairly straightforward and largely 9-to-5. We could quickly get out into Northumberland and it wasn't all that far to the Yorkshire Dales or the Lakes. Phil Baines was still in the North East, married now to his long-term partner Leslie, and it was through Phil that I met a crowd of other local climbers. Most significant of these was Bruce Stelling from South Shields. Bruce was an electrician who had always worked down the pit. He'd really got into his climbing during the miners' strikes of a few years earlier. He was such a character and a real pleasure to go out with. On the one hand, very much like Phil, he was a fiery individual with a short fuse – a few years later, during a really pleasant evening at another friend's house where we were having dinner with our partners, some seemingly innocuous comment even resulted in Phil and Bruce squaring up to each other out on the street! – but, on the other hand, he could sometimes be incredibly gullible, which made him easy meat for a good wind-up.

In the officers' mess at camp there was the inevitable mixed bag. Most were very easy-going, down-to-earth and good fun. There were others who were a bit up themselves. Top of this league was our adjutant. During a memorable mess meeting, with all the officers present, those who were single and lived in the mess and the married officers (known as the 'pads') who lived in quarters on camp, were having a discussion about how to encourage the married officers and their wives to come into the mess in the evening and use the bar – important for raising mess funds as well as just being sociable. The main sticking point for the pads was the dress code. They didn't want to come to the mess if it meant having to wear a tie. (The dress code for dinner every night was a suit and tie!) There was agreement that the dress code could be relaxed. I suggested that perhaps we could relax the dress code for everyone in the mess and dispense with the need for a suit and tie for dinner. Cue a sharp intake of breath and outrage. "But surely, you dress for dinner when you're at home, don't you?" spluttered the Adjutant, after regaining his composure. The irony was blindingly obvious. If the married officers in the room had dressed for dinner, we wouldn't have been having the debate in the first place!

The Commanding Officer (CO) in place when I arrived was something of a cartoon caricature of a colonel – a bombastic character who liked nothing better than to try and remove the cork from a magnum of champagne with a swipe of his sword during a Mess Dinner Night. I invited Phil along to one of these grand evenings. I lent him my dinner suit and Leslie, his wife, found him a new white dress shirt to wear with it. We had a great evening. Dinner was fabulous and there was a lot of drinking. Phil enjoyed the spectacle and the chance to mix with a different crowd of people.

After dinner, as often happened, we had a game of 'mess rugby'. In the large anteroom, all the furniture was moved to the side and a cabbage placed in the centre of the room. Jackets were removed, as were spurs where applicable. Two sides were formed – subalterns and their guests against the more senior officers. The resulting melée was a free-for-all, with the simple aim being to get the cabbage to the opponents' end of the room by any means possible. Phil was in his element. He was someone not unused to a brawl and had the strength to ensure he would nearly always come out on top. He considered it a badge of honour that his brand-new shirt was ripped from his back in the ensuing madness. At one point in the drunken fracas, there was a brief halt in proceedings. The dentist and the CO retired to the gents so the former could apply sutures to his boss's wounded eye. It was only later that night that Phil piped up in his strong Sunderland accent "I got that old fella good and proper!"

In one significant respect at least, my time at Ouston proved to be quite life-changing. Also living in the mess was someone who became very special to me. She was young, lively and utterly gorgeous – a Yellow Labrador named Hannah! More importantly, she was owned by an equally gorgeous and lively young nurse called Karen, who was to become my wife, four years later. Karen had trained in the army and spent her nursing career up to that point on postings at various hospitals. Currently, she was employed as a Liaison Officer, going into schools and colleges around the area, talking to young girls about a career in the army. She'd been a cross-country champion and was still very active and a keen runner. We shared a lot of common interests. She wasn't a climber but she loved to be out in the hills.

We also went to lots of concerts and ballet in Newcastle and on one occasion went to see the Royal Ballet perform their brilliant *Still Life at the Penguin Café* in Manchester. It seemed like a good idea to stay overnight with some of my relatives in Burnley as it was only an hour's drive to Manchester. By this time, my mother was living in Scotland, so I asked her older brother and his wife – Uncle Frank and Aunty Barbara. This is East Lancashire – they will always be Uncle and Aunty! I had asked if I could come and stay with a friend and had explained we were going to Manchester. "No problem, you're always welcome. You can use the spare room. Plenty of room for two in there." Only problem – I hadn't thought to mention that this friend was of the female variety! There was some panic when we arrived – it wasn't quite the done thing then for an unmarried couple to share a room. The jungle drums were busy that evening as word went round about 'Nicholas and his lady friend'!

Nicke Book

p. 48, "A Year Off before Univ.

Next p. 49 2nd parag.

P 117 top of page

P 109 Top of the pg

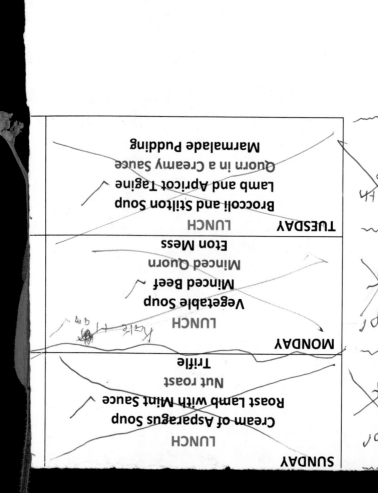

SUNDAY

LUNCH

Cream of Asparagus Soup
Roast Lamb with Mint Sauce
Nut roast
Trifle

MONDAY

LUNCH

Vegetable Soup
Minced Beef
Minced Quorn
Eton Mess

TUESDAY

LUNCH

Broccoli and Stilton Soup
Lamb and Apricot Tagine
Quorn in a Creamy Sauce
Marmalade Pudding

Naturally I got out climbing with Phil, Bruce and their mates as often as possible. They introduced me to the crags of Northumberland or 'the County' as they called it. The climbing in any area of the UK will have a unique character and that's certainly true of the North East sandstone. The rock is quite fine in texture – more fine than gritstone but still providing good friction. Trusting that friction in the absence of more positive holds is often the secret to success, particularly on the harder lines. Routes often require a bold approach and although the crags are not usually that high, a fall will often be serious. I spent a lot of time getting familiar with Bowden Doors, Back Bowden and, my favourite, Great Wanney.

I had a memorable revisit to Wanney with Phil many, many years later. I was working in the North East with BAE Systems so arranged to meet Phil after work in order to get a few routes in. I was climbing quite well at the time, unlike Phil who hadn't done much recently, spending most of his time mountain biking. Phil was happy to be dragged up a few routes, so I led an E2 as a warm-up, followed by an E3. Both were great routes but felt very comfortable. There was time for one last route, so I suggested a good-looking E4. Up I went, again finding the climbing well within my comfort zone albeit with very limited protection. I wasn't bothered by the paucity of gear, but down on the ground, looking up, Phil was clearly worried. He kept insisting that I try and find something to protect myself. I had to shut him up! At that point, he didn't have a completely clear view of me. Slightly out of view of Phil, I tied a thin sling round a wispy bunch of heather sprouting from a crack and clipped it to my rope. "I've got some protection, Phil," I shouted down. "Is it any good?" he asked, his mind still not at ease. "Oh yes, I'm happy to go to the top from here now that I've got this," I replied, in all honesty. Phil now satisfied, I made the crux moves up the blank wall and pulled over onto the top. I'll leave you to imagine the none-too-complimentary comments as he discovered just what had been protecting me for that last section as he seconded up the route.

John Wilson visited me at Ouston for a long weekend of climbing on one occasion. He was accompanied by two strong Scottish climbers who I'd met through John when we were climbing at Dunkeld. They were Mark McGowan, known as Face, and Paul Loughlin, known as Frodo. We met up in the Lakes first, with a visit to Langdale. I'd been wanting to lead *R 'n' S Special* for some time. An amazing, bold trip across a wall with delicate climbing helps to explain why this was a worthy inclusion in *Extreme Rock* along with its neighbours *Tril-*

ogy, to the left, and *Fine Time*, coming straight up through steep ground below *R 'n' S*. I led it that day with Face and John and have been back to repeat it on many occasions since.

That wall on Raven Crag overlooking the Old Dungeon Ghyll Hotel in Langdale, small as it is, packs in some great climbing. I went on to climb *Trilogy*, up the steep corner on the left with Phil in 1991 and would complete the set with *Fine Time* a few years later with Helen Davies. Also on this excellent piece of rock, I did *Centrefold* with Glenn Sutcliffe in 1993. It goes up the middle of the wall before it veers off to the right while *Dawes Rides a Shovelhead* keeps going straight up. Glenn and I both fell off on our first attempts, as we tried to figure out exactly where to go. I guess I was lucky that it was my turn to have another go when, between us, we'd finally worked out the sequence.

After our trip to Langdale, John and the boys came back to stay at the mess so that we could climb in Northumberland the next day. It wasn't unheard-of for people to have guests to stay but most people's guests weren't like Face and Frodo. It was a first for them and the mess, with their shoulder-length hair, ripped climbing tights and vests and unintelligible Glasgow accents. But they were my guests and, up to a point, that was respected. The Scottish connection also helped. Half the officers in the mess were from Scottish regiments and so felt obliged to try and find some affinity with their fellow countrymen. Sometime later our adjutant commented to Karen, "Nick does have some… interesting friends, doesn't he?"

The following day at Back Bowden, I did *The Tube*. It's a superb E4 that traverses a long way rightwards along a thin break before surmounting the naturally sculptured, capping wave of the buttress at its weakest point. I really enjoyed the moves, however, when John came to second it, he got wrong-handed and ran out of steam. Now, the traverse isn't that well protected, at least I hadn't put much gear in, thinking only of John and trying to avoid the need for him to hang around and take it out (typical of me – always thinking of my second!). Before his arms turned to jelly and gave up on him, he made the schoolboy error of trying to climb back to the left in order to reach some better holds. When, eventually and inevitably, he could hang on no more, the pendulum was impressive, made bigger by his retreat leftwards away from the gear. He missed a fencepost by inches as the swing took him sailing past. The crowd loved it! A similar situation arose some years later, climbing in Gordale with Dominic Donnini. I'd just led the second pitch of *Jenny Wren* quite comfortably. This involves something of a precarious traverse leftwards across a fairly blank ramp of perfect limestone to reach the belay stance of *Face Route*. Once again, it wasn't terribly well protected

Neil Stabbs on *Trilogy*

and I'd been in no mood to hang around and fiddle something in; after all, it didn't feel that hard. Dom, not having the best of days, didn't find it quite so easy. The resulting fall resulted in another huge swing – so far, he came back with an Irish accent. Once again, the crowd went wild!

One of the benefits of being in the army is that they run all manner of training courses that anyone can apply for and attend during working time. In November of that year, 1987, I enrolled on the Joint Services Rock Climbing Instructor course. By that time, the Golf had sadly passed away and I was currently relying on a Honda CX 500 motorbike – a classic model, most favoured by couriers at the time due to the shaft drive and renowned reliability (but sadly another vehicle they wanted parking round the back of the officers' mess!). I made the long journey down to Tywyn in mid-Wales in pretty atrocious November weather but well wrapped up in waxed-cotton waterproof kit. I met the rest of the course candidates, along with the staff. I was comfortably climbing E5 at this point so was paired off with the next best climber in the group. He was a well-meaning bloke from the Navy who'd get dragged up HVS on a good day. The young instructors on the course were all good fun and, I think, delighted to have someone with my climbing background and experience with them for the week.

Their boss, the Chief Instructor, wasn't quite as pleased to see me. I tried my hardest to get on with him. I didn't make a big deal of the routes I'd done. When the standard of climbing became apparent, I really did try to play down my own achievements and not talk about the routes I'd done – unless asked. We all had an interview with the boss to let him know what experience we had, what type of climbing we'd done and also to study our 'logbooks' that, no doubt, we'd all kept since attending previous, lower-level courses. I explained that I didn't have a logbook as such but did produce my little red notebook as an alternative. It only showed the extreme-grade routes, but I hoped it would satisfy his curiosity. After several minutes of reading through the various entries, it was obvious he was determined not to be impressed and there was even a hint of disbelief. When he started quizzing me about some of the entries, clearly trying to catch me out, it was my turn to be unimpressed. "Who did you climb *Central Wall* at Kilnsey with?" "What grade is *True Grip* on the Cromlech?" "What did you write about *Main Event* at Hodge Close?"

We were all at a crag in the Moelwyns one day, practising our rescues on different easy routes in small groups. At lunchtime we gathered in the boulders below the crag to eat our packed lunches. One of the young instructors pointed out a boulder problem they'd all tried and not yet managed to work out a successful sequence to get up. "Show us how to do it" one of them said to me. I looked at the moves, could see what was required and did it, much to their delight. When their boss arrived a few moments later, they were keen to tell him that the long-standing problem had finally been solved. "Hmm, bet you couldn't do it again," was all he could say. I got up to repeat it for his benefit when he stopped me in my tracks. "Aren't you forgetting something?" he asked, tapping his cumbersome, army-issue helmet. I sat back down. "I'm sure you can work it out for yourself." I was not about to start wearing a helmet to do a short, simple boulder problem.

I did get a chance to do one decent route that week. We were at Tremadog on our last day. It was a day of climbing simply for the pleasure of it. No instruction, no pretend scenarios, just pick a route and enjoy yourselves. After a week of climbing at Diff and Severe level (all very easy), I asked my allotted partner if he'd mind if I chose a route. I would do my best to get him up after me. He agreed and so we made our way to Stromboli Buttress where I climbed the rather impressive *Hitler's Buttock*. I'd previously climbed its two similar neighbours: *Sexual Salami* and *Cardiac Arete*, both E4, so had seen what it looked like. It's a step-up from the previous two, a tough E5, relying on micro-wires to protect the technical moves on the tiny finger holds. I was delighted to get up it cleanly. My second, on the other hand, was blown away, having never been on anything even close to this. It's interesting to note that my report following the course commented that I was "a competent climber, capable of climbing E4 on-sight...". Oh well, I'd attended, passed the course, got the certificate and it certainly beat working for the week. Why should I care about the insecurities of someone else?

The rest of my time in the North East was full of climbing adventures in Northumberland and the North Lakes with Bruce and Phil, pushing the boat out as far as possible on most days out at the crag.

I also had the now-familiar summer climbing trip with John, split between North Wales and the Lakes. It was on that year's week-long trip to the Lakes that

"I don't know about this," says Nick as he tugs at the rather pitiful wire. Time for a rethink. He climbs back down for a chat. This is not like him. Something's spooking him.

Nick's had *Creation* on Raven Crag above Thirlmere on his list for a while. Trouble is, so have many others, but to most it's just 'on the list' and never actually gets done. A photograph of it had featured on the front of a guidebook a few years ago – it looked outrageous. We'd all heard about it but no one that we knew had done it. The feeling is that it's well under-graded at E4. Everyone suspects it's good E5... possibly harder?

I can see Nick is trying to rationalise it. It's only 30ft of hard climbing. It has some protection but it's only one, maybe two, really thin wires low down at the start of the hard section. The best runner is a tiny Chouinard No 1 stopper, maybe 2mm thick. This is the runner that Nick had just placed and was testing. The crux headwall is clean, the holds and moves look obvious but there's no let-up. It's 80ft up in the air, leaning out at an awkward angle and committing as hell. Once you set off up the hard section it's difficult to come back, the holds aren't good enough to reverse.

"OK so what if you do fall? Will the wires hold?"

"They should do but not if you fall too far onto them. But I think the hard bit's just above that runner."

If they do pull it's going to be a long fall, off the headwall and out into space. Not nice, really not nice. So, the runners under the headwall have to hold. These need to be improved. The old peg needs to be backed up. The belay can be moved further up the groove to reduce drag, improve runner alignment and give a better load angle.

That's it. Nick has his head round it now. He looks totally focussed as he optimises the lower runners. I try and reassure him that I'll hold the fall no matter what – as long as the gear holds. I'm not sure he's listening.

He checks the thin wire at the start of the headwall and commits...

Like a machine, he reads all the holds in front of him, works out the sequence as he goes. This is all on-sight. He storms up the wall in minutes – no more runners, no more hesitation, just execution. It's cool and precise, impressive to watch. A joyful whoop from the belay ledge signals the successful outcome.

Now it's my turn to follow. I have a rope above me and I'm still worried at the prospect.

Looking down at me from his belay ledge as I survey the crux section, Nick is smiling. "Well, what do you think?" It's a loaded question, he knows what's coming and he's seen the look of concern on my face. He knows exactly what I'm thinking – bastard!

"It feels bloody hard. I really don't know how you led this. E4 my ass!" I'm on the headwall, relaxed now that I'm on the finishing holds. A lot of expletives pour out with the relief and we laugh loudly and openly about it.

Nick's performance on this route clearly demonstrates the bold but calculated nature of his climbing more than almost anything I can think of. It was hard and it was dangerous, yet it was all thought through, made as safe as possible and executed perfectly.

As it turns out, the route was subsequently upgraded to E5 and 30 years later the current UK Climbing consensus is pushing it up to hard E5/E6.

Phil Baines

we visited Raven Crag, Threshthwaite Cove for the first time. This is probably the best single-pitch climbing venue in the area, provided you are climbing E3 and upwards. Every route provides top quality climbing. I ended up writing the guide to the Eastern Crags, which include this amazing crag, many years later, describing it as having *"more stars than a night at the Oscars"*. I would also add my own route, *Road Rage* (E7), some years later.

That year I also met up with long-lost Sandhurst friend, John Vlasto. He was based at Catterick briefly, which meant we could climb together again. He suggested I come over to the Lakes with him on one occasion as he was attending a

Mick Johnson, *Running on Empty*, Raven Crag, Threshthwaite

pre-expedition meet in the Beech Hill Hotel on the shore of Windermere. John was part of a joint military and civilian expedition to the Himalaya and this was to be their initial get-together. He'd also suggested another friend came along – Brian Davison. John and Brian had been on a previous military/civilian trip together. In their own different ways, they are as barking mad as each other so made a great combination. Brian and I weren't part of the official team so had to keep a low profile over the weekend but still managed to spend the couple of days eating and sleeping in the hotel as well as making full use of their facilities. Nobody was going to notice another couple of climbers. The staff just assumed we were with the main party. Since then, I've climbed extensively with Brian and been on many, often ridiculous adventures.

The climbing later that year included numerous trips to Aberdeen where John was now living. The sea cliffs on the coast north and south of Aberdeen are fantastic. I soloed a lot of E2 and E3 routes as well as climbing many others with John and his local mates. That year we also hit many of the bigger crags in the Lakes: Eagle in Borrowdale, Dow, Dove, Pavey Ark and Scafell, and we visited Chapel Head Scar for the first time, another crag that I'd come to spend a lot of time at and, later, write the guide to.

After the summer holidays with John it was back to Germany to rejoin my battalion, albeit not for very long, thankfully. It was just long enough to partake in some more useful non-military training on our doorstep. Just up the road, almost adjoining, was the smaller town of Sennelager, home at the time to many military ranges, a large training area and, most importantly, the Army Sport Parachute Centre. Courses were available for military personnel at a fraction of the price in 'civvy street'. I lapped it up, quickly rising through the various stages from a static-line jump (where your parachute is deployed automatically) to long periods of free fall.

The timing couldn't have been better. We were soon to deploy, en masse, to the prairies of Canada for large-scale, live-firing, battle group scale exercises. This training was something to behold in its own right with mechanised infantry fighting alongside tanks and supported by artillery, but on this trip I had no involvement with the military manoeuvres. I had a much more important job to do. I was in charge of running the post-exercise Adventure Training in the Rockies for anyone who wanted to partake. If that sounds like my ideal job, it got even better when I arrived and met the PT (Physical Training) Corps captain stationed there whose job it was to organise everything! "So, what's my job?" I asked him when we met. "Just get the names and let me know who wants to do what!" he replied. This was going to leave a lot of time for checking out the activities beforehand and exploring the area on a motorbike borrowed from another regimental colleague.

The icing on the cake was that my new best friend, the PT Corps captain, was really into his skydiving and had introduced this as one of the options that the soldiers could opt for in their choice of activities. He was delighted to discover that I was already trained and had been jumping back in Sennelager. We spent a lot of time at the DZ (drop zone), a small airfield outside Calgary at a one-horse town called Beiseker. The sky diving centre was run by two laid-back dudes whose approach was very different to my previous army-related experiences.

They were still safe and ensured everything was done correctly but they didn't let the red tape get in the way. If you showed you were competent, they let you get on with it and weren't afraid of pushing the boundaries just a little.

I was there one day when the wind was blowing a gale. Too much for any jumping, well, by the beginners anyway. Was the pilot prepared to fly? "Hell, why not? I've been up in worse." The guys hatched a plan – fly to 13,000 feet and four of us would jump out. This was a normal altitude to get a couple of minutes free fall – but not today. "Soon as you jump, deploy your rig

Instructor Gordon Bennett dispatching a trainee from the Cesna at Beiseker DZ

and see who can get blown the furthest!" What could possibly go wrong? Down on the ground, a pick-up truck was driving East across the prairie tracks, keeping up with where we might land.

I went approximately 25km before coming in to land. For someone flying a parapente wing that distance might appear insignificant, but these were high performance sport parachutes with low glide ratios. Coming in to land in those conditions was exciting! Turning into the wind took off some of the speed but I was still being blown backwards by the wind at an alarming rate. Other treats during that time were night jumps and particularly, the RW (Relative Work). This is when multiple people jump out together and manoeuvre themselves around to link up. Having someone else in the air with you provides some perspective, something to measure yourself against and really emphasises that you are flying and not just falling.

It didn't always go according to plan! On one occasion, I was offered the use of someone else's fancy parachute, just to see what 'really good' felt like. Up I went in the small aircraft, along with others, including Gordon Bennett, one of the laid-back instructors. The plan was for me and Gordon to jump out together and do some RW practice on the way down. It all went well, with some turns, somersaults and successful linking-up before we waved-off in preparation to deploy the 'chute. Not all parachutes are the same; there are various designs, not only of the wing but the way in which you pull the rip-cord. I was used to a fairly standard handle on the right side of the harness at chest height. The rig I had borrowed had what is affectionately known as a 'dildo'. This is a sausage-shaped handle that tucks into the bottom right-hand side of the pack. When it comes time to deploy, you just reach down and right, grasp the handle and extend your arm forwards once more. Simple!

Only when I reached my right hand down to where I expected to find the small, rolled-fabric handle... it wasn't there! I fumbled around, knowing that it must be there somewhere, all the time heading towards the ground at terminal velocity. Eventually, I had no option but to deploy the reserve parachute. This is not a pleasant experience. The reserve is packed in such a way as to deploy very quickly and as a result the deceleration is incredibly quick. I was left winded and gasping for breath as I approached my landing. This is also more severe under a reserve as the 'chute is smaller and less manoeuvrable. Still, I was down in one piece and the only downside was the hassle for my friend, the owner of the rig, who'd have to get it sent away for the reserve to be repacked. Back at the DZ I was quizzed as to what'd gone wrong. When I explained about the dildo not being in its place, and not being able to find it, Gordon calmly commented "Oh yeah, I saw it fluttering about behind you as we were coming down together". He didn't think to point it out!

On return to UK, I had a few more jumps, including at the small airfield at Cark beside Morecambe Bay, just across from Humphrey Head at the south end of the Lake District. This was the most fabulous location with wide views of the Lakeland fells in one direction and the expansive sands of the bay in the other. Sadly though, it soon became apparent that sky diving was an expensive game when not being heavily subsidised by the army. And anyway, I was about to be offered another fantastic opportunity in a very exotic location.

QUESTION

Q *The 'Adventure Training' opportunities within the army sound pretty good. Were they?*

A This was probably one of the best parts of army life. They were very generous with opportunities for getting off to do all manner of exciting things – all in the name of character building as well as giving us a chance to relax and have fun. There were so many chances to do things, especially if you were prepared to organise it yourself. In my last year in the army I was part of a trip to Northern Ontario for two weeks of dog-sledging and cross-country skiing – all paid for by the army. It was a fantastic experience that would be prohibitively expensive in civilian life.

Dog Sledging in Northern Ontario

8 - Lost Colonies
E3 6A HIGH CRAG, BUTTERMERE
Life in Zimbabwe

"Do you want to go to Mozambique?" "Yes," I replied without hesitation. "Where exactly is it?" I'm in the adjutant's office, back in Germany in late 1989, and he's trying to find a position to slot me into. It turned out that it wasn't Mozambique at all but Zimbabwe, where I was to spend six months with the Mozambique Training Team, hence the confusion over the location.

At that time, Mozambique, an ex-Portuguese colony, was still in the grip of a long and terrible civil war. The Marxist FRELIMO government had long been supported by the Soviet Union, while the anti-communist RENAMO, supported by South Africa, were still fighting a guerrilla action against the one-party state in pursuit of democracy. Sponsored by the FCO (Foreign and Commonwealth Office), our role was to train the FRELIMO soldiers in Zimbabwe so that they could return to their own country to fight the terrorists. "Sorry, could you just run that past me again? Which side we are on? Surely we're in favour of encouraging democracy?"

It was complicated – a tripartite arrangement between the UK, Zimbabwe and Mozambique. Zimbabwe, a land-locked country, needed a secure route to a coastal port for imports and exports. To their south was the apartheid regime of South Africa so the only option was to go east, through neighbouring Mozambique. The UK, unlike some ex-colonial powers, wanted to do everything it could to support Zimbabwe's burgeoning economy, ten years on from independence. All the soldiers that we were to train would return to their homeland and be part of the force protecting the railway line that ran along the Limpopo River to the Mozambique coast, which had been a popular target for the RENAMO guerrillas. As a result, Mozambique would have better-trained soldiers, Zimbabwe its route to and from the coast and the UK would be seen to be doing the right thing. Everyone was happy! Just to add to the picture, we were only permitted to provide 'non-lethal aid' – advice and training, not weapons and ammunition (all supplied by the Soviet Union). Complicated? That's international diplomacy!

Prior to the move, I'd been back and forth between Germany and England. By now the relationship with Karen had matured into something more serious. She'd recently left the army and bought a house in the North East. She was studying at Newcastle University to become a District Nurse, which she then did, to great effect, in the east end of Newcastle. On one return visit I'd driven from Paderborn to the airport at Dusseldorf, a good two-hour drive, only to realise I'd forgotten my passport. Rather than go back, missing my flight, I managed to blag my way through the airport checks with just my army ID card. It was more of a challenge on arrival at Manchester, and even more so when trying to return at the end of the weekend but it worked. How times have changed!

All the arrangements were made for my posting to Africa. Certain perks came with the new job, many of which were down to being on 'Loan Service' from the Ministry of Defence to the FCO. In return, the FCO paid 35% of our salary on top of our normal income. They also paid for us to travel Business Class to our destination. Having said that, Business Class on Air Zimbabwe wasn't much to write home about! I packed all my kit, including some limited, basic climbing kit: boots, harness, chalk bag etc. I wasn't sure whether I was going to find any climbing when I got there. I also took my latest acquisition – a super-lightweight, aluminium Cannondale mountain bike. One of the benefits of being in Germany was that we could use the American PX stores, the equivalent of our NAAFI. These places have all manner of equipment and provisions at bargain prices and I'd bought it at one of those.

When I arrived in Harare, it turned out that not quite all the arrangements had been made correctly. There was nobody there to meet me. So I queued at length through immigration and customs like everyone else and when it came to collecting my luggage, my bike was missing. I was told it had been impounded and I'd have to pick it up from the warehouse later. I did get it back, albeit rather the worse for wear, in due course, but I later realised that none of that would have happened if I'd been met. The officials at the airport respected a uniform. In future, whenever we had a new member of staff or even a guest arriving, we'd turn up at the airport wearing our army uniform, with the little Union Flag sewn onto our shoulder, and we'd be held in the highest regard and more often than not saluted by the officials. We'd be able to stride through all the barriers, meet our new arrivals on the tarmac as they stepped off the plane and accompany them out again just as easily. Wearing that uniform turned the whole process into a quick and easy, rubber-stamping job!

Zimbabwe – what a place! I was struck by how well-ordered it appeared. Harare was clean, tidy and had an air of cosmopolitan modernity. The Harare Sheraton, our regular base in the city, was a fabulous, up-to-date hotel with all the mod cons. Ten years on from independence and the place appeared to be running well. Sure, there were undoubtedly all manner of inefficiencies and underlying problems and, of course, the white Rhodesians weren't altogether happy with the situation they'd found themselves in. But why shouldn't the indigenous population run their own country? They were doing their best and Britain was giving them all the assistance it could. It contrasted starkly with other ex-colonial powers in neighbouring countries, such as the Portuguese in Mozambique who, once the struggle to maintain control was lost, simply packed up and left with nothing but carnage and confusion trailing in their wake.

When I did eventually manage to arrange to be picked up, I was taken to HQ where I had a very encouraging interview with the brigadier, the officer in overall charge of all the British military teams in the country. I got a warm welcome and a good introduction to the country and why we were there but what I remember most was that he told me to make the most of the opportunity of being in such an exotic location, to do the work required but also to enjoy my time in the country. And it is a truly magnificent country – potentially one of the richest in Africa with a wealth of resources and a fabulous climate. It's been tragic to see the decline in the subsequent decades. We can only hope that, in time, Zimbabwe can get back to how it was when I was fortunate enough to spend time there.

Our base was at Nyanga in the Eastern Highlands near the border with Mozambique. Thanks to the recent civil war, the road network was quite good – it's much harder to plant landmines in tarmac! As I was driven out to Nyanga on that first occasion, I was in awe. There were granite outcrops everywhere with huge potential for routes. The countryside was green and flourishing and every now and again I'd catch side of the abundant wildlife. This was going to be amazing!

First things first, I clearly needed more gear. This was long before email and internet and even the phone lines were limited so I wrote a letter back home to get more kit sent out. The first delivery arrived without a problem. Sometime later I needed to send another request. The harsh, rough granite was playing havoc with my already well-worn rock shoes. I wrote to John Wilson. It was a brief, hand-written letter with words to the effect of: "Please buy and send a new pair of rock boots. I think a pair of Fires would be best." I opted for the Boreal Fire because they were a bit less dependent on a perfect fit. John sadly understood the instruction as: "I think a pair of **fives** would be best." Reading this and immediately assuming that I would want another pair of the Asolo Runout shoes that he knew I'd had previously used and really liked, his immediate reaction was to think: "He doesn't take size 5… I'll send him a pair of 5½!" He duly bought them from Rock & Run (based in the Lakes) and sent them out. I was overjoyed to receive his parcel and tore it open in anticipation. Imagine my dismay at having to squeeze size 7½ feet into 5½ shoes… but I managed!

The impressive rock architecture beside the road to Nyanga

Bouldering near Nyanga in my new rock shoes

Life at Nyanga was idyllic. In colonial days, the area had been a summer holiday retreat for escaping the oppressive summer heat of the lowlands. There were still a number of great hotels with bars and restaurants and we were living in lovely ex-holiday homes, typically sharing three to a house. Each dwelling was allocated a couple of staff. Ours were Memory, a sweet local girl who did the housekeeping and would prepare food for us if we wanted her to, and Lazarus who looked after any maintenance and tended the garden. Lazarus also got us our own chickens to run around the grounds and provide a regular supply of fresh eggs. He also used to wash our vehicles most mornings. We'd been provided with Mazda pick-up trucks to drive from home to the camp and also to get us out and about around the training area. We could also use them for our own personal use. They did get pretty grubby after all the use they got, especially in the dusty conditions of the training area, so one day I asked Lazarus to clean inside the cab as well as doing the outside as usual. I headed out of the front door after breakfast, ready to make the 20-minute drive to the training camp, to find Lazarus stood by the open driver's door, hosepipe in hand, spraying water into the cab! "STOP!" Then again, how would he know any different?

Unsurprisingly, once again one of my biggest challenges was finding someone to climb with. My colleagues weren't keen, but it turned out that our mechanic, a sergeant called Chris Holdsworth, had done a bit of climbing so he was quickly recruited. I'm not sure he was quite aware of what he'd signed up for. I spent a lot of time on my own, abseiling down crags and giving the potential lines a good wire-brushing as they were often covered in moss and lichen. Underneath were some marvellous lines on rough, crystalline granite. Once clean, or occasionally on-sight, I would drag Chris along to hold my ropes while I

New routing at Windrush Crag

did the first ascents, mostly in the E1 to E3 range.

We'd been out on one such day, creating a fine E3 5c at an area called Sanyat-we. It was a good, varied line consisting of a slab, crack and wall, with not a lot of gear in places. On our return to the village, I had a visit from our Commanding Officer, David Black, who by coincidence was from the same regiment as me. He'd come to give me the news of the tragic death of a good friend of mine from our regiment, Dominic Swift. He'd been climbing in Glencoe when his abseil anchor failed, resulting in a long, fatal fall. I named that day's route *Dominic's Route* in his memory. I wrote to his mother and his girlfriend to pass on my condolences and let them know about his lasting memorial in the African bush. They were delighted.

Some of the other route names had special significance at the time. On a smaller crag that we called Windrush (the farmstead below was called Windrush Farm), one of the routes became *Ten to One*. This refers to the mythical foreign exchange rate that everyone sought. The official rate between the Pound Sterling and the Zimbabwean Dollar was around two dollars to the pound but in reality, nobody ever changed their money through official channels. There were so many people in the country who could see the way the economy was going. They wanted foreign currency as a safeguard for the future and were happy to do a deal at a better rate. Everyone found their own local contact to go to for local currency. Mine was called Charles and he worked at the Sheraton in Harare. He'd approached me on one of my first stays there and for the next six months we did good, mutually beneficial business. At the time I was getting a rate of six to one, but it was said that some were getting the elusive ten to one.

Another new route at Sanyatwe was named after an interesting experience at a concert in Mutare, the nearest large town to the east of us with a border crossing to Mozambique. One of our Zimbabwean army staff, a Sergeant Major Chamunorwa, had asked me whether I wanted to take a trip to Mutare where British reggae band Misty in Roots was due to play. Chamunorwa was a fascinating character. During the war of independence he'd been in the Selous Scouts, a predominantly white, special forces unit of the Rhodesian Army with a ferocious reputation that is claimed to have been responsible for 68 per cent of all the 'terrorist' deaths during the long, bloody conflict. Those 'terrorists' were now his Zimbabwean Army colleagues.

I leapt at the chance to go to this concert with him and we drove over in the afternoon to the football ground in Mutare where the band and their support were due to play. There was a strained atmosphere from the outset that I didn't really understand. There was also a strong police presence, which didn't seem entirely appropriate. After the support act had finished, before Misty in Roots had had a chance to come on, some trouble kicked off and the police came in with an overly heavy-handed response, ultimately firing tear gas into the crowd. As we were engulfed in the gas, we did the only thing it's possible to do in the circumstances and that's to run. It was chaos as the crowd tried to get out of the enclosed space. We climbed a fence and ran to the car and got away as quick as we could – all quite unlike any other concert experience I've had before or since. Several days later I created a new route and named it *Tears For Misty*.

Nearly all the new routes were climbed using my Trad rack for protection and in most cases this was sufficient. I'd also spied a coupled of excellent looking lines that had no natural gear – just-off-vertical walls with crimpy finger holds. It's one thing winding your neck out on a crag at home but doing the same thing in the back of beyond in a place like Zimbabwe with no rescue facilities and no nearby medical resources would be reckless. The alternative, other than choosing another route, was to place a bolt. I'd had a rudimentary hand-drilling kit sent out, along with some self-drilling spits, so I set to work. This manual approach to bolting is hard work and slow progress at the best of times and putting bolts into the super-hard granite of those crags was desperate. It would often take several

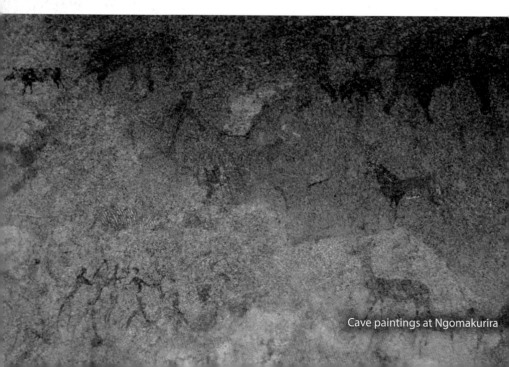

Cave paintings at Ngomakurira

spits to create a hole of adequate depth as they were often blunt before they'd done their job but it was worth it. They helped create some stunning routes.

It wasn't all new routes that I was climbing at the time. There were some established climbing areas, particularly closer to Harare. I met up with two locals – Ian McDonald and Andy Michalowski – who introduced me to a number of good crags including Canon Kopje, Christon Bank and Ngomakurira. At the latter I did a tough new route called *Terribly Clever Expatriate*. It was named after the vehicle registration numbers on all expat vehicles that included the letters 'TCE'. During that visit to Ngomakurira, a 30km drive north east of Harare, we were somewhat humbled by the local wildlife. We'd climbed another easier new route, maybe HVS we thought. As we were packing up our kit at the end of the day a troop of baboons literally ran across the wall that we'd just climbed. Maybe it wasn't a 'first ascent' then! There's some remarkable rock art nearby but I've heard there's been significant vandalism recently. It's a tragedy to see these national treasures desecrated.

Much closer to Harare, in the suburb of Epworth, is the amazing collection of boulders known as the Epworth Balancing Rocks. These provided awesome bouldering and some more committing solos. One of the formations, which consists of three boulders stacked on top of each other, features prominently in the design of Zimbabwe's banknotes. The face that appears on the notes helpfully provided a great mini-route, which I soloed.

Also posted to Zimbabwe at the time was another keen climber, Chris Field. He had a training role at the Zimbabwean Army's Staff College in Harare, so we met up occasionally when I was visiting the capital to get out climbing. Chris and I did a number of new routes at Chris-

Climbing on the 'Banknote Boulders', Epworth Balancing Rocks, Harare

ton Bank, north of Harare.

Often the simple adventure of prospecting for new crags and routes was sufficient for a great day out, especially in the Nyanga area. I'd try and persuade a couple of colleagues to join me for a trip out to a likely-looking crag that I'd spied in the middle of the bush while out training with our recruits. Armed with an AK-47 each, in case of trouble with wildlife, we'd bash our way through thick undergrowth, trying to make enough noise to frighten off snakes, leopards or baboons. The target crag, once reached, didn't always reward us with some climbing. Many showed great promise but have probably never been visited since.

Sometimes I'd go prospecting on my own, especially to crags I knew. One such was the Sanyatwe area that I returned to regularly. One evening I was sat at the top of the crag, having just cleaned a new line. I was enjoying the peaceful calm of the evening, watching the sunset when I noticed, several hundred metres to my left, a troop of baboons, similarly sat on top of their own buttress apparently also enjoying themselves just watching the sun go down. It felt like a magical moment of connection.

The training that we were providing felt worthwhile. Irrespective of the crazy international politics, we were given these raw recruits, some of them looking too young to be there, and they were our responsibility. Thankfully, the conflict

Sunset baboons

back in their homeland was drawing to a close but if we could give them sufficient skills to keep themselves and their companions alive, that would be a job worth doing. Coming from Mozambique, they spoke a range of different African dialects, but most had a pretty good understanding of Portuguese. We were provided with interpreters for all our lessons in camp and training in the field. I chose to go one step further and taught myself sufficient Portuguese so that I could speak to them directly and dispense with the need for translation. The first time I ran a lesson in Portuguese, the reaction was hilarious, the assembled group in front of me fell about laughing. I turned to my interpreter and asked "What did I say? Did I get something wrong?" "No," he replied. "They are just so happy that you are making the effort to speak to them directly. No white man has ever done that before! There were one or two mistakes, but don't worry about that".

The training wasn't like back at home. We only had these raw recruits for 12 weeks but in that time we taught them the basic military skills to defend themselves from terrorist attack and fight back. We taught them to build a defensive position that could withstand an assault, how to use communications equipment and, of course, how to use the weapons at their disposal. As these were all supplied by the then Soviet Union, we had to familiarise ourselves with them first. I'd never used an RPG-7 rocket launcher, and although I had used a Kalashnikov rifle, most British officers and NCOs hadn't. Most Europeans and Americans would be a bit sniffy about the Kalashnikov or AK-47. It doesn't match up to the technical standards of the American M16 ArmaLite or the British SA80 but then it's serving a different market. It's long been the weapon of choice for the guerrilla, bandit or terrorist for a very good reason – it's considerably more robust than the lightweight, plasticky, western creations that need disciplined cleaning and maintenance. You could leave your AK-47 lying around in a humid muddy jungle or in dry dusty bush for days and be pretty sure it wouldn't let you down.

There was some scope for confusion with the Russian ammunition. One day we were introducing our recruits to the hand grenade. These were Russian stick grenades with a fist-sized warhead mounted on a wooden stick. To use them, the soldier would unscrew a cap at the bottom of the handle from which a ring-pull on a cord would drop, pull the ring and throw. Four or five seconds later it would explode – simple! They came packed in wooden crates, which were helpfully labelled in Cyrillic. Some comedian pointed out that "Of course, they produce one version of these with an instantaneous fuse… for use with a trip wire. But don't worry, they are clearly labelled." Well, seeing as none of us could read a word of Russian, that added a bit of spice to using the first one!

AK-47 familiarization

Bayonet training

My trusty pick-up

Assault course

RPG-7 rocket launcher

Russian stick grenade

We used our pick-ups to get around and they were good, reliable vehicles but everyone had a tendency to abuse them somewhat. One morning, one of the sergeants turned up with significant damage to his truck. It looked obvious to everyone that he'd been overdoing it on one of the rough tracks and hit a tree. "No, honestly," he protested, "a huge kudu jumped out at me and I hit it." A kudu is a large antelope with characteristic, twisted horns. They were fairly common in the area and some were the size of a horse. "So, what happened to the kudu?" we asked. "It ran off." Sorry, but we just didn't believe it. Good try, but why not just admit your driving wasn't up to scratch? It was only a week or so later that a small group of us had piled into someone's vehicle for a trip down the valley to one of the hotels. On our return, late at night, with three squeezed into the front and the rest sat in the open back, we were banging along down a straight stretch of road at a good lick when a huge bull kudu suddenly appeared from the bush at the side of the road and leapt straight across our path. We missed it by inches. Maybe he'd been telling the truth after all. It's a testament to the remarkable ability of the local craftsmen that when the damaged pick-up was taken to a ramshackle workshop in the village, it came back in pristine condition. Despite the lack of access to spare parts or approved colour schemes, the damaged bodywork was expertly panel-beaten and filled and the paintwork matched perfectly.

Part of my role was to train the officers who were to lead the rest of the com-

With some of the Mozambique officers I was training

pany of soldiers we were training. In addition to the same basic soldiering skills, they also needed to understand and develop their leadership skills if they were to command loyalty and respect. They were a great bunch of guys, a bit better educated than the rest and a couple of them spoke a little bit of English. We ended up learning each other's language in tandem. I took them out climbing a couple of times to help build trust and confidence but mainly just to have a bit of fun. I've often wondered what became of them. I suspect that some of them are running the country by now!

To add a bit of spice to the training, someone had found a supplier of locally made pyrotechnics. He was a larger-than-life American in Harare. He supplied all manner of flashes and bangs to add a bit of realism to mock battles and assaults. They were certainly a lot louder than anything that any of us had come across before. There was one exercise that we did with each intake that involved a simulated attack with live ammunition being fired, quite safely, over the heads of the trainees as they were hunkered down in a defensive position that they'd constructed. Our Engineer colleagues – another captain and sergeant – were responsible for the sound effects. One of the things we had was a mock-up of mortar fire. Charges were buried in the ground around the trenches which would simulate the rounds landing and exploding, while off to one side, out of the way, a linked set of explosions would be set off to simulate the rounds being fired. It turned out that our Engineer colleagues were parked up in their pick-up with all the explosives in the back. The sergeant ignited a salvo and threw it away from the vehicle. However, because the six charges were linked, as one exploded it jumped like an over-powered firecracker prior to the next one detonating. At some point one of these jumped into the back of the truck. The sergeant saw this and instinctively grabbed it intending to throw it clear and so prevent the disaster of all the rest being detonated. As he reached for it the next charge went off, taking a thumb and first finger with it. He was evacuated immediately to the nearest hospital in Mutare where the medics did a fantastic job of limiting the damage and saving the rest of his hand. The subsequent investigation uncovered the fact that these pyrotechnics were made with det-cord, not the usual, low-explosive black powder or gunpowder. Det-cord is incredibly powerful and usually used to set off other high-explosives. That explains why they were so loud! With typical squaddie humour the sergeant was henceforth known as "Fingers".

The wildlife in Zimbabwe was amazing. Of course, everyone was eager to see elephants, hippos, rhinos, big cats and all the classic large mammals, but we didn't have many of these in the Eastern Highlands. What we did have was a remarkably rich array of birdlife and if you looked out for these, you could have a fantastic wildlife experience every day. It used to amuse me when, after a trip out into the bush, I'd be asked: "Did you see any wildlife?" "Yes, masses," I'd reply enthusiastically, reeling off a long list of exotic bird species. "Oh, right," they would say, disappointed. "But did you see any animals?" From the large and impressive fish eagles, auger buzzards, secretary birds through the peculiar hamerkop with its odd-shaped head, and the hornbills with their oversized bills, the ugly marabou stork with its bare neck and head to the colourful lilac-breasted roller and the diminutive sunbirds, there was so much to see in every different type of habitat.

Lilac-Breasted Roller and Hornbill

Out in our training area we'd often see Secretary Birds. These birds of prey have a distinctive shape and appear to be wearing knee-length breeches on their very long legs. We'd also hear, more than see, the 'Go-Way' bird, the Grey Lourie with its distinctive call that appears to be saying "Go away. Go away." On a canoeing trip on the Upper Zambezi, above Victoria Falls, I had a couple of memorable experiences. Firstly, our small group had paddled into a small lagoon out of the main stream of the river for a lunch stop. As we sat eating our picnic, a huge elegant fish eagle landed in the branches of a dead tree nearby. This is the iconic image of this stunning bird and it was only added to when a second bird, perhaps the mate of the first one, landed in another tree on the opposite side of the pool and they started calling to each other with their haunting cry. After that treat, as we headed on downstream, I heard a persistent knocking coming from a tree that was overhanging the river. I gently steered the canoe towards the sound and slowly drifted beneath the canopy of leaves. There above me, sat on a branch, was a large pied kingfisher with a fish in its bill. The sound was the bird repeatedly whacking the fish against the branch – whether to kill it or to soften it up I'm not sure but it was a privilege to see.

I was quite new to birding, so every trip out brought new discoveries. Karen will happily tell anyone that I am capable of Olympic-standard bullshit. I like to think of it as confident guesswork and a great example was one time when we were on a safari in Hwange National Park. Karen had come to stay and we were having a few days in this beautiful area, guided by one of the rangers. All morning we'd caught sight of many different birds as well as bigger game animals. At one point the ranger stopped the vehicle, pointed at a bush and asked "So, have you any idea what that bird is? It's quite rare." It was a medium-sized black bird with a bright red chest. I had no idea. I'd never seen one before but figured it looked vaguely shrike-like in its shape, with a large bill and the chest was too distinctive to ignore. "That will be a crimson-breasted shrike" I stated with great confidence, having no idea if such a bird existed. "Wow, you do know your birds don't you?" he exclaimed, clearly impressed. I'd hit the jackpot – with all the skill of buying a lottery ticket. Karen looked at me knowingly, seeing through the façade and clearly not at all impressed.

Another bird-related experience that sticks in my mind was from a climbing trip. I was sat at the top of a crag belaying when a Black Stork slowly and effortlessly drifted by. These birds are all wings – wide with squared ends that allow the birds to glide and soar effortlessly. Protruding out at the front is a long, thin neck and similarly scrawny legs trail behind. It looked like something from prehistoric times. Then, to my utter delight it lazily brought one of those long legs forward and scratched its head while continuing its slow drift towards wherever it was headed.

For all the bird life, the big mammals were usually the highlight of any trip. Karen came out to visit twice during my stay and we had several trips – the one to Hwange in the north west, near Victoria Falls, and also a fantastic five-day trip down the Lower Zambezi through the area known as Mana Pools. At this point of the mighty river's journey towards the Mozambique border and the ocean, it widens and lazily ambles through game-rich savannah. We were a small, self-contained group of five plus a guide in three open canoes. We camped overnight on the sandbanks beside the great river, cooking on an open fire and sleeping under mosquito nets. It was magical. We would steer around pods of hippos in the river and had elephants coming to the banks to drink. I was keen to get some great photos and on one occasion, with a large elephant in the reeds at the side of the river, I was paddling closer and closer as Karen was back-paddling faster and faster to get us further away. "It's flapping its ears, that means it's about to charge." "Yes – but think of the photo." We woke up on several mornings to find crocodile tracks in the sand near where we were sleeping. Apparently, they only take their prey when they're in the water. We certainly hoped so.

It was on this canoe safari through Mana Pools that I proposed to Karen and we agreed to get married the following year. I recognise that I was incredibly fortunate to have got to know her. She was petite but full of energy, which she put into her running with great success. She was very intelligent, well-read, had similar tastes to me and loved being out in the wilds. Like me, she'd left home straight after school and done her nurse training with the army in Germany making her very independent and equally focussed on whatever she was doing at the time. I recognised how professional she was in her role and she was to become a brilliant leader of the District Nurse team for which she was responsible for many years.

Karen has also been incredibly tolerant of my commitment to climbing. At the time of our wedding, one of my older female cousins from East Lancashire

Preparing to set off on our Mana Pools safari

approached her and said: "I guess you'll be putting a stop to all this climbing he does, now that you're married." Karen was mortified at the thought. "Why on earth would I want to stop him? That's who he is. If I didn't like him climbing, I wouldn't have married him in the first place." As we found on many future climbing holidays with other couples, not everyone is that relaxed and partners can often expect a lot more together-time. More recently we've had many cycling holidays to France and Mallorca. We'd both get ready in the morning for a day out on the bike then Karen would go one direction and I'd go the other. We might try and coordinate a meet-up for a coffee or lunch, but Karen would be the first to say, "I have no intention of riding with you. Why would I want to do that? We both know neither of us will be happy with each other's pace." As a result, we both get a great day out and meet up later in the day to share our experiences over food and drink.

Over the years, something of a ritual has built up between me and Karen, whether I'm off on a trip abroad, going out for the day or even just heading off for a session at the climbing wall. The last thing she'll say to me before I go out climbing is, "Be careful." Just that, no embellishments. I'll inevitably reply, "I will – you know me." "Exactly!" will be her final comment, with a knowing look. The point is, she does know me. She recognises that I will sometimes not hold back and others might think I was being careless. But she also understands that I'll approach anything I do with care and consideration.

Inevitably, my time in the paradise that was Zimbabwe had to draw to a close. At least I felt like I'd made the most of the opportunity. There was one last benefit. The Foreign and Commonwealth Office paid for Business Class travel back to London, but this could be traded in against a lower of class ticket to go further afield. One popular option was to buy a 'triangular ticket' from Harare to Australia and back to London via a Far East stop, with the third leg, back to Harare, left unused. We had to make up the difference in price but bear in mind that it was paid in Zimbabwe dollars, acquired at a favourable rate, so it was still a real bargain.

So, having finished my stint in Zimbabwe, I naturally flew to Australia for a climbing trip – sadly one of my least successful foreign forays. I made my way out to the world-famous Arapiles. "It'll be fine," they said. "You'll find loads of people to climb with," they said. It was August, the middle of winter, and conditions seemed perfect to me but, apparently, people don't climb at Arapiles in winter – it was as good as deserted. I spent one night in the ghost-town of a campsite, soloed a handful of routes and hitched the 1000km back to Sydney. That was some hitching experience! I stood at the end of the road leading to the campsite with thumb out. Eventually a car pulled up. "Where you going, mate?" "Sydney," I replied, hoping they were going that direction. "So are we, hop in. Hope you don't mind doing a bit of the driving on the way." The rest of the trip to Australia was redeemed by a combination of two fabulous productions of Puccini operas – Turandot and La Boheme – at the Sydney Opera House followed by a week learning to dive on the Barrier Reef. A fair swap.

On my return from the African adventure, I was given a job setting up and running something called an AYT (Army Youth Team), based in Preston. These small teams were set up around the country under the control and budget of the Recruitment and Liaison branch. Having said that, there wasn't any overt recruitment taking place. The whole thing was more of a marketing exercise trying to raise the profile of the army among young people through sporting and adventurous activities. To many of my more ambitious colleagues, this role was seen as a dead end with no benefit to personal development or a future career. To me it was a dream job. I didn't want a future career!

I had a great team to work with, another mixed bag. My dependable second-in-command was Colour Sergeant Paul Salt. 'Salty' was an old-timer. He'd been around a long time and knew everyone. He was a wheeler-dealer, a bit of an Arthur Daly character. If you needed an item of kit, then Paul would be able to get his hands on it – just don't ask where it came from! Next up was Sergeant Pete Shipley. He'd done some covert work in Northern Ireland but had also been Drum Major of the Regimental Band – not two trades that would naturally go together. He walked with a limp having had his leg broken by an overweight sergeant jumping on it after a mess dinner. The team also had two corporals: Corporal Swanson ('Swanny') who was happiest sat in a kayak. He was probably the most qualified when it came to outdoor activities. The other corporal was Bernie Catterall. Bernie had been a Guardsman but was now a member of the Queen's Lancashire Regiment TA (Territorial Army). He was initially seconded to us for six months, but I managed to get him back into the regular army, where he stayed for the next 16 years. Bernie was also someone who got on with any job you gave him, and it was him who, more often than not, was given the job of belaying me when I wanted to get out climbing. Also seconded from the TA was Private Gary Mackeral who became known as 'Billy the Fish' or simply 'Billy', named after the sporting hero in the Viz comic. Finally, we had the female element in the form of the effervescent Lou Cunningham, a soldier from the WRAC (Women's Royal

Army Corps). On her first day out with a group, she went mountain biking with Bernie and a group of kids. The day was pretty terrible – wet and misty. They'd been riding along a ridge on the moors above Widdop. Bernie was out in front when they came to a stop to let everyone catch up. Bernie pulled up and put his foot down to steady himself. Lou, new to mountain biking, did the same, except she put her other foot down – only to find herself falling down the grassy bank and landing in a bog. She hadn't seen the drop in the mist but she had managed to cheer up the despondent group and keep them laughing all the way back to the transport. Bernie and Lou became an item and were married some years later.

We spent that year taking groups of kids climbing, canoeing, mountain biking and walking as well as running fun activities at their own premises in the schools and youth clubs of Lancashire. During the summer we created a base at a campsite in Coniston and the groups would come up to us for a few days or a week. Between all the team, we'd got enough skills and knowhow to provide a fantastic experience for the kids – if any of them ever thought about joining the army, that would be a bonus, but it certainly wasn't something that we dwelt on. Just being given the chance to introduce these youngsters, often from deprived areas in deepest Lancashire, the chance to experience the outdoor world was a privilege and all credit to the army for doing it.

In 1989 I was serving in the TA after leaving the regular army when I was offered a secondment to a new recruiting initiative, 144 Army Youth Team. I wasn't doing much else in my life so decided I just had to give it a go.

It was good to be back in the army full time. I'd never really fitted into my civilian lifestyle. This was different, though. It didn't really feel like work – just one trip out after another, doing a job but a hugely enjoyable one. We'd take kids from all sorts of social backgrounds from college to young offender Institutions out for activities from mountain biking to climbing and during the week we'd often go into schools to run sessions of games or initiative exercises getting them to figure out how to cross the 'crocodile-infested swamp' with a couple of planks and a barrel.

Louise and I were out mountain biking with a group on the day the Iraq war broke out. This benefited the team as I managed to manipulate one of the young soldiers out of a key for their recruiting caravan which was sharply commandeered and dispatched to Coniston Hall campsite for the summer.

It wasn't much like the army either. The team was small and friendly, led by Captain Nick Wharton. We all had our jobs to do and as long as we did them he'd let us get on with it. He'd always listen to whatever anyone in the team had to say, whoever it was. I found this really taxing at times – democracy in the army, it'll never catch on! We all had a clear idea of what the team was trying to do and we worked well together. Freedom to think and to make decisions made the team successful and we all had a good time while we were hard at work. The Boss was a good listener and he'd always make sure everyone was alright. Before he left, he got me an extension back into the army full time after my initial spell of six months with the team, and I stayed for another 24 years!

When we were at Coniston for the summer, we'd have all sorts of adventures like doing a sump dive from an underground lake back out into the fresh air at Hodge Close Quarry. You didn't tend to do that sort of thing on other army adventure training. We did this with no proper gear, just an army issue torch in a clear plastic bag, a piece of old climb-ing rope and a kayaking helmet. The Boss  would often use me as a belay machine so he could climb some of his harder climbs. I'd get dragged up after him, then I'd get to have a go on something more sensible. It was a good time in my life. Me and Lou eventually got married. I had a reverse vasectomy and fathered four children. Who says miracles never happen?

Bernie Catterall

Karen had already left the army and, having qualified as a District Nurse, was living and working in the North East. She'd sometimes come over to Coniston for the weekend, along with Hannah the labrador. Like most labs, Hannah liked her food and, for her, life on a campsite was heaven. She'd creep out of the tent at night and forage for scraps around the site. Many people would cook an evening meal and leave their dirty dishes outside their tent, intending to clean them in the morning only to find that the washing-up fairy had visited overnight and left them spotless.

It was during this last year that I was given an ultimatum by the army bigwigs. Having already twice extended my Short Service Commission for additional time, I was given the choice: "Either convert to a Regular Commission (and stay forever) or leave at the end of the current engagement". I didn't want to stay forever so I chose to leave.

9 - Cream

E4 6A CRAIG BWLCH Y MOCH, TREMADOG

The best the UK has to offer

Over the years I've climbed all over the world. I've been to climbing areas with diverse styles and disciplines as well as many different rock types. Naturally, the two tend to go hand-in-hand. The way in which climbing develops in an area is to some extent determined by the rock available. But it's always a pleasure to get back home, to what's on offer in the UK.

Climbing here isn't the highest, nor the hardest. We don't have the best crack climbing nor the steepest, most expansive face climbing. The rock isn't the grippiest and the crags certainly aren't always the cleanest. Our climbing venues aren't always the most scenic, they don't always give us the best views or atmosphere and we're often climbing in less than favourable weather. What British climbing does have, however, is a wide selection of all the above, packed into a relatively small area.

We've all got our personal preferences. Some like the long runouts above a solitary bolt on a steep, slate slab while others relish swapping leads on a small stance on a long multi-pitch route in the mountains. Some like the challenge of trying to find and place their own, sometimes marginal, protection while at the same time trying to work out a sequence that will get them up the next section of route. Others would rather just clip a line of bolts and concentrate purely on the technical difficulties. Meanwhile, at the other end of the climbing spectrum are those who are happy to spend all their time barely leaving the ground on a boulder problem. There's plenty for everyone.

Just take North Wales: easily accessible climbing on classic mountain-style crags of volcanic rock in Llanberis, Ogwen and other valleys; arguably the best sea cliff climbing in the world across Anglesey at Gogarth; and, to the north, the fingery limestone of Pen Trwyn and the Ormes. Go south instead for the road-side fun of Tremadog, quite different again, or stay in Llanberis and visit the slate quarries for a completely different climbing experience, requiring a whole new set of skills and mindset.

The same could be said for the Lakes. I remember one particularly varied day out with Stuart Wood ('Woody') that just evolved from one adventure to another as the day went on. We started with a trip to the sandstone at St Bees on the west coast of Cumbria. With the benefit of the bolts, we were both able to quickly lead five routes from 6a+ to 7b including the superb *Dreaming of Red Rocks*. Having knocked those off we drove inland and up idyllic Eskdale to Hare Crag – granite territory. I can't remember what Woody climbed but I did *Where Dogs Run Free*, a short, but quite hard, E5 finger crack. Continuing up the valley, at the top of the pass we went to Hardknott Crag, which is made of typical Lakeland volcanic rock. Here I led both *Powerglide* and *Caesar*, tough routes that aren't particularly well protected.

By now a pattern was emerging and that probably spurred us on to think of another venue and another change of rock. We opted to drive down the Duddon Valley towards the coast where we made a call at the esoteric Donkey Rocks, a small, obscure outcrop of haematite, a reddish-brown rock that has similar properties to slate, near Broughton-in-Furness. Here we tackled a further two routes on very peculiar rock. That might have been enough, but as we were heading back to Ambleside so I could drop Woody off, we took a final detour up the road to the spectacular slate quarry, Hodge Close, for a final ascent of *Limited Edition*. One day out, 11 routes on five crags and five very different rock types. If we'd planned it, we could've headed back down towards the coast, to the South Lakes Limestone and added yet another substrate, but we hadn't. So much variety in such a tiny patch!

As I've said, that variation in rock types affects the styles of climbing that can be done. Sandstone is a sedimentary rock with a fine grain that often pre-

Al Phizacklea on *Sky*, Hodge Close

Glenn Sutcliffe powers up *Toxic Rock*, St Bees

sents smooth, rounded faces with few positive holds, particularly where it's been worn down by wind or water. The lack of holds is compensated, to some degree, by good friction from the individual sand particles, but the absence of distinct cracks often makes finding natural protection challenging. That's why the cliffs at St Bees, for example, have succumbed to the bolt.

Granite is igneous (formed from magma) and so very hard and usually coarse-grained but it can vary significantly. The crystal size can affect the coarseness but so too can weathering. In Chamonix, glacial action on the lower section of cliffs has worn the rock very smooth but, by contrast, the short outcrops in the lower part of the Eskdale valley are rough and provide excellent friction.

Most of the crags in the Lake District are formed from volcanic rock. This is often cracked and highly featured, generally with ample positive holds and gear placements but fewer as the grade goes up. But again, there is variation even across this small region. In some cases, Lakes' rock is smooth and slatey, while in others it can be very rough and textured.

Haematite, the penultimate rock type of that day out with Woody, is pretty rare but very similar in nature to its more common cousin slate. Slate itself is completely different to other common rocks. This smooth rock is made of fine-grained muds, ashes and volcanic tuffs that have been compressed. Unlike other rock, with slate it often feels as though there either is a hold or there isn't with nothing in between. These holds maybe very small and often require a great deal of finesse to use them. There's very limited friction from the smooth surface and woe betide anyone caught in a rain shower mid-route as the surface will turn to glass in an instant. Most slate climbing in the UK is on rock faces exposed by quarrying, which introduces fractures. Tree roots and the effects of freeze-thaw cycles mean that much of it is unstable and liable to movement, rockfall or even catastrophic collapse. Recent decades have seen significant changes in, or even total demise of, several once-popular routes.

Another memorable trip that involved the incomparable Woody was a weekend in Scotland in 2000. With us that time were Dave Birkett and James McHaffie. Dave is an undisputed legend within Lake District climbing, and far beyond. His hard, craggy features make him look as if he's carved out of the local stone that he spends his days working with. Part of the formidable Birkett dynasty with grandfather Jim Birkett, the strongest climber of his generation, and his uncle Bill, well-known climber, writer, photographer and raconteur, Dave still

Nick on *Copenhagen*, Hardknott Crag ◉ David Simmonite

lives in Little Langdale, at the heart of the land that he so clearly holds so dearly to his heart.

Young James, as he was at the time, is also the product of a fine climbing tradition. His father, Ray McHaffie, was a prolific climber, especially in Borrowdale where he famously climbed the Classic Rock route, *Little Chamonix* wearing boxing gloves and roller skates. Caff, who bore a striking resemblance to a young Harry Potter at the time, was working with Woody at Rock & Run in Ambleside.

Woody had filled Caff's impressionable young mind with many tall tales of 'The Captain's covert activities' while in the army. Soon after I'd picked the three of them up and we were heading north, young Caff asked, rather sheepishly, "How many people have you killed?" Playing along, initially I asked, "What, me personally or those where I've ordered others to do it?", going on to say, rather sternly, "I can't disclose that sort of information." Later in the journey, as we were passing Hamilton on the motorway, I rather clumsily sped past a police car doing well over the limit. Predictably, the blue lights went on and he pulled me over. I got out to speak with him, to be told, "That was blatant cheek! Did you not see me?" I was full of apology explaining that I had seen him, albeit at the last moment, and considered that it would've been more dangerous to slam the brakes on. I explained we were going climbing in Glencoe and how sorry I was to have allowed my speed to creep up and so on. Eventually, he let me go with just a warning to be more careful.

When I got back in the car, the guys wanted to know what had happened. I nonchalantly explained that I'd told the policeman who I was, and he'd immediately apologised for inconveniencing me. Caff looked in awe but the other two recognised the sweet smell of bullshit wafting round the car!

The following day we climbed non-stop on Tunnel Wall on the side of Buachaille Etive Mor. We were all climbing really well and swapping leads on all sorts of routes. I did *Risk Business* with Caff, *Twilight Zone* with Tim Emmett, who'd joined us, *Waltzing Ostriches* with Woody and *Uncertain Emotions* with Dave. I was already a very long way up *Twilight Zone*, a runout E6 6a without any runners, when GP Mark Garthwaite turned up at the crag, asking who the lunatic was without any gear? "Things are looking up," I shouted down. "There's a doctor at the crag!" That evening we also met up with John Wilson and a team who'd driven over from Aberdeen. It was quite a night in the bar of the Kingshouse, with Dave McBirkett holding forth expansively, his attempted Scottish accent growing stronger as the night went on and the beers went down.

I climbed with Nick Wharton, aka the Captain, between 2000 and 2002. He's undoubtedly one of the boldest climbers I've ever climbed with and has a super-cool head. At a shakeout, before a hard section of a climb, most people ponder, deliberate and take time to psyche up and commit. With Nick it's the opposite – he jumps straight into a hard sequence with total commitment. I don't think I've seen anyone commit to something so quickly, which, when you think about it, is the most efficient way to do it, even if the sequence isn't always perfect. There were plenty of stories of Nick scaring partners by running it out with no gear and big serious leads. Around 2000 I'd on-sighted my first few E7s and was doing more solo climbing in the Lakes than had been done there previously but Nick still seemed to have a better head than me for committing to bold runouts nonchalantly.

I was working at a climbing shop in Ambleside, Rock & Run, at the time and me and Nick would often do after work trips to places like Dow Crag and Pavey Ark. On a day off I remember going to *Tophet Wall*, high on the side of Great Gable. I had a stinking hangover so wasn't so keen to climb but I recall belaying Nick on some E5s before he went for the tough Pete Whillance route *Incantations* (E6). It had recently lost a critical peg, so the protection was even more sparse than usual. He got pretty high before a hold broke and he took a big lob onto some pretty dubious gear.

On a trip to Scotland with Nick, Woody and Birkett I was sharing a tent with Nick and on the drive up it had been discussed about how often Nick had killed people when in the army. I was concerned he'd have some flashbacks at night and try to kill me. Having Woody with us, we got pretty drunk when we arrived. Next morning Nick and I did *Risk Business* to warm up then some E6s on the left and I remember him not putting in any gear for the first 20m on one of the E6s!

The last time we climbed together was on a trip to Pembroke in 2002, he picked me up and we flew down at high speed. I was labouring for Cumbria Stonework at the time and felt pretty fit. It was a really great trip, out early and climbing till 8.30 in the evening, often doing ten routes or so. I remember doing *Abandon Ship* (a bit damp and it felt fierce), *Orange*

Robe Burning and on the last day jumping on *Souls* (a tough E6) as a warm-up first route of the day and it feeling pretty easy.

After the epic I had on *Master's Wall* on Cloggy I could have stopped climbing but first time out after it was climbing with Nick on Raven Crag, Thirlmere, and I think some of his confidence must have oozed into me again. No doubt, he's one of the UK's boldest climbers operating in the last 30 to 40 years.

Nice one, Captain.

James McHaffie

Woody was to become a regular climbing partner over the years but even more importantly he became our 'Gentlemen's Outfitter'. After many years of working at Rock & Run he went on to manage The Mountain Factor, just down the road, and, later, to set up and run the Epicentre, also in Ambleside. The top-quality Patagucci bargains were regularly snapped up by his climbing mates, who were always warmly welcomed in the shops with large doses of raucous abuse. Not all his customers knew how to take this kind of language – it isn't perhaps what you normally hear from behind the counter. Occasionally, the more awkward customers would be told where they could go, which, allegedly is what, sadly for us, led to his ultimate departure. "You can take the boy out of Barrow, but you can't take Barrow out of the boy!"

When it comes to varieties of climbing, most people will have their likes and dislikes, dictated by their strengths and weaknesses, past history and what's available. It's also a matter of taste. Some choose to throw themselves into bouldering or Sport climbing while others prefer to pursue the Trad approach. We could look even more broadly and throw into the mix Alpinism or mountaineering in the greater ranges. In fact, why bother going outside? Some choose to spend all their time climbing on indoor climbing walls.

We're all climbers. No group has a monopoly on that term and any sense of superiority from making one choice or the other is surely misplaced. Just as runners can be sprinters, track-racers or fell-runners, so climbers might tackle an 8000m peak or an 8ft boulder. We all have our preferences. Mine is usually Trad climbing on mountain crags but I love to clip a few bolts from time to time just as I've enjoyed regular trips to Fontainbleau for a bout of bouldering. I really can't see the appeal of going to a beautiful, crag-rich location like Llanberis Pass to climb a boulder problem, but I can see that others do and are incredibly talented at it. When it comes to Sport climbing, I've struggled to get into the right mindset and commit to the style. I enjoy a sporty spring trip to Spain or France with the chance to clip bolts in the sun while getting some valuable early-season time on the rock. I have, at times, been drawn more deeply into the Sport climbing approach and made multiple attempts to get up a particular route – even over a couple visits to the crag. But the concept of working a route, grinding it into submission, is one that I've never truly embraced. I prefer a quick hit and then on to the next thing.

This is illustrated by my record on sports routes. My best achievement on-sight was graded 7c, a route on the Wild Side at Sella in the Costa Blanca. I did that just after flashing (climbing straight off, ground-up) a 7b+ on the same crag. My best performances as a red point (climbing after some degree of practice) were, for many years, 7c+ (although one of those was later upgraded to 8a – it made my day when I heard!). As I understand it, this one grade difference between on-sight and pre-practised success smacks of a lack of commitment and a failure to enter into the spirit of things.

This preference for on-sight climbing comes from my Trad upbringing and is hard to shake off. It was just the way we did it. On a few occasions I've tried a hard Trad route on top-rope prior to leading it, sometimes encouraged down that line by someone else. In most cases, I've been left feeling that this pre-practice has detracted from the final outcome and on at least one occasion I can remember really chastising myself for being drawn into what I still consider a less-than-ideal ethic. For me, it cheapens the experience.

But, as I've said, it's a personal choice, no better or worse than anyone else's. It should also be said that there is a level of difficulty where it might be considered reckless not to have some inkling of what is coming up. Climbing ethics can be a minefield, particularly somewhere like the UK where the different styles of climbing take place right next to each other. Different points of view get quickly polarised, even more so now in the age of social media, with some very forceful exchanges. Providing that one person's approach is not to the detriment of an-

Nick climbing the bolts at Malham; *Free 'n Easy* 📷 Adam Hocking

other's, let's just allow them to get on with their climbing while we focus on ours. I saw a post on Facebook recently from a highly-respected old-timer who was berating the modern approach. The post referred to "how we did it in the 50s" but climbing in the 50s and in 2020 are as far apart as exploits in the 50s are from those of Victorian gentlemen climbing in their tweeds. I'm sure that WP Haskett Smith and his pioneering chums would no more understand the climbing ethic of the 50s than someone from that time would understand the current style.

In my opinion, it's the British tradition of placing removable protection while on the lead, Trad climbing, that sets this approach apart from many others and it'd be tragic to see that eroded away by creeping fixed protection. We currently have a pretty good consensus as to what is and isn't acceptable, but many grey areas certainly exist.

Hodge Close Quarry near Coniston is a good example. It's an old slate quarry – a large, man-made hole in the ground. On the walls and slabs of this great venue there are scary, runout Trad routes sitting alongside fully-bolted Sport routes. If someone eyes up a new line, should they bolt it or climb it as a Trad line? If they put in a peg, why not a bolt? If their new line crosses an existing Trad route, should that restrict where they can place fixed protection? I don't entirely agree with retro-bolting any of the classic lines that already exist and have been climbed many times over on scant protection.

For example, *Life in the Fast Lane*, a brilliant Pete Whillance 1980 creation that goes at E5 6b, has a move off the belay, onto the initial arete, that feels desperate – mainly because it's unprotectable – fall off and you'll probably miss the ledge and drop down the wall to the side with your rope going directly to your belayer. Drill a bolt at head-height and that move would be rendered much easier. But that is part of the beauty of Trad climbing, overcoming the doubts and committing to the move. Of course, placing a secure point of protection doesn't actually make the climbing easier, it just feels more difficult when unprotected. On the same wall further to the left is the superb line of *Stage Fright* at E6 6b, also by Pete Whillance from a few years later. The route finishes with a very long runout up a beautiful top slab above two pegs. If, at some point in the future, those pegs were replaced by bolts, would that diminish the climbing experience?

Another saga that involved the mighty Pete Whillance took place on the North Stack Wall at Gogarth and ended in the creation of *The Cad*. Both Pete and Ron Fawcett had simultaneously been given the nod about the line and both headed down as soon as possible. Ron got there first and bagged the first ascent but with a bolt placed halfway up the wall to protect the long, fingery section above. That bolt definitely had no place on a cliff like Gogarth. When I came to lead the route with Brian Davison in 1994, I took great delight in not clipping the bolt, relying instead on the lower gear behind the slightly creaky flake. It was well accepted that using the bolt would reduce the grade from E6 to E5. Having the bolt there and not clipping it is probably, psychologically, harder than not having it there in the first place. Not clipping it is an active choice that the climber has made to increase the risk when they don't have to.

I love the rock at Gogarth, and the North Stack Wall is the perfect angle for me: not too steep, requiring balance and good use of body position. The holds are fingery and as a result the climbing is technical. There is no place for brute strength on routes like *The Cad*. Add to this, the lack of protection and that makes this one of my favourite routes of all time.

QUESTIONS

Q *You are recognised by many as having a particularly bold approach. What is it that enables you to climb like that?*

A That's a really complex question. It's probably a mix of all sorts. Some of it may just be a natural ability to not be fazed by the situation, to focus on what's really important. It's tempting to think that I've benefitted from my military training along with some of the dangerous situations I faced, yet my climbing was quite 'bold' from the start. In recent years yoga has certainly taught me how to control my breathing and remain calm – but again, that's a recently acquired skill. There's something about an optimistic confidence, a self-belief in my ability to make a move, get up a route and succeed. That doesn't always work out, so it needs to go hand-in-hand with a willingness to fall off occasionally. But am I being 'bold'? That's just a perception. I don't actually consider myself as especially bold. It's been said that I'm better described as 'single-minded'. When on a route, my mind is focussed on the upward progression, not on looking for protection and as a result I'll find myself – often quite happily – further from the last gear than most others would be comfortable with.

Q. *So what's going through your mind when you're above your last piece of gear?*

A. That would depend on the situation – and how good that last piece of gear was! I can think of a recent example where I was climbing an E4 in the Lakes. I was faced with a tricky, committing move – there would be no second chance once I'd started on the sequence. I had a reasonable, but not bomb-proof piece of gear below my feet and off to one side – it wouldn't be a pleasant fall and I'd have preferred something a bit more secure. I remember the thought process: the runner is probably good enough and I'm pretty sure I can make this move but I can't afford to faff around or I'll get pumped. I didn't let the circumstances get on top of me so having weighed up the possibilities just launched into the move with the determination to get it right. I knew that on that day I should be able to get up a route of that grade – and I did. This is why accurate grading is so important.

Q. *Do you think anyone can have that bold approach?*

A. Some people are naturally a lot more risk averse – they wouldn't want to put themselves in a situation that felt 'out there'. But if people want to push themselves then I think they can practise to some degree and get more used to these situations. It's a bit like leadership – anyone can be trained to be a *better* leader, but they must have some foundation on which to build.

10 - One Step Beyond

E3 6A GOUTHER CRAG SWINDALE

Climbing abroad

For all that our British Isles have to offer the climber, it's still great to get away on a foreign trip, whether that's for a new style of climbing or just some better weather. Different venues appear to have gone in and out of fashion. In the 1980s and into the 90s it was the south of France – Buoux and Verdon being the most popular. After that it was all about trips to Spain, in particular, around the Costa Blanca near Benidorm – El Chorro down in the south near Malaga or on the island of Mallorca. Since those days, the Greek island of Kalymnos appears to have taken over as the destination of choice for early or late-year trips and other popular options include Turkey, Morocco and now many more areas in Spain.

Like many other Brits at the time, I had a trip to Buoux with Phil Baines, Bruce Stelling and a crowd of others from the North East in the spring of 1988. It was probably the most badly behaved trip I've ever been part of – even before we got on the ferry at Dover as I cheekily parked my car in a residential street in the town before meeting up with the lads. We sampled far too much local wine and beer and as a result of the subsequent high spirits we got thrown off the municipal campsite in Apt part-way through the week. But it didn't stop us knocking off a lot of great routes, using a combination of Pete Livesey's *French Rock Climbs* and a set of hand-drawn topos.

Three years later, Phil and I went back, with Karen and Lesley. That was a much more sensible and sober affair. We'd booked a gite just outside Apt. During the day, Phil and I would knock off a lot of routes while the other two went walking or cycling. I recorded over 30 routes of all grades, including several graded 7b. In nearly all cases they were either flashed (climbed straight off - ground-up) or red pointed (climbed after some degree of practice) on a second attempt. It never crossed my mind to spend longer working routes that were harder – that's just not the way I climb. Phil was knackered by the end of the week with battered and bloodied fingers from stuffing them desperately into the many finger pockets and there was just a hint of tension in the air – I suspect Lesley hadn't imagined that Phil would be out climbing all day, every day.

The following year Karen and I were back in France with a slightly altered itinerary, accompanied this time by John and Alison Wilson. We visited the magnificent Ceuse for the first time, spending three or four days there, ticking 22 routes up to 7b+ before we moved on to Verdon for the rest of that first week. The Gorge du Verdon, 25km long and up to 700m deep, is a stunning location with seemingly smooth, vertical limestone walls. The routes are immediately exposed and it's often committing to get into position. You have to abseil down from the top for several pitches and then pull the ropes down behind you, leaving you no option but to succeed in climbing back to the top. The climbing is often fingery and not always terribly well protected. Add the baking midsummer sun and it's easy to see why we sensibly dropped our target grades a few notches.

For the second week of this particular trip, we were booked into a comfortable gite not far from Buoux. On day one, John and I headed off to the crag while Karen and Alison planned a short bike trip. We were on our fifth route when, as John was lowering off one route and swinging across to put the clips in the adjacent line, he unclipped his final piece and swung to the side with some force. He put his foot out to stop himself but the outstretched limb hit the rock with more of an impact than expected. I lowered John to the ground. The damaged limb couldn't bear any weight and it was obvious he'd done some real damage.

We got back to the car eventually, with me supporting him and carrying the rucksacks, and drove to the gite, expecting to find the others back from their ride. No sign. Maybe they'd decided to go a bit further despite the heat. I got John settled with some strapping and ice on his now ballooning ankle before heading out in the car to have a scout around – still no sign of them but then I'd no idea where they'd been heading. It turned out that the two of them had had no real idea where they were heading either!

Our gite was located on top of a hill and they'd headed down the far side, not planning to go very far. After many small French villages that all looked the same, they'd lost track of where they were and which direction would bring them back home. By now, Alison, a pale-skinned Scot, was burning up. Apparently, they went from one village fountain to the next, plunging themselves into the water to cool off. Eventually, they found a garage and Karen sneaked a look at a map on one of the shelves to figure out where they were and how to get back. They arrived after dark, exhausted and sunburned to find John with his leg up in some discomfort. Oh, and it was John and Alison's first wedding anniversary, too!

With John out of action, Karen belayed me at a number of different crags in the area and a little further afield at a crag in the Ardeche. "Let's go for a day-trip to the Ardeche," we said. "It's not far," we said. "Oh yes, it is!" came the reply and, true enough, it took us hours to get there in stifling temperatures and busy holiday traffic. We just had time for two short routes before it was time to face the drive back. When we got back to the UK, John finally went to get his ankle checked. He'd knocked the edge off his ankle bone – no wonder it was painful.

It was just Karen and me the following year but we still managed to get some climbing done at Ceuse. I was taking longer than expected to solve the complexity of the superb, sustained *Berlin*, a 7c with quite a long runout before the crux moves. I kept taking long falls and meeting Karen on the wall as she was pulled up to the first bolt. Karen was doing a fine job of belaying, using an old Sticht plate – a very rudimentary belay device – but once she worked out what everyone else was using, she put her foot down – "I want one of those," pointing at a Grigri being used, effortlessly, by the adjacent team. "They're very expensive," I protested. "If you want me to belay you, you buy one." And so it was – a small step down the slippery slope to becoming a modern sport climber – something I managed to resist!

One of our most significant adventures abroad was a trip to California. The main objective was two weeks in Yosemite but we'd planned for an initial week at the Needles, in the Sequoia National Forest, relatively close by in American terms. The complete team comprised Karen and a three-year old Flora, Greg Fell, Dom Donnini, Helen Davies, Andy Stockford and Colin Downer. We also met up with a young Leo Houlding while we were there. Greg travelled out with me, Karen and Flora and I planned to do all my climbing with him. As we were camping, we had quite a lot of kit and when we went to pick up the hire car it was obvious that the four of us, along with all our baggage, would struggle in the car we'd booked. The only other vehicle available was a 15-seater minibus – it would have to do!

When we got to the Sequoia National Forest for that first week, we pitched our tents at a deserted Quaking Pines campsite on the main road. Every morning, Karen drove me and Greg up the rough track from there to the trailhead to begin the long, but lovely, walk-in. The Needles is a stunning climbing venue, hauntingly beautiful, and it was really quiet when we got there – perhaps because it was late summer or because of the length of the walk-in. We even left our kit at the crag after day one. One morning as we headed up the track, Flora was listening to one of her tapes and the delightful, catchy tune "Supercalifragilisticexpialidocious" was playing as we pulled into the parking area. There were a handful of other climbers camping up here, at the trailhead, and as we got out of the van, with the music blaring, they looked our way and exclaimed in a Vegas drawl "Jeez, you guys! You Brits knock me out. You're into Mary *Poppins*?" (The tinted windows of the van meant they couldn't see Flora.)

That week's climbing was brilliant. The scale is nothing by comparison with Yosemite but the rock is a finer-grained granite that produces great climbing on faces and cracks. The atmosphere is a little bit eerie – it's no wonder the different buttresses have names like Witch, Wizard and Sorcerer. It's also easy to understand why the local, indigenous Indians considered the Needles to be the hallowed ground of Inyo, the mighty spirit. We climbed mainly on the Sorcerer Needle and Witch Needle which have a mixture of fine cracks and face climbs. The best of the bunch was definitely Scirocco, a soaring arete with immaculate finger edges and a few well-spaced bolts. While Greg and I were climbing, Karen and Flora would go for walks in the forests and mountain trails – only later seeing the posters warning of potential mountain lion attacks. Most days they'd call in at the local store, the Ponderosa Lodge, for drinks and cake where Flora, with her wild, blonde hair and bright blue eyes, was adored by the locals.

From there it was less than 200 miles to Yosemite. Approaching on the Wawona Road, the view from the aptly-named Surprise View was breathtaking. All the books and photos were no preparation for the immense scale of the scene laid out in front of us. This is probably the high point as, once you descend to the valley floor, the traffic and commercial development, however tastefully done, detract from the surrounding natural beauty to some degree. We planned to stay

Nick on the brilliant, delicate arete of *Scirocco* at the Needles, California

at the rough and ready Camp 4, the spiritual home of Yosemite climbers, but we weren't prepared for just how rudimentary it was. In addition, the Park Service appeared to go out of their way to complicate matters, making everyone queue up at a certain time in order to book a pitch – a process that had to be repeated several times during our stay. In fact, the impression we got was that the Park Service would rather not have climbers there at all, despite the clear enjoyment tourists took in gawping up at the vast walls with climbers camped on portaledges during their multi-day ascents.

Flora was in heaven – left to enjoy a feral existence around the campsite, frequently calling for 'Stocky' – the exuberant Andy Stockford, possibly because he, too, had wild, blond hair. All credit to Stocky, not accustomed to children, for his tolerance. Little did we know then that he suffered from depression, and would tragically take his own life a few years later.

Flora grew up on this style of holiday, most often in climbing areas. Over the years she got more and more involved herself, from bouldering on the children's circuits at Fontainebleau to joining me on routes in Ailefroide in the Ecrins in the southern Alps. We had several multi-family trips to this beautiful area. One day, Flora and I, along with Iain Cole and his daughter, Flora's schoolfriend Mari, headed up the valley to climb some easy, multi-pitch routes. Flora did well on the climbing. When we reached the top I explained, rather matter-of-factly, "Right, time to abseil back down". It was only at this stage, several hundred metres up the buttress, that my lack of parental guidance came to light. "How do we abseil?" asked Flora. Ah! No time like the present to learn, then. And she didn't stop at climbing. Growing up she watched us both regularly going out running and cycling. We encouraged her to compete in the local fell-running series and she was out on her bike with us from an early age. We felt it was important to get her involved in the things we loved. As Alan Plater put it in his brilliant TV series *The Beiderbecke Connection*: "If we don't share our passion with our children, how will they ever learn to be passionate?" We take a great deal of satisfaction from the way that our daughter has developed into a young adult with a passion for the outdoors, zealously pursuing her own activities with great success.

At Yosemite, Greg and I got stuck into the climbing, which was subtly differ-

Young Flora enjoying the via ferrata on holiday in the Dolomites

Very young Flora getting to grips with bouldering at Font with expert guidance from Karen

ent from the previous week at the Needles. We climbed up and down the valley on single and multi-pitch routes, inspired by years of poring over the classic picture book, *Yosemite Climber*. We bridged up the long corner on *Bircheff-Williams*, jammed up *Serenity Crack* and teetered up the slabs of *Stoner's Highway* where the holds on the smooth, worn granite required a good deal of imagination and great faith in the friction. The *North Face of the Rostrum* was a brilliant multi-pitch outing, but the best day out was undoubtedly *Astroman*. With 12 varied pitches of superb climbing up Washington Column, it's no wonder this is considered by many to be one of the best free routes in America, let alone Yosemite. I was so fired up for the Enduro Corner that I flew up it, barely stopping to place any of the many options for protection. This pitch is 50m of continuous corner-climbing using jams and laybacks and occasionally getting a good bridge across the corner with splayed legs, which enables you to draw breath. I think that the way I climbed it so quickly and, on the face of it, so effortlessly threw Greg somewhat. I'd made it look so straightforward and I guess he expected to find it easy, which it isn't. The result was that he was pretty blown away by the end of the pitch and left me to lead most of the rest of the route.

The whole route is tremendous, but the only other pitch of real significance is the famous Harding Slot. After a desperate sequence to get established, you're left squirming up a body-width, bottomless shaft with many hundreds of metres of fresh air below. It was slow progress, udging up a few inches to slip back a couple. There came a point where I genuinely thought I was stuck – I couldn't move up and there was no going down. I could let go with both hands and both feet at the same time and not move, being wedged by my chest. I could feel a sense of panic lurking somewhere nearby. I needed to give myself a good talking to! I remember that internal dialogue: "There is no way that you are the largest climber ever to have done this pitch. Others have got up, which means you can fit through! Now calm down and get on with it." It was all that was needed. I relaxed, reassessed the position and was soon climbing out the top of the slot onto normal climbing terrain. But I had needed that conversation, that opportunity to stop, calm down, take stock of the situation and recognise that there was no need to allow the encroaching panic to get any closer. What a fantastic day! *Astroman* still remains one of the best routes I have ever climbed outside the UK.

It appears I am in illustrious company. The poet Samuel Taylor Coleridge recorded a very similar experience in 1802 during a 9-day trek around the Lakes 'wandering lonely as a cloud' as his mate Bill might have put it. On the fifth day of this epic trip he found himself on the summit of Scafell and wanting to get to Scafell Pike. He made a descent of Broad Stand heading for Mickledore. Nat-

Pete Robinson climbing high above the idyllic campsite at Ailefroide, France

urally he describes his experience in more poetic terms, but the situation is the same. He got himself in a bit of a pickle in terrain that was beyond his experience and he started to panic. He was terrified by the prospect of the next drop onto a narrow ledge but he couldn't climb back up the sections he'd already dropped down. It was only when he stopped and rested and took stock of the situation, even laughing at himself and the situation he'd got himself into, that the tension was released and he could proceed.

It was during this trip to Yosemite with its endless finger cracks that I first became aware of a significant kink in the little finger on my left hand. You might think you'd notice such a thing, but it was only after repeatedly trying to jam my digits into thin cracks and finding the offending little finger wouldn't go in that I started to take note. I was developing a Dupuytren's contracture. This is the result of a thickening of the palmar fascia, the layer of connective tissue beneath the skin that overlays our muscles, tendons and other working parts. It makes the finger slowly start to bend and, if left unchecked, it can contract all the way to the palm, drawing the adjacent fingers after it. The only solution is surgery to open up and peel back the skin, allowing the thickened tissue to be cut and scraped away. The operation is relatively simple and returns the finger back to normal, although it does return with time. I have, to date, had three procedures on the left-hand little finger, one on the right-hand little finger and one on the left-hand ring finger. I now have a lot of scar tissue and limited feeling in that little finger on my left hand, something of a nuisance to say the least.

I came back to Yosemite with Dom Donnini and Ross Purdy in 2005. That time the plan was to do some Big Wall Aid climbing routes. The training and preparation back at home was great fun – something a bit different. We practised setting up the portaledge at Hodge Close, aid climbed

One of my Dupuytrens-deformed fingers – a nuisance when it comes to finger jamming

up pre-existing pegs and bolts at Gordale and became more proficient at placing and removing pegs in a granite quarry near Shap. This quarry was still in use, which meant we had to go under cover of darkness, further adding to the adventure, but it was good to be able to practise in granite and in rock that was about to be blown up anyway. We wouldn't have wanted to desecrate genuine cracks with our amateur hammerings. It was also an opportunity to get used to placing copperheads – lumps of soft metal on a wire that you hammer into a small depression in the rock before trusting your body weight on it – a terrifying proposition to start with!

Sadly, the trip itself turned into a succession of minor catastrophes. Our baggage was delayed, possibly due to it being somewhat overweight. There was a landslip on the road between the accommodation we'd booked, just outside the valley, and the Park entrance, meaning we had to take a huge detour to get to the valley. Eventually, after several days of preparatory outings, we had changed our objectives and we set forth on *The Nose* on El Capitan. I was part way up the Stovelegs pitch when it started to snow quite heavily! The weather was coming from the north, over the top of the 3000ft cliff, so we couldn't tell whether it was a passing shower or something more sustained. When lots of teams on other routes around us started to retreat we thought we ought to do the same so started the multiple abseils back to the ground. The bad weather then set in for a few days and the impetus was lost. In truth, I don't think I'm truly suited to the laborious process of aid climbing – the slow progress, the hauling of the bags and the jumaring up the ropes (a method of rope climbing using extra bits of kit to get up Big Walls).

Another memorable foreign trip was one of many adventures I've had with Brian Davison over the years – a two-week climbing trip to Oman. With us on that occasion were Geoff Hornby and David Barlow. They'd been before and Geoff had a contact in Muscat, Rob Gardner of Oman Adventure, from whom we hired a 4x4 vehicle. Climbing on the sharp, pristine limestone was excellent and the country was a delight. The people are just the friendliest and most welcoming you could ever hope to meet. Even in the back of beyond, with only rudimentary language between us, they'd regularly invite us to join them to share a few dates and a small cup of delicious Arabic coffee.

Most of the time we were prospecting for new routes and added a significant number for the guidebook that Geoff was working on. We camped out in the de-

Brian Davison emerging at the top of the crux pitch of *Cobra* on first ascent

sert most nights, although we once found a fabulous, shady oasis of palm trees, fed by simple irrigation channels from a meagre stream, where we stayed for several days, giving many of our spare provisions to the local family in exchange for the freedom to camp on their patch. One day, while we were based here, Brian and I had climbed a long, rambling ridge line with several steep pitches along the way. We eventually emerged onto a seemingly deserted, scrubby plateau and set about identifying the best descent route. We hadn't been looking for long when a local shepherd appeared, seemingly from thin air, happily pointed us in the right direction and went on to lead us down a hidden path. He refused to accept anything for his troubles. He just seemed happy to have helped.

There is so much good quality rock to be climbed on, all over Oman, with only limited development so far. Sadly, even though I've been back to Muscat on numerous occasions for work, I haven't had the chance to climb there again.

I've had several other short, sunny Sport climbing trips with Brian, which in itself is something of a contradiction. Brian is one of the most traditional climbers I've met. His reliance on ancient gear that has been superseded many times over and his refusal to use chalk, even on the hottest of days during continental climbing holidays, sets him apart from most others. Although I shouldn't be too critical. When it comes to old kit, I've got previous. Chris Gore reminded me recently of a climb we did together at Gordale. I was doing *Pierrepoint* and had just clipped the first bolt. He was berating me for the state of my quickdraws as the gate of the karabiner didn't close properly after clipping the rope through. What made it worse was that the krab at the bolt end of the 'draw was still open as well!

One trip to Calpe on the Costa Blanca brought Brian's disdain for chalk into sharp relief. The gang this time was myself and Brian, Rob Knight and the above-mentioned Chris Gore. Rob, like me, has climbed extensively in the Lakes and beyond for many years but is also someone who'll do whatever's appropriate and happily spend time clipping bolts when Sport climbing. On one particular day out climbing together in the Duddon Valley, I remember him having a go at me for not placing enough gear on some hard routes. But he was a fine one to talk about taking risks, having tried his hardest to scare the living daylights out of me as he pushed his powerful motorbike to the limit driving out there that day.

Chris on the other hand is very much embedded in the Sport style. He moved from the hotbed of elite climbing in Sheffield to somewhat sleepy Kendal in 1995. We were introduced by mutual friend Neil Foster and over the years

Nick on *Magic Flute* on a crag high above Benidorm – the photo that adorned the cover of the Rockfax guide to the area 📷 John Wilson

we've climbed together in the Lakes and abroad, but predominantly on Sport routes in Yorkshire. Chris has served his time on Trad routes, with many hard ascents under his belt in the Lakes, North Wales and elsewhere, but these days it takes a lot of persuading to drag him away from the limestone.

So Chris and Brian could not be more different in approach – opposite ends of the spectrum. Thanks to this, our trip to Calpe had an added, entertaining dimension. It was a particularly hot week, which meant Rob, Chris and I were fighting to get on routes before Brian, whose chalk-free hands would leave crux holds sweaty and slippery. All that said, it was a great trip with a lot of climbing achieved. Also in the area at the time, in their campervan, were Kendal-based Mark Glaister and Emma Williams. Their main interest was the shower facilities in our tiny apartment – not really designed for four burly climbers. On arrival, Rob made some bellicose statement to the effect that he hoped nobody was going to be snoring and keeping him awake. But, naturally, only one person proved to be a regular snorer – and that was Rob.

Another limestone climbing trip was a long weekend to the Tre Cime in the Italian Dolomites in 2012 with long-time, Lakes-based climbing partner Woody. We'd hatched a plan to make a quick hit on the *Brandler-Hasse* route on the north face of the Cima Grande. This is a big route with a fierce reputation. We trained hard to make sure we had sufficient strength and endurance for this 23-pitch outing. It's hard to give it a British grade, but it's probably the equivalent of an E5 with three pitches of 6a climbing (French 7a and 7a+) in the middle. It was only a brief visit. Flying into Venice on the Thursday, we hired a car and drove up to Misurina for a few supplies before continuing up the road to the car park near the Rifugio Auronzo and the short, flat walk to the Rifugio Lavaredo. Having settled ourselves, in we went round to the base of the route. We'd heard of many people getting the start wrong, so wanted to do a recce before the early morning start planned for the next day. "Time spent in reconnaissance is seldom wasted," as they say. Just as well that we did, as we ended up making the same mistake as others had.

The problem is that the obvious line and the fixed gear keeps leading you upwards, when in reality the route traverses off to the left, far earlier than expected. It's a different route that continues straight up. We just did the first two pitches then abseiled to the ground and returned to the hut. Later that evening, as we were turning in, we asked the hut guardian if he'd leave some breakfast out for us as we were planning on an early start. He asked what our plans were and when we told him we were going to do the *Brandler-Hasse* he looked us up and down, seeing two middle-aged, unlikely looking contenders. "Are you sure?" he asked with some concern in his voice. "It's quite an undertaking," he added, still doubting our ability. "We'll be fine – what could possibly go wrong?" With a shrug and a look of disbelief in his face he wished us good luck.

The next morning dawned fine and although it'd rained a fair bit during the night, that wasn't going to cause a problem on the steep north face. We were soon underway, buoyed by knowing where we were going at the start. We swung leads comfortably and made fast progress. The route was clean and even had a few new pegs in place since Alex Huber, the German climbing superstar, had soloed it the previous year and had clearly spent a lot of time in preparation, ensuring the line was as free of loose rock as possible. The crux section starts nine pitches up. After steady F6a-6c climbing, there are two F7a pitches in succession followed by the F7a+ crux, all of which climb through even steeper ground. They're still pretty straightforward and well protected. The whole route is adequately supplied with a mixture of pegs, slings and the odd bolt. Those, along with a slim rack of

Woody getting some brief respite on *Brandler-Hasse*

our own, meant that it never felt anything other than safe. There are certainly enough old pegs to clip that at least one of them is bound to hold in the event of a fall. As it happened, we didn't need to test the security of the gear. We made pretty quick progress, slowed only by the very wet conditions on the top four or five easier pitches due to a large snow patch that was still sitting on the top. This snow was melting and running down the top of our line. We were soon stood on top, looking for the descent, which is a few straightforward abseils into a snow-filled gully.

We were back at the hut drinking welcome beers by late afternoon. The guardian was blown away. He apologised for ever doubting us and gave us celebratory drinks to make up for it. He then went on to say that we really must climb a route called *Yellow Wall* (*Muro Giallo* or *Gelbe Mauer* depending on your choice of language). This, it turned out was a 12-pitch straight line up the 400m, south face of the Cima Piccola, an impressive wall overlooking the hut. It lies to the left of its easier, older and better-known partner *Spigolla Giallo* (*Yellow Edge*). Towards the top of the route, the hardest and most spectacular pitch is a roof that has to be surmounted. This is apparently one of the sections of climbing

Nick topping out on *Muro Giallo* with a big grin that lasted all evening   Stuart Wood

Woody with a well-earned beer after the *Brandler-Hasse*

used in the opening sequence of the Sylvester Stallone film *Cliffhanger*. We see the muscular form of Stallone soloing effortlessly around this roof – although it was actually the well-known German climbing star Wolfgang Gullich, who sadly died in a car crash not long after the filming.

We were shown the line and provided with a topo and sufficient enthusiasm and encouragement to get anyone up it. Once again, the day was fine and we set off for the route, just getting to the bottom before a younger, local team who were clearly concerned that they were about to get stuck behind us. I'm glad to say we left them standing! The route was magnificent. Twelve consistent pitches, all clean and well-equipped, the first nine all graded between 6c and 7a+, with only the minority at the top being a couple of grades easier. As previously, we swapped leads and every pitch was dispatched on-sight with ruthless efficiency. Naturally, we had to do the one-arm hang off the lip of the *Cliffhanger* roof. The quality of the climbing was superb, vying with Yosemite's *Astroman* for the top spot on my list of all-time best routes outside the UK, fine praise indeed for a Sport route!

Once again, back at the hut we were greeted like heroes by the guardian and his staff, who'd been watching our progress off and on during the day from the rifugio terrace. We were plied with extra drinks all evening while our new best friend told all other guests of our exploits. The following morning, after a well-earned lie-in, much needed after the excesses of the night before, we packed up and headed back to Venice to fly home that afternoon – one of the best, most productive, short climbing trips I've ever had.

I'd climbed with Nick for years, mainly in the Lakes but also on lots of trips around the UK. I'd also had my fair share of foreign climbing trips. This was to be a trip to remember. We were going to the Dolomites for a long weekend to do the *Brandler-Hasse*.

I had nothing to do with the planning. The Captain organised our itinerary with military precision and it all worked like one of his well-planned, brilliantly-executed covert operations. He said he'd booked us into an Alpine hut near the crag. That sounded a bit primitive. I was a bit concerned it might not even have running water, let alone any beer. How was I to know it was as good as a hotel with waiter service and a well-stocked bar?

I'd been under strict orders to get fit so set about getting back to fighting weight and climbing strength. I was training down at Leo Houlding's wall in Staveley – the Fly Cave – a superb little facility that soon got me up to the required fitness.

All that training paid off. Between us we crushed the route – despite the reservations of the bloke in the hut. Little did he know what the Wharton-Wood combination was capable of. Apart from the piss-wet pitches at the top, it was a breeze, and we were back at the hut 'in time for tea and medals'. The Italian was well impressed and pointed up at the wall overlooking the hut. "Tomorrow, you climb that... is special... you enjoy!"

He was right. Next day the Captain had us up bright and early as usual and we had a superb time on the Gelbe Mauer, scene of Wolfgang Gullich, in place of Stallone, at the start of the film *Cliffhanger*. Of course, we both had to do the one-arm dangle off the massive jug on the lip of the roof when we got to it. That night was a real bender. The Italian and his staff kept giving us drinks. Capitano Nico and Maestro Woody were the heroes of the hour.

The thing that stands out about climbing with Nick is the attitude that anything is achievable. Nobody else has the same drive to try and perform like him. He has 100 per cent commitment, and he expects it from you as well – no excuses. He did the second ascent of *Paths of Victory* (E6 6c) on Dow Crag straight after I did the first. Okay, he'd watched me, but it's a bloody hard sequence and he still did it first go. Both Caff and Ian Vickers apparently fell off first go. I love the dry humour. It's always good value. I've never had a bad day out with him. But the ridiculous early morning starts... it must be an army thing!

Stuart Wood

QUESTION

Q *What other destinations have you got in mind?*

A Where to start? Definitely back to Morocco – there is so much fabulous climbing to go at there and such a lovely country. I would be interested to go and climb in Saudi Arabia. I've visited for work on numerous occasions and always found the people to be very hospitable and it looks like there's some great potential for climbing – currently largely untapped. One other place I'd love to climb is South Africa. I went to Cape Town on a work trip a few years ago and arranged to hook up with a local climber through an introduction from Mary and David Birkett. Sadly, on that occasion the weather put a stop to proceedings and I didn't get anything done but it looks amazing.

Nick and Steve Scott at top of Hanibalturm, Furka Pass –
the bus stop and bench examples of local humour!

11 - Lakeland Cragsman
HVS 5A SERGEANT CRAG SLABS
Life in the Lakes

The English Lake District – what a fabulous place. Who wouldn't want to live there? There's certainly something very special about it: the lakes, the hills, the tiny villages nestling between them. Okay, it can get quite busy at times but that's really only around the honeypot areas and the weather isn't always great but then if it didn't rain, we wouldn't have the lakes and then it'd just be 'The District' which would be a rubbish name! The wagon-wheel layout with the valleys radiating out like spokes from a central hub means that getting from one area to another can involve a bit of a journey and the walk-ins are often quite an effort. It can be quicker to get from home to some of the crags in North Wales than it is to get to some Lakeland crags. But for all that, Lake District climbing has a special quality of its own. It's just a shame that the vast majority of climbers stick to the same handful of crags. It's a bit of a vicious circle – not many people climb the routes, so they get overgrown and dirty and because of that not many people climb on them… And so it goes.

After I left the army in 1992, we sold Karen's house in Boldon Colliery and moved to our permanent home in Kendal, just a few miles outside the Lake District National Park (LDNP) to the southeast. I got a job in a management training centre near Windermere and Karen got a job locally too. We'd made the move to the Lakes and intended to stay. People often say, "Oh, you are lucky to live in such a beautiful part of the country" but luck has got nothing to do with it. It's a strategic decision. If you want to live here, just do it. Buy a house and get a job. Of course, the house might be a bit more expensive than in other places and don't expect finding a job to be easy. One of the reasons this is such an attractive corner of the country is because there isn't much industry and so there aren't many jobs, and even fewer that pay well.

The job that I'd found was okay. It involved a lot of time outdoors, doing teamwork and leadership-based activities before debriefing the clients and drawing out the lessons back at base. It meant a significant drop in salary and some long hours, but we were living where we wanted to be. The next change of direction came about as the result of a chance conversation with Mark Lardner, a regular climbing partner at the time, while we were sat at the bottom of Chapel Head Scar. I think I'd just flashed the brilliant *Song For Europe* (7b+). Mark and I were both having a grumble about our respective jobs when, out of the blue, he made a seemingly random suggestion. "You've got a science degree. You should become an Environmental Health Officer," adding that, "They're having trouble recruiting them at the council." He knew because his wife, Sonya, worked for South Lakeland District Council and had mentioned they were having trouble finding people to fill these well-paid, interesting-sounding roles. I was sufficiently intrigued to not let it pass by. "What the hell is an Environmental Health Officer?" The following day Karen had a day off, so I asked her to call in at the Job Centre in town to see if they could throw any light on the topic (before the days of a quick internet search!). She came back, furnished with a very dated-looking leaflet that, despite its rather dull appearance, described what sounded to me like a fascinating role: Food Hygiene, Pollution Control, Noise Monitoring, Health and Safety, Housing Standards. On further enquiry, it transpired that if you had a science degree you could replace the standard four years of training with a two-year masters. Within a couple of months, I was enrolled on the appropriate course at Birmingham University. Having spent all that time since my undergraduate days working, coupled with the fact that I was paying for this myself, I approached the course with great enthusiasm and a very different mindset to most of the other students who'd come straight from an undergraduate course.

I was in Birmingham all week and home at the weekends, which was not ideal, but it meant I could throw myself into the work and still have time to run every day and go to the newly-opened climbing wall in the city. Each Saturday I worked for Alan Steele at Inglesport, the caving and climbing shop that he'd set up in Ingleton with his wife Deanne, many years before. By coincidence, Alan had also been an EHO or Sanitary Inspector as they'd been called in his day. It was a 'Sani-man' job with Settle Rural District Council that had brought Alan and Deanne to the area from Bradford originally.

Moving to Kendal and getting involved in the Lakes climbing scene was a new experience. In the past, whenever I'd relocated, I'd already had some established climbing partners in the new area to call on. This time, although I knew the area well, I didn't. I'd still meet up with Phil, who'd regularly drive over from the North East, but to make some new connections I went to Rock & Run, the climbing and running shop in Ambleside, set up by Rick Graham and Andy Hyslop, and ended up arranging to go out with Rick for the day. Rick is quite a Lakes legend, probably responsible for as many hard, new routes as anyone else, so it felt like quite a privilege to be climbing with him.

Our venue was Goat Crag in Borrowdale. Rick was happy to let me do most of the leading and we started off on *Athanor*, a fantastic E3, both technical and steep as is typical of this great crag. Next up was *Mirage* (E5 6b), which Rick had first put up in 1981. My approach to leading had always been to get the essential protection and then just get on with it and go. No sooner had I set off up the first pitch, feeling quite comfortable, when Rick called up from below, in his quiet, understated manner, "There's a good Rock 4 just to your left". I didn't really feel the need for a runner but thought I ought to place it as Rick had been kind enough to point it out. Another move: "Good placement out to your right." Okay, maybe there isn't anything after this for a while. One move up: "Rock 1 there, in that crack". And so, it continued move after move. I'd never placed so much gear and was soon running out. I was also left wondering how the hell he remembered all these runner placements. It wasn't as if he'd only just done it. The route is superb, one of the best on the crag, with a delicate, technical first pitch followed by a steep and strenuous second, best experienced by combining the two into one magnificent long pitch, as I did that day. We finished off a great day with a relatively easy ascent of *Praying Mantis* (E1). It was after this day of climbing together that Rick started referring to me as 'Skimpy Rack' referring to the limited assortment of gear that I'd routinely take on my harness.

Shortly after the day out with Rick, I was put in touch with Steve Scott, another one of that Lakes crowd. Only recently has Steve pointed out to me that Rick had obviously discussed our day out with his inner circle: Ted Rogers, Johnny Adams, Ken Forsythe and others and come to the conclusion that it'd be best

Mark (Ed) Edwards stepping of the (now sadly departed) Android tree

for all involved if this eager, over-enthusiastic, young buck was foisted onto Steve for future outings. The following weekend Steve and I made our acquaintance with a visit to the marvellous Raven Crag, Threshthwaite Cove and so began 30 years of climbing together. A few days later, we arranged to climb at another Raven Crag, this time in Thirlmere. Steve picked me from work and introduced me to someone waiting in the car: "This is Glenn Sutcliffe. Hope you don't mind me bringing him along. I'm pretty sure he won't slow us down!" Something of an understatement. Glenn was possibly the strongest man in the world and a member of the GB climbing squad. That evening, we did *Blitzkrieg* – a well-positioned E4 up the steep centre of the crag – marking the start of another regular climbing partnership. And that's how it works, one connection leads to another until a whole network has been established.

The phone rang… On the other end was a bloke I'd never heard of asking if I'd go climbing. Being able to trust yourself is a good trait to have when strangers ask you to go climbing with them. We met up as arranged, the bloke introduced himself ("I'm Nick"), we shook hands and off we went to Raven Crag at Threshthwaite Cove. Talking on the approach it turned out that he had been out with Rick recently and Rick and the other locals decided that he should be pointed in my direction.

Nick, being well-mannered, offered me the lead. I set off up *Baby Driver* (E3), the warm-up route, but quickly ran out of gas about halfway up, where it gets pumpy and a bit runout. I came down for a pit stop. This didn't bother Nick. In fact he seemed revved up. He tied on the sharp end and screamed off the grid to make a racy finish in some style – I was impressed. Satisfied that we weren't going to die together we went on to climb *Boy Racer* (E4), no problem for Nick, on/off for me, and, finally, *High Performance* (E5). On the difficult thin initial crack Nick showed his ethical mettle – first time, gritting his teeth and straining until he fell off and then coming down, resting, pulling his ropes through and getting back on and doing it!

That commitment and punishing mental strength was demonstrated again a few weeks later when we visited Blue Scar in the Dales. *Priapism* (E5) had four crap pegs and a thread in its tough 27m, a disappointingly protected yet brilliant route where you don't want to fail, and fall. Watching from the other end of the rope I could feel the tension of Nick's commitment to continue moving upwards, stringing steep sequences together on fantasy friction, using his imagination to link one set of fictional holds to the next. It wasn't always pretty but he climbed with utter determination and total confidence. And that's how he approaches everything…

Steve Scott

It wasn't all about climbing in the Lake District National Park. Being located in Kendal meant relatively quick and easy access to Malham, Gordale, Kilnsey and the other crags in Yorkshire or we might make flying visits to Pen Trwyn at Llandudno. Ridiculous as it might sound, we could be climbing on Pen Trwyn in less time than many of the high Lakeland crags due to tortuous drives and long walk-ins. I made a lot of these trips to North Wales and Yorkshire with Mark Lardner.

Mark was a very different breed of climber. He was quite new to the game, having been an accomplished paddler previously, but he threw himself into his new-found activity with great gusto, albeit almost exclusively Sport climbing. He had soon built his own wall in his garage. It was immaculate, a work of art. The 8ft square board was hinged at the bottom and suspended from chains, allowing the angle to be changed. It was covered in a mixture of holds – both purchased and lovingly home-made. We would work out all manner of problems, some of which extended onto the horizontal roof beams before returning to the board. They would all be given a name and a grade. All this resulted in Mark becoming very strong, very quickly, which he made use of on successful ascents at Chapel Head and on Yorkshire Limestone. But his enthusiasm only lasted a few years. Having climbed at 8a he gave it all up and moved on to other interests.

Occasionally I would persuade Mark to venture onto the Trad but that usually meant I did the leading. One very memorable day we made a visit to the mighty Dove Crag, home to some amazing, steep routes, particularly on the North Buttress. Mark was more than happy for me to be on the sharp end all day and that was fine by me. I climbed *Fast and Furious* followed by *Fear and Fascination*, both brilliant E5s created by Rick Graham. Not satisfied with those I then went on to wrap up the day with *Bucket City*, a much harder proposition at E6, initially done by Martin Berzins and my old friend Neil Foster. That was a very good day out!

Neil climbed a lot at that time with Martin and the two of them had created many fantastic hard routes around the Lakes, including many classics at Dove Crag. A couple of years later, Martin was going to be in the area and looking for a climbing partner. Neil put the two of us in touch and we arranged a day up at Dove. Wow! I was going to Dove with Martin Berzins – the man was legendary. He was always extremely strong and many of his routes were very bold. We had a great day out doing a handful of routes each, finishing with the *Flying Fissure Finish* of *Fast and Furious*. This route is an alternative to the original line, but that makes it sound like a minor variation. In fact, it's a significant addition with superb, airy climbing, just a touch harder and more sustained than the original.

I wanted to do it but then Martin, who had seconded Neil on the first ascent, said he was also keen to lead. "No problem," I suggested "I'll lead it, then abseil off and you can lead it on my gear". Agreement was reached. Up I went, in my own, usual style, climbing fast and light, only placing what I considered to be the essential protection. I found it very straightforward albeit extremely good. I returned to the ground and pulled the ropes, leaving my runners in place for Martin to use on the lead. He didn't take any other gear with him as mine was already there. As he got higher, his mood darkened, and the expletives got louder with him shouting down and asking why I hadn't placed more runners in the obvious placements. He still got up but didn't seem terribly pleased with me. Oops!

Three big routes in one day at Dove Crag with Mark was not all that untypical. I have always got as much out of a day as possible. Around this time, I was also climbing regularly with Cliff Fanshaw and one day, along with Alan Steele, we had visited Burnt Crag in the Duddon Valley. The Duddon is a lovely backwater in the south west of the Lakes. It's a beautiful valley and probably benefits from not having a lake to draw the crowds. The climbing is made up of many, much smaller crags than elsewhere in the district. Burnt Crag is the jewel in its crown. Superb, clean, compact rock with an array of single pitch routes from E3 upwards. This was my first visit and I was like a child let loose in the sweet shop. Given free reign by Alan and Cliff to do all the leading I raced from one to the next, notching up three E3s, an E4 and two E5s. A few weeks later, Cliff and I had a similar day at Blue Scar in Wharfedale when I notched up an exhausting two E3s, two E4s, two E5s plus an E6. My little red notebook records: "An excellent day out in the sunshine at Blue Scar".

The weekend after my trip to Dove Crag with Martin Berzins I was climbing with John Fletcher from Lancaster. We always used to rib John about his 'advancing years'. He was, at that time, only in his mid- to late twenties, but he came across as very sensible: '26 going on 50'. It turned out that we had both been at the Grammar School in Lancaster at the same time except he was in his first year when I was in the sixth form. He was a good climber, always very calm and steady, whatever the situation. On this particular day, both of us managed to climb *Hell's Wall* in Borrowdale. It's a very tough, fingery route that is graded at E6 6c. Protected by numerous pegs, it is also given a French grade of 7c, albeit the pegs are well-spaced in places and it is no clip-up. Needless to say, we were both over the moon to have done it, but not satisfied with that we drove round to Reecastle in Watendlath where I also climbed *Penal Servitude* and *Daylight Robbery*, both good E5s.

Many of the harder Trad routes in the Lakes are now given a French grade to help give some indication of what to expect. When I was writing the *Eastern Crags* guidebook in 2011 with Al Davis, we introduced French grades for all the harder routes at Dove. I thought it only fair to let subsequent visitors know what they could expect from these routes, so I added the following warning for inclusion in the introduction:

"Where French grades have been assigned in brackets, these do not suggest a clip-up! Far from it. Most of these routes are very serious undertakings unlike the 'cheese-eating, surrender-monkey' routes that normally attract these types of grades!"

Sadly, the editor did not appreciate the classic *Blackadder* quote, so it had to come out.

I've already admitted that the weather in Cumbria isn't always perfect for climbing outside. It's essential to have an indoor alternative. When I moved to the Lakes, there had been a rudimentary wall, by today's standards, at Charlotte Mason College in Ambleside for some time. The underside of the bridge at Sedgwick, just south of Kendal, that takes the A590 over the river Kent, also provided some excellent traversing. The next, nearest wall was in the Yorkshire Dales at Ingleton. Alan Steele had built a great facility in the village and continued to develop both the bouldering and leading available.

One day, while I was working in Environmental Health at South Lakeland District Council, a planning application was passed to me for comment. It was a plan to develop the old Milk Marketing Board milk drying plant in Kendal into a climbing wall. Being a tall and open space, the building would be perfect for a climbing wall and pretty useless for anything else. The only problem appeared to be a lack of funds for the capital investment in the project, putting the whole venture in some doubt. Not long after, by pure chance, I was at the wedding of my old Sandhurst friend, John Vlasto to his lovely wife Catherine. Brian Davison and I, along with our partners, were sat on a table of his 'climbing friends' and a few others. At some point during the reception, someone at our table came out with the unexpected statement: "I have loads of money and want to build a climbing wall. I just don't know where." "I know just the place," I was able to reply. I explained the situation in Kendal and it grabbed the attention of this potential climbing wall entrepreneur, who turned out to be Jeremy Wilson. I put him in touch with the original guys with the ideas but no money and so was born the Kendal Wall. Jeremy's sister-in-law, Kate Phillips, was appointed manager and has been doing a brilliant job of running the place ever since the doors opened in December 1995. Over the years the wall has evolved, keeping up with demand for bigger and better facilities and providing a tremendous resource for the area. Jeremy's empire now includes a further seven bouldering walls in London, all with the same attention to detail and providing first-class training facilities.

Over the years, I went on to spend a lot of time with both John and Catherine Vlasto. They are some of the most generous and welcoming people I know. Whenever I was in London for work, I would stay with them in Hampstead, or at the 'Chateau Vlasto', their beautiful chalet in Chamonix. They were such a lovely family. Catherine, also a highly competent climber, was very welcoming and a good climbing partner both out on the crags and frequently at the London climbing walls. I had a fabulous trip to the Verdon with Catherine for a week one summer, where we ticked many lines but suffered with the heat and the tough grades.

Once on a climbing holiday to Turkey with John, disaster struck early in the trip. It was only our second day and we were up at the crag early. I led up a line and left the clips in for John to repeat. As he reached the penultimate bolt, I saw

Nick on the desperately fingery *Daylight Robbery*, Reecastle ☐ John Fletcher

him slump onto the rope. "Get back on and give it another go," I shouted up. "No, lower me down," he said. I didn't understand – the climbing wasn't hard there. "You might as well finish it," I tried to insist. "LOWER ME DOWN," was the emphatic response. I lowered him to the ground to find him in considerable agony with a mis-shaped shoulder, which had dislocated as he was making an awkward move (something that had happened a few times before because of some inherent weakness). Eventually we got him to the hospital in Antalya where the shoulder was reset but he was clearly going to be out of action for a while and flew home the next day. I stayed on, finding plenty of other partners to climb with for the rest of the week.

John and Catherine subsequently went their separate ways but remain great friends. And it's always a pleasure to catch with both of them, their new partners and their three boys.

It's not only the crags and their routes that define an area for me, but also the people and the Lakes has always had a lot of true characters, many of whom I've had the pleasure of climbing with. Of particular note in the South Lakes are the collective *Barrow Lads*. This disparate group of climbing mates included: Keith

Some of the Barrow Lads beneath Chapel Head L-R: Ian Cooksey, Steve Merry, Dave Geere, John Hudson. Mark Greenbank, Keith Phizacklea. Tim and Cherrie Whiteley behind.

Phizacklea, Steve Merry, Stuart Wood, Andy Rowell, Stevie Whittall, John 'Thin John' Hudson, Brian McKinley, John Holden, Greg Fell (a temporary local) and Steve Hubbard. There were also the local climbing aristocracy including Alan Phizacklea and Rob Matheson.

They were an eclectic collection. The enigmatic Keith, legend had it, didn't exist in any official capacity – no National Insurance number nor NHS number (although many years later he did eventually get a passport so there must have been some record somewhere). Stevie Whittall was a plumber, specialising in doing work in the combat zones of the world. Al Phiz, the other phamous Phizacklea (no relation to Keith but just as good looking, if not quite as follicly challenged in his later years) was a draughtsman in the shipyard at Barrow while John Hudson, Managing Director of the same shipyard, was responsible for overseeing the construction of the UK's nuclear deterrent.

Turning up at any crag to find a collection of this gang present guaranteed some strong performances as well as a day of hilarity. (For me, the hilarity reached its pinnacle when the lads would turn up at the crag with a golf club and a handful of balls and proceed to compete with each other to see who could drive the furthest.) All of them have been involved in a lot of the recent developments in the area and the creation of some of the best routes around. I got to know many of them through Dominic Donnini and Helen Davies, another strong climbing partnership. Dom had recently left the army and the pair were living in Kendal. I spent a lot of time with both of them. Helen eventually moved to Colorado but Dom has stayed in the Lakes. Dom not only had very strong arms but also a very powerful personality. He has talked his way into and out of many situations over the years, very self-assured and full of confidence. He became a great friend, in fact for many years our families celebrated Christmas together, particularly when Flora was younger.

Another activity which many of the South Lakes climbing crowd were unsurprisingly involved in was the production of the local climbing guidebooks. Climbing guides to the Lakes area have been produced by the Fell & Rock Climbing Club (FRCC) since 1922. When I first got involved, guidebook production was a much more democratic, if chaotic, process, particularly when it came to photo selection. A couple of times a year the unruly masses would gather in the back room of the Golden Rule pub in Ambleside to discuss aspects of the upcoming guidebooks and argue about grades and descriptions before moving to

Dom Donnini and Tim Whiteley on *Tophet Wall* – best route in the Lakes?

the highlight of the evening – the photo selection. A projector and screen would be set up and slides would be viewed with cries of support often mixed with howls of derision depending on personal preference and no small amount of favouritism and bias. Somehow, I got dragged along to one of these meetings by Dom and Helen and so began a long association with the Fell & Rock and their guidebooks. In fact, it was at a subsequent guidebook meeting that Al Phizacklea presented me with a Fell & Rock application form, already completed and just requiring my signature. I needed four letters of support from existing members in addition to my proposer and seconder. They were all obtained that evening.

My involvement in the guidebooks moved up a notch when I became Photo Editor around the time of the 2000 *Borrowdale* guide. This was a time when guidebooks were needing to change. They have been evolving since they were first introduced but the appearance of *Rockfax* really put a rocket up the backsides of the main club-based producers. In addition, the expectations of the buying public were going up. Action photos had to match the incredible standards seen each month in the climbing magazines and crag diagrams needed to be dragged into the modern age. In the Lakes, Al Phiz had done a brilliant job for many years with his sketches of crags that showed the route lines. For the first selected climbs guide in 2003, *Lake District Rock*, we added colour to Al's line-drawings, which at the time seemed innovative and exciting!

The front cover of that book uses a photo of mine. It shows Dom Donnini and Tim Whiteley climbing the classic *Tophet Wall* on the Napes with Wasdale in the background. I had envisaged this shot for some time, so the guide gave me a good excuse to drag the other two up there to act as models. It was just a week before I completed my successful Bob Graham Round so I was naturally feeling very fit. I legged it up to the crag from Seathwaite in Borrowdale, carrying most of the kit, dropped the climbing gear at the foot of the route then scouted around, further up the hillside, for the best vantage point. When the lads arrived, they got their gear sorted and set off up the route. Once the photos were taken, I left them to it. In the meantime, I ran back to Styhead Tarn then on up to the summit of Scafell Pike via the Corridor Route before retracing my steps. By the time I got back Dom and Tim were just finishing a second route, just in time for us to head back with me getting to lead a couple of routes at Kern Knotts on the way. A good use of a day.

Producing guidebooks can be a thankless task. There is such a lot of work that goes on in the background to try and create the best possible reference book but when they come out, they are quickly pored over for even the smallest error or oversight. In most cases, all this work is done by volunteers and the meagre profits ploughed back into the local area or some relevant charitable cause. In the case of the FRCC some of the profits go back to the club for the upkeep of huts but sizeable donations are regularly made to charities connected to the outdoors. A substantial amount of the proceeds has gone to the Cumbria Bolt Fund, which aims to keep on top of the fixed protection in the quarries and other Sport climbing venues of the area.

I really don't remember volunteering or even agreeing to write a guidebook, but somehow I found myself responsible, along with Al Davis, for creating the *Eastern Crags* guide, published in 2011. We roughly split the job between us, with me getting the crags with predominantly harder routes and Al the rest. As a result, for a while I spent nearly all my climbing time on the crags in this area. Thankfully, there were many others who were very keen to help out with providing and checking route descriptions and other relevant information, particularly about some of the harder recent additions to places like Dove and Iron Crag. Active at the time was a strong team from the North Lakes, made up of largely non-working individuals including Mike Norbury, Mick Johnston and Al Wilson. Known as the North Lakes Job Club, they worked their way round many of the major crags cleaning routes, replacing in-situ pegs and slings. Among their targets were: Dove Crag, Raven Crag at Threshthwaite, Raven Crag at Thirlmere, Iron Crag and in Borrowdale they cleaned up Goat Crag. This sterling effort was helped by generous donations of equipment from Stephen Reid at Needlesports in Keswick, FRCC Guidebook Editor at the time.

By now we had moved on from Al's line drawings of crags to using photo diagrams. This meant an added level of work pressure to get the crag photos in the most appropriate light. It also meant that the lines on the photos had to be absolutely accurate as guide users are likely to rely on what they see on the picture when deciding where to climb. This approach was then rolled out to all other guides including the new Winter Climbs guide, creating a major challenge. Getting a suitable photo of every crag in good winter condition, in the right light, to be able to show the winter lines could take years of effort. We had to come up a cunning plan and we did – a helicopter!

The good folk of the FRCC Committee agreed to the funds so, in March 2005, during a short spell of cold, clear weather and the right conditions on the crags, we hired a helicopter from Liverpool airport. It was to be piloted by local climber Justin Gwyn-Williams who duly collected the aircraft and flew it up to

Al Wilson of the *North Lakes Job Club* on assignment, Raven Threshthwaite

Kendal and parked it in a mate's field. The following day was the photo-shoot. I was to sit in the passenger seat and get the required shots around the eastern side of the county in the morning before handing over to Dave Willis who would capture the western crags in the afternoon. We arrived to discover that our aircraft was little more than a plastic bubble with a short stem sticking out the back, powered by what looked like a lawn-mower engine. Justin suggested I remove the passenger-side door. It wasn't the removal so much as his instructions that I found alarming: "Just pull out that single split pin and it should lift off," he explained calmly. I had hoped it might be a bit more difficult to take the structure apart! In fact, once we were airborne everything went smoothly and we got some fabulous shots. Along the way we passed by Rampsgill Head just as guidebook writer Brian Davison was climbing a new route. It was later named *Friends Above* (V), in reference to our presence. It was a fabulous experience to fly round the mountains getting all the shots we'd planned.

I was pleased with the *Eastern Crags* guide and so somehow found myself taking on the South Lakes element of *Eden Valley & South Lakes Limestone*, published the following year in 2012. Once again, it meant spending most of that season on these crags. The best of these is Chapel Head Scar on the western flank of Whitbarrow in the beautiful Witherslack valley. I've spent a lot of time at Chapel Head over the years, climbing nearly all of the routes on this tremendous, steep limestone escarpment. Possibly the best route on the crag is the magnificent *Wargames* (7b). First climbed by Al Phizacklea during the boom

Dave Willis (right) and Justin Gwyn-Williams (driver) in the helicopter for the Winter Climbs guide photo shoot

in development in 1985, it combines steep, thuggy jug-pulling at the start with more refined, delicate climbing towards the top, all on superb, solid limestone. I've climbed this many times but the most memorable was on a day at the crag with the mighty Glenn Sutcliffe. We'd both done a number of other routes and thought it would be a good wheeze to see if we could get up *Wargames* in the flip-flops we were wearing at the bottom of the crag between routes. It says something about the lack of a need for good footwork that we both managed it!

QUESTIONS

Q. *For many people, climbing your own new routes is their ultimate goal. Is this the same for you?*

A. Not really, certainly not as much for most other climbers I know. Sure, it's nice to create your own line, name it and leave it as a legacy for others to enjoy in the future, but I've never been all that driven to seek out new routes. Both of the major additions I created in 1995, and several others over the years, were suggested by friends. It wouldn't cross my mind to have gone looking for them in the first place. I've identified a few obvious lines through my guidebook work and gone on to produce new routes to plug the gaps. For me, the pleasure is in the act of movement over the rock, whatever the route, whatever the history of it.

Q. *What are your top three recommended routes in the Lakes?*

A. There are so many of different character on such a wide range of crags – long, short, high mountain, valley and so on. And so much depends on grade, so I'm going to give one easy, one medium and one hard:

> *Tophet Wall* (HS) on the Napes, Great Gable, Wasdale
>
> *Gormenghast* (E1) on Heron Crag, Eskdale
>
> *Woodhouse's Arete* (E6) on Dow Crag, Coniston

Ian Cooksey on *Route of All Evil*, Chapel Head

12 - High Performance
E5 6A RAVEN CRAG THRESHTHWAITE COVE
Some of my best years (so far)

For many reasons 1995 was a special year. It was the year that I graduated from Birmingham with my Masters in Environmental Health and South Lakeland District Council created a new post so that I could move from student/trainee to full-time employment in my new career. It was the year that our daughter was born. And it was also the high point of my Lake District climbing, in fact my climbing career in general. But 1994 wasn't exactly shabby on the climbing front either.

I ticked off a lot of routes all around the country, making frequent visits to Gogarth and Llanberis in North Wales, Pembroke in South Wales and enjoying a laugh-a-minute week in Cornwall with Alan Steele. One particularly monumental day out that year took place on the fabulous granite sea cliffs of the North-East Outcrops, by then local to John Wilson who'd moved up to Aberdeen. Karen and I were on a trip to Skye where it rained so incessantly that we decided to abandon ship and head over to the east coast where, as usual, the sun was shining. The day after we arrived, John and I headed out for a day on the crags. We went to Earnsheugh, a sizeable crag with some big routes, with no particular plan. John had done most of them before so he generously gave me the opportunity to take the lead. With barely time to draw breath between routes I

knocked off *Necromancer, Prehistoric Monster* and the best of the bunch and aptly named, *Thugosaurus*, all weighing in at E5. But that was not the end of it – we
were only just getting going. John suggested a change of location, so we headed
a short way down the coast to Craig Stirling where I added three more routes to
the tally for the day – *Yahoochie, Yerteezoot* and *Running Wild* – another three
E5s making a total of six for the day. I was delighted, some years later, when John
pointed out that our exploits had made it into the historical section of the local
guidebook.

By default, Nick has always been a fast climber. He believes there's no
need to dither. If the gear you placed several feet below you and several
moves ago means that safety is assured for a few more moves, then press
on. This makes him a bold climber and makes for a bold watch too on occasion. If you're going well, why bother to stop and place gear? If you're a
little bit off your best form, then stopping to place gear will be futile. Save
energy for moving rather than stopping to fiddle and faff. Failing will
surely follow fiddling and faffing, whereas moving gets the route done.

It helps if you have a sparse rack of gear. This eliminates faffing,
necessitates economy of placements and reduces failure. Those who
climbed with him, in the early days particularly, will tell you that Nick
was mischievously happy with a minimal collection of kit. A luxury item
like a camming device was appreciated for the speed that it could be
placed but that was never enough to merit ownership. Having a full set
of cams on the harness, three Friends in those days, would have been a
special occasion for a particular route and they were usually borrowed
from the team at the crag.

Nick's preference for sparse protection and confident but realistic
assessment of his own form and abilities has served him well over the
years, matching his strong preference for action. It's only when there's a
satisfactory tally, of suitably challenging routes, that the day is done, the
belayer can stand down and value for money has been achieved.

That day on the North East Outcrops in 1994 is a case in point. I knew
Nick was in a run of form so Earnsheugh was a good choice for a day of

memorable mileage. We would be able to get a couple of routes in if not more. It's a big cliff with a foreboding atmosphere, a committing feeling, and a place that commands respect. The routes all have a well-deserved reputation for not giving up their prize easily. They respond especially well to the positive approach of a confident climber, so my own battling performances often resulted in a flawed ascent.

There's a grassy ledge at about one-third height that I reached from the boulder beach by the E2 first pitch of *Prehistoric Monster*. This served as a warm-up for the day ahead, a rare thing for Nick. From the ledge, many of the much sought-after prizes of the main wall are in play and usually climbed via beefy crux pitches topped off with a short exit pitch to the top of the cliff.

Or you can cut the faff, head for the sky, and run it out. If you minimise your gear and your belays, you'll get the miles in if you've got what it takes. This was a perfect venue for us and the odds were stacked heavily in favour of a day that would leave a lasting memory.

By mid-morning *Necromancer* (E5 6a), *Prehistoric Monster* (E5 6b) and *Thugosaurus* (E5 6b) were all felled by the deadly combination of merciless efficiency, a handful of runners and a convenient abseil back to the grassy ledge.

Knowing that we would probably be looking for a good return on the day I had a vague plan that the accessible collection of high quality E5s at Craig Stirling could be needed once the Earnsheugh visit had gone well. I also knew that the cliff's notoriously fickle conditions were favourable.

Yahoochie, *Yerteezoot* and *Running Wild* are steep, single-pitch routes with quick access and a perfect belay platform just above the sea. *Yahoochie* was the only route of the day that I hadn't done before, and it justified its bold reputation which has now been recognised with an uplift to E6 6a. It was in my mind to lead it after Nick, but the morning mileage was nagging in my mind. The bold nature of the route meant that, for me it would be a new milestone on the sharp end, one that I would need to be fresh and focussed for to succeed.

Yerteezoot (E5 6b) was quickly dispatched as the afternoon warm-up followed by *Yahoochie* which I declined to follow so that I could have my moment on the sharp end. Twice I'd got through bold moves to a good hold only to reverse to the ground lacking the commitment and confidence to press on, things that just came naturally to Nick. Given what had gone before I must have had the physical fitness to do the route had I approached it fresh but in truth I didn't have the head for it. We finished the day with the photogenic, bold arete of *Running Wild* (E5 6b) which, after a technical start, gave a thrilling finish to an outstanding day

Each one of the routes that day might have been a season maker at the time for many local climbers. Indeed, they are the kind of routes that carry a reputation that draws climbers to these cliffs from further afield. Certainly, working through two or three over a summer would have confirmed your progression though the grades and marked the year out as a successful one. To cruise up six of the gems of the north east coast in one day of on-sight climbing was an outstanding effort that to this day is still talked about. In fact, there was a 26-year wait for a repeat performance and that was by Scottish hot-shot Robbie Phillips.

John Wilson

I was climbing a lot at that time with Alan Steele and also with John Fletcher. I felt like I was climbing well and an obvious route that needed my attention was *Lord of the Flies* on the Cromlech in Llanberis Pass. I'd done many of the other routes on these iconic walls and it was the next step. A day trip to the Pass was arranged with Alan and John, *Lord* being my main objective.

The first ascent of this famous route by Ron Fawcett in 1979 was filmed by Sid Perou and shown as part of the TV series *Rock Athlete*. I can remember watching this on a big TV one lunchtime at school. It was probably the first climbing film I'd ever seen and it's a classic of its time. Ron, dressed in his matching green running shorts and vest, with his corny, "Come on arms, do your stuff" routine for

Nick with last protection at the girdle ledge on *Lord of the Flies* 📷 John Fletcher

the benefit of the camera. In the film, when Ron is on the top section, he places a really good runner. "What a bomber that is," he shouts down to Chris Gibb, his belayer.

It is funny how our memories work, but I could have sworn he says it's a Moac Original. So, come my turn to face up to the great route, I made sure I had the aforementioned piece of gear ready on my harness to protect me on the hard, final moves. The Moac was a large nut, mine was threaded on quite thick red and purple cord. The climbing on the right wall of the Cromlech is amazing with ample edges, cracks and pockets. *Lord of the Flies* at E6 6a is very similar to *Right Wall*, which gets E5 6a. It's just a bit more sustained and the gear a bit more spaced. I made good progress up the steep wall using the mixture of edges and pockets that characterise this rock to reach the line of the girdle traverse at two-thirds height. I got some reasonable protection in at this point, got a half-decent shake-out of the arms and braced myself for the headwall.

As I moved up, I had in mind the promise of the bomber Moac placement. A couple of moves up from the poor resting point there was a reasonable nut placement but, hey, I had the good gear below. "No need to stop, just keep going," I told myself. Past another potential runner, same again, press on. Now I can see the dependable Moac slot approaching, another possible placement but, "Keep going, you'll get the Moac in a couple of moves." Finally, a long way above my last gear, with several missed opportunities for additional runners, I reached the pocket where I knew I could get the bomber nut to safeguard me through the final moves to the top. I got the Moac off my harness and slotted it in place... but it slipped right through. Puzzled, I tried again. It still didn't fit and I had nothing else that would take its place. "Watch me here, Alan, I'm going to have to go for the top." And so it was. I made the most unnecessarily bold finish the route has probably ever seen. If ever it was a Moac Original that fitted in that pocket, it clearly wasn't now. Maybe the slot had got slightly worn, maybe it was never that runner that Ron had used – rewatching that film, he never did say which runner it was – but I had it so fixed in my mind it was a huge disappointment. As it was, by not stopping to place those previous runners my arms were probably fresher and so more able to power up the final few hard moves. It was a brilliant route, and still one of the best I have done. The day was only improved by adding its neighbour, *Precious* (E5 6b), a more direct version of *Right Wall* to the tally.

The summer of 94 was a great time for me, climbing with Nick. We had many adventurous days on the rock, mainly hard classic Trad. I asked Nick how he could press on with scant or poor protection. He told me he wasn't strong enough to hang about putting gear in, so best not to waste energy on it. Not quite true, he is physically strong, but his greatest strength was his presence of mind, keeping calm and under control. All climbers know you can work on strength and you can develop technique. For most of us confidence is hard to gain and so easy to lose; Nick's self-confidence was tops. I can clearly remember the *Lord of the Flies* day 26 years on. It was a masterful display of controlled climbing, no headspace for panic or fear, totally focused on the climbing.

I have been asked by some climbers, "Did you not find him intimidating?" The answer is not at all. The partnership worked well. Nick was not hogging the show. He would inspire and, importantly, encourage and his confidence was infectious. There have been a few days that could be worrying and some that were very tiring, running between routes, but I honestly cannot remember a bad day out.

Alan Steele

All the routes on these striking walls are fabulous and there was a time when I had done every route from the corner of *Sabre Cut* round to the left, all the way round to *Hall of Warriors*, round the corner to the right, until a few newer harder ones were added. The routes on the left wall of the corner lean back, just a touch, so are a bit less strenuous, but often still fingery and in some cases well runout, particularly the filler-in routes such as *True Grip* and *Tess*. The right wall is pretty much plumb vertical. Both walls offer a mix of flakes, pockets, thin cracks, tiny spikes, all generally quite positive and where there is gear it tends to be good.

John Wilson and I were in Llanberis Pass on one of our trips. I think we'd been climbing on the Grochan but were camping out in the cave amongst the boulders below the Cromlech. When we got back to our cave, we could see someone climbing on the Cromlech way up above us. We watched with interest as best we could as we were always interested in seeing what other teams were up to. The person we could see was climbing on the right wall but we couldn't make out where their second was belaying them from – they should have been visible from where we were stood, albeit we were way below them. After a while it became apparent that whoever was up there was on their own and soloing *Right Wall*. In utter amazement we scrambled up the steep hillside as quickly as we could. It was Phil Davidson making his monumental ascent – the first solo of *Right Wall*. There was no-one else around, no audience, no photographer, this was a very understated act. By the time we reached the base of the crag we just found his shoes at the bottom of the wall. Eventually he came wandering back, appearing almost embarrassed that we had caught him in the act yet obviously very pleased with what he'd just managed to pull off. This was a massive achievement at the time by one of the most unassuming climbers the UK has ever produced. He would return sometime later and repeat the feat, with a photographer on hand to capture some truly iconic images.

1995 got off to a flying start, albeit on bolted routes, with one of my early-season trips to Portland with Alan. The drive to the south coast is a six-hour epic so it makes sense to make the most of it. In March, a team of us headed off for a long weekend to a static caravan on the island of Portland. The resultant tally for myself was 30 routes from 6a to 7b+, all flashed. Alan also did most of them. The following year, on a return trip, there was a bit more pressure as we couldn't get away until the Friday evening. It was the last weekend of March and so the clocks were going forward early on Sunday morning. This is always a momentous time of the year as the extra daylight gives us all an additional hour of climbing in the evening. As we pulled onto the M6 for the long drive south, I made the suggestion that we put our clocks forward by one hour there and then, giving us an extra hour of climbing on the Saturday and I managed to get overall support for the cunning plan.

That Saturday I led 17 routes followed by 19 on the Sunday before we had to pack up and head home. Also there that weekend and staying in an adjacent caravan on the same park was another Lakes team with Ken Forsythe, Johnny

Adams and others – rather fortuitously as it turned out. I was up early on the Sunday morning, eager to get going. I'd made everyone an early morning brew when, disaster, the gas cylinder ran out. It was too early to get a refill from the site owner, so a covert operation was launched to swap our cylinder with that of our compatriots next door, who hadn't yet stirred. It was with great satisfaction that we watched someone emerge sometime later with a puzzled look on their face as they shook their cylinder to find it empty.

Hot on the heels of the Portland escapade came a fabulous week over Easter in the sunny Ardeche with John Fletcher, John Wilson and a team of his mates from Aberdeen. As usual, the routes were flowing at the various limestone crags up and down the valley. There is very much a holiday atmosphere in this part of France with a river never far away and a lovely gite to return to each evening. Next up was the May Day Bank Holiday when we went to North Wales, staying at the Rucksack Club hut in Nant Peris. The forecast for the Saturday was looking good so it made sense to head up high to Cloggy where I did *Serth* (E2), which is useful for gaining access to the upper part of the crag and the magnificently positioned route *The Axe* (E4). Now that we were well and truly warmed up, it was time to step it up a gear and tackle the classic wall climb *Midsummer Night's Dream* (E6). Another typical Pete Whillance route, it is fingery, runout and thoroughly absorbing. The following day it looked like the best option would be to head across Anglesey to Rhoscolyn or Gogarth. As it was, we went to both. We ticked off a couple of good routes at the former before heading round to its big brother in the afternoon.

I had my eye on Andy Pollitt's awesome-looking line on the main cliff, *Skinhead Moonstomp*. It's basically a very direct line through *Positron* in a mind-blowing position. I'd seen the photos of Andy on this route and they were probably my main inspiration. There he is, looking as cool as ever in a vest and Lycra with a bandana round his head to keep his long hair under some degree of control. He is laybacking up the blind flake with nothing but a thin bit of cord looped over the top of a rounded boss as his only protection for a long way. Dom and I made our way to the bottom of the cliff at sea level. From the belay at the end of the excellent first pitch, the route disappears round a corner then over a bulge onto the steep headwall. With your belayer and last gear out of sight, and nothing but the sea visible a long way below, the climbing is thin and tenuous, using typical Gogarth holds – tiny, often creaky flakes of quartzite – to reach the

Climber on *Grand Prix*, Raven Crag, Threshthwaite. *Road Rage* steps right from here to climb the blank wall. *Internal Combustion* goes up the centre of the shield"

rounded, blind flake, desperately looking for at least some marginal micro-wires to give protection but just having to keep pushing it out. You follow the flake, which does provide some purchase on its right-hand side, to its top where the pathetic excuse-for-protection bit of cord is looped over the hold. It has to be thin cord – anything thicker would simply roll off. From this brief respite, a series of well-spaced, flat jugs lead up to the crack of *Positron*. This is climbed, through its crux sequence, before heading straight up to a comfortable bucket-seat belay and relief. I sat on that belay, looking out over a calm sea with the sun dropping towards the horizon, a good mate at the other end of the rope, having just climbed the most amazing piece of rock. What a feeling! That is the best route I have ever climbed, anywhere in the world. The route is a fitting tribute to one of the true superstars of my generation who sadly died in 2019.

The following day we were in the slate quarries, dodging the odd shower before heading back home well satisfied.

The weather during that summer was brilliant. The sun seemed to shine every day hitting new temperature records as the year went on. We made the most of it, getting up to the high crags as often as possible. There were some new routes to be climbed as well as lots of classic hard routes. The first of the new routes was at Raven Crag, Threshthwaite. The most striking feature of this crag is the large shield of rock high on the left side of crag. This is home to Pete Whillance's *Top Gear*, site of his monster fall when he slipped off the top ramp on the first ascent and just brushed the ground on the stretch of the rope. That route climbs the right side and then makes a rising traverse across the shield, while *Internal Combustion* is a much harder line up the centre. My new route was to take another direct line up the left side. I abseiled down to brush it clean and check the potential protection as it looks very blank. I put in one peg as the only protection for most of the hard section. I felt like there was a good chance of success, but we would need to return later that week.

So it was, one day, mid-week after an early finish at work thanks to flexi-time, we headed over Kirkstone Pass for the tiny hamlet of Hartsop with Dom driving us in his usual aggressive style. Also with us were Helen Davies and Paul Clavey. We walked up the initial valley, a little pensive with the prospect of some very hard and sparsely-protected climbing. As the crag came into sight, I could see another team heading for the crag, not altogether surprising as conditions were great and this is one of the finest crags in the Lakes. However, paranoia immediately set in. "What are they doing? Is someone going to steal my new route? What an outrage." We had to get there quickly. I raised the pace. The mystery team stopped below the shield. "Why are they stopping there? They're underneath my line!" By this stage I was almost running up the steep slope beneath the crag. As we made our final approach, I could see that the offending team consisted of the highly talented Mike 'Twid' Turner and a mate, clearly a very strong team, quite capable of getting up my new line. "Hi lads, what are you planning on doing?" I asked. "One of these harder routes," came the reply from Twid. One of these routes? Which did he mean? There was only one hard route there currently. "Do you mean *Internal Combustion*? Yeah, it's a brilliant route. There's a good peg just over the lip of that roof. Take care on the upper section, the climbing is excellent but a bit thin," I garbled quickly. I had to get him interested in that and hence steer him away from my own line.

Persuaded by my sparkling sales pitch they opted for the established route. I could relax and focus on my own effort. I set off up the easy, initial section and placed the excellent gear in *Grand Prix*. At this point, the straightforward but enjoyable E3 goes left, whereas I was committed to heading up and right. The first few moves at least have some positive holds, albeit small, but then the rock becomes blank with only marginal, sloping finger holds to even hint at a way forward. On the first attempt I took a substantial fall onto the solid runners in *Grand Prix*. With no chance for another look at what was to come, having fallen to well below the tricky section, I returned to the ground to adjust my cap and try again. I quickly got back on, this time making it through the fingery, crux section to the security of the peg and beyond, completing the new line – *Road Rage* (E6 6c), named after Dom's inimitable style of driving. It was fingery, technical climbing on small, less-than-positive edges with not a lot for the feet and although the real difficulties are contained within a 15ft section, it packs quite a punch and feels very committing. I graded it E6 because that was all I knew. Ten years later when it was repeated by Dave Birkett, he immediately suggested that it should be E7. Just recently, I was back at the crag repeating *Top Gear* and a few other routes. Descending from these via the abseil point at the top of the crag takes you down the line of *Road Rage*. I was blown away at how hard it looked: the lack of positive holds and the scanty protection.

Thanks to the long spell of dry weather, we made several trips up to Scafell. On one of these visits Dom pointed me at the incredibly steep prow below the upper arete of *Edge of Eriador*. Dom had previously placed a couple of pegs, but it was soon apparent that he wasn't going to be able to lead a new route there. He generously handed the project to me. It took several visits and many attempts, but eventually, after a protracted labour, the route was delivered, another healthy E6 6c and christened *Entonox*. Once again, this was upgraded to E7 on being repeated.

Falling off first attempt at *Road Rage* 📷 Dom Donnini

I don't know how many days' climbing I've had on Scafell – one or two hundred maybe. I used to think that if I got ten days in a season it had been a good year. I do know that I'll never really have had enough. It's not just about the climbing. The whole journey from Little Langdale over the passes, through Eskdale to Wasdale, is always full of hope, maybe because spring comes sooner to those west-facing valleys. Seeing the Eskdale primroses, a good three to four weeks before they appear in Langdale, is a real tonic. The flowering gorse at the head of Wasdale is so beautiful. I tell my five-year-old daughter that it smells like coconuts – and that fragrance as you set off on the start of the walk is wonderful.

I always stop at the beck crossing at the bottom of Brown Tongue and drink as much water as possible and once again at the Woolworths boulder to fill my water bottles. The next section to Mickledore is in the shade and quite often still frozen in spring. It makes you question whether there's any point in trying to rock climb today and then you hit the ridge and the sunlight and see the whole glory of the East Buttress and it's as though life starts again.

I don't know how best to describe the East Buttress. I'm a stonemason and all day long I pick up stones and every so often I pick up one that I think is bonny, and then turn it over and think it's dead bonny on the other side as well. This is the East Buttress. Whatever side or angle you look at it from it's beautiful.

There are two main bases for the East Buttress. One is at the small shelter beneath Nick's route *Entonox*, and the other is further down and round on grassy ledges beneath *Ichabod*. From either place the difficulties of climbing on the East Buttress soon become clear – it's steep, really steep. Some routes like *Great Eastern* cleverly weave their way through the overhangs. All the others attack the overhanging barrel shaped buttress straight on. And, if you walk back from the ledges beneath *Ichabod* towards the shelter at the base of *Entonox* you see the profile of it – it's a powerful sight. No other route on Scafell tells the story of how steep it is quite like this one. And every time I look at it, I ask myself the question – why didn't I climb it first?

Ed Luke

Dave Birkett

And that wasn't the only 'protracted labour' of the summer. Our daughter Flora initially fought hard against making an appearance but eventually arrived at the end of August, after much use of gas and air (or Entonox), hence the name of my new route on Scafell. The birth did prove to be quite an ordeal. Karen was in labour for over 20 hours and because we were in Westmorland General Hospital, a quiet outpost of the NHS in Kendal, there was no consultant cover. The unit was midwife-led, which is great when everything is going smoothly but not so good when the going gets tough. It was also Bank Holiday Weekend so nobody would come in to help. Karen ended up being taken by ambulance, lights flashing and siren wailing, down the motorway to Lancaster. Within five minutes of arrival, the consultant delivered the baby with the help of rotational forceps. At least it meant she got to be born in Lancashire, like her Dad!

The local authority, my employers, were very generous with paternity leave so when mother and child had to return for a few days in hospital, that left me with the opportunity to get out to Gordale on several occasions.

By December we were able to take three-month old Flora on her first climbing trip. We all went to Mallorca, along with John Wilson and Liam Grant and their respective families and John Fletcher. A perfect end to a momentous year.

QUESTION

Q. *Throughout you have referred to the names given to routes. Could you explain – for a non-climber – how that naming process works?*

A. Whoever does the first ascent of a new route is responsible for giving it a name by which it will be known in future. Over the years there have been many and varied names given to climbs by different climbers. Sometimes the name will simply describe the route: *Right Wall* and *Left Wall* are the names given to the routes on the respective walls of Dinas Cromlech in Llanberis Pass. On the same crag, between these two, the corner is called *Cenotaph Corner* – referring to the feature it follows but also giving it a distinctive name. The route between *Cenotaph Corner* and *Right Wall* was named *Lord of the Flies* - a well-known book title that is very relevant to the route as the climber might look like a 'fly on a wall' and maybe at the time Ron Fawcett, rightly, considered himself Lord of aforementioned flies.

My own new routes described in this chapter both had some relevance to me at the time. *Road Rage* described Dom's driving and most other routes on that crag have driving connotations. *Entonox* referred to the gas and air used during childbirth – used by Karen (and me!) It also sounds a bit like *Equinox* – a route nearby.

13 - Beyond the Pail
E6 6B DOVE CRAG
Other Adventures

It's wet – I'm crawling along a river. It's cold – the water is largely made up of melting snow. It's dark – it's the middle of the night and we're in a tight, underground passage lit by a headtorch on its lowest setting to save power. Every now and then I try to get some relief from the pain in my knees by switching from a hands-and-knees crawl to a low stoop-cum-shuffle, but the passage is too low for that to be comfortable for long, so I end up back on my knees. The several kit bags jammed full of ropes and wire ladders that I'm dragging behind me snag on the same lumps and protrusions that moments before I've caught my knees on. At least the effort is keeping me warm – until we stop and then the icy water soon takes over again.

At some point respite will be provided by a flat-out squeeze or, best of all, some soft mud to slither over. Later, we'll be going deeper, sliding down the rope into the darkness to find the next horizontal bedding plane along which to crawl, the only benefit being that each set of ropes and ladders left behind at each vertical pitch as our lifeline to the outside world is one less burden to carry. We're in Yorkshire and I've been persuaded to resurrect my caving career. Why do I let myself get talked into these things? All in the name of a good adventure I suppose.

They say that, "all work and no play, makes Jack a dull boy". Following that principle, perhaps it's even better if Jack were to add some variety to his play. Climbing can be all-absorbing, but there's no harm in trying something else from time to time. Over the years I've had a go at a number of different outdoor activities – sometimes because I fancied them, sometimes after a bit of arm-twisting.

During my last job in the army, I was initially based at Weeton Camp, between Preston and Blackpool. The Battalion doctor was Louise Holden and she was married to Javed Bhatti. Javed and Louise had been at Leeds Uni together, where they got involved in ULSA, the university caving club. Javed was a force to be reckoned with underground – small and strong, a great combination. He's also one of the most sociable people you could ever hope to meet and he managed to rekindle my interest in caving. So after a quick refresher of Single Rope Technique (SRT) – a method of getting up and down vertical sections of cave – we planned a trip down one of the big, grade 5 caves in Yorkshire – Pen-y-Ghent Pot. This is an impressive, classic trip, not to be underestimated, and one hell of a challenge. I'd read somewhere that this trip was described as a "tiring day underground". Well, we were going to do it overnight so surely that wouldn't apply!

We'd chosen to go at night because it was the middle of winter and the surrounding hillsides were covered in deep snow. Going overnight would reduce the risk of the snow thawing and flooding the cave. Four of us parked up at Brackenbottom near Horton-in-Ribblesdale and distributed all the gear we needed which was quite a lot. It was well after nightfall but the combination of a cold clear night and a blanket of snow meant that we had good visibility, even without lamps. The challenge was wading through the thigh-deep snow as we made our way up the hillside and then finding the entrance. Having Javed as guide made it much easier, but we still needed to excavate a lot of snow to access the actual entrance.

We scrambled down into the cave at around 10pm, then stooped and crawled until we met the stream. This is where the fun really begins. What follows is the idyllic sounding *Canal*, in fact the start of a 1000ft of awkward low stooping and flat-out crawling along a passage that is 4ft high and 2ft deep in water. After this delightful introduction, there is a short pitch to descend, but thankfully that then leads to the Easy Passage – I should've guessed that the name was ironic. There wasn't going to be anything 'easy' about this trip. There are many other pitches to descend, some of which could be climbed down, others involving longer abseils. All needed ropes to be left in place, which of course made for the large amount of equipment.

At one point, we got well ahead of our other two companions and they ended up turning back when the going got a bit too tough. Eventually, Javed and I reached the bottom. It was a fantastic feeling to have achieved our objective, like reaching the top of a long and arduous, multi-pitch climb. Now all we had to do was repeat the whole experience in the opposite direction; in climbing terms, the equivalent of down-climbing the whole route! This is where it becomes even more physical, battling against gravity and climbing up the ropes that we'd left in place. All with the delightful prospect of that 1000ft of crawling back along the Canal as the icing on the cake. We re-emerged into the gloom of the pre-dawn at around 6am. As the Four Seasons might have put it, "Oh, what a night" (maybe they'd done a similar trip in "Late December back in '63"?)

There were other trips with Javed, none quite as long, but just as exciting. *Black Shiver* on the northern slopes of Ingleborough is a good example. I remember a lot of water, some big, free-hanging abseils and several tight crawls. The most significant memory of that trip was the start. It commences with a 15ft climb down a fairly narrow, vertical shaft. Imagine a couple of thinner-than-normal telephone boxes stacked on top of each other. Getting down was fine. It was at the bottom of this initial descent that the fun began. I stood, totally encased by rock walls, with my feet in a shallow stream with no apparent way on. The trick, it appeared, was to follow the water that disappeared into an uninviting, flat-out crawl at shin-height. With chest in water and pushing my helmet ahead of me to allow free-passage, I was left wondering what on earth I'd let myself in for. And we had only been going five minutes!

I'm in awe of the early pioneers, exploring these cave systems without any prior knowledge of what they might discover and driven by curiosity and a desire for adventure. I'm all in favour of adventure, but I do believe that when there is a guidebook available, it is probably best to consult it – or at least I am now...

Some years later, when I was working at South Lakeland District Council, a few of us decided it'd be fun to reacquaint ourselves with the 'joy' of caving. The team was Mark Richardson, Andrew Tomlin, Scott Burns and me. Mark had done a fair bit of caving before and, through his diving, he knew many of the cave divers in Yorkshire. Andrew had done it once or twice in recent years, but Scott hadn't been since schooldays. It was decided that we would do a simple through-trip to reduce the kit required and settled on Swinsto Hole in Kingsdale. This is a great trip, starting at the top of the hillside, abseiling down a number of pitches with some easy-enough crawls in-between, and eventually exiting from the Kingsdale Master Cave by the road. What could possibly go wrong?

After work one day, we parked near Braida Garth, halfway up this remote valley, and headed up the hillside in search of our entrance. Now, it'd been a while since I'd done this trip but I felt reasonably confident that I'd know it when we found it and in the twilight we finally found an entrance that looked about right. In I went and at the first pitch I rigged an abseil through the resin-fixed anchor bolts that would easily pull-through once all the team was safely down. Mark was first down so he set up the next abseil as I pulled the rope down the first pitch. As I was checking Scott's abseil technique on the second, shorter pitch, Mark called back up to ask where the route went from there. "Just look around," I shouted back above the noise of the water cascading down the first pitch. "Follow the water." But it appeared that we'd reached a dead-end. There was no way on. We'd gone down the wrong hole.

This left us with a bit of a challenge. We were on a ledge with a 30ft, slightly overhanging chamber above us, down which a waterfall was falling. We'd pulled down our only connection with the top. The other three all looked at me. "Right, only thing for it, I'd better climb back up!" I offered, surveying the slightly alarming route that would take me back to the top. Luckily, perhaps, I was climbing steady E6 above ground at this point – just not normally in wellies and boiler suit using a caving harness and static ropes. 'Static' rope is absolutely not designed to protect a climber who falls. It's meant to be abseiled on or climbed up using mechanical devices as it doesn't have the stretch that's required to absorb the impact of a fall. Even a short fall on such a rope could be catastrophic.

I duly set off, nominally protected by Mark as he belayed me with the caving rope round his waist. I managed to get a sling over a stumpy stalagmite for protection halfway as I battled with the greasy, overhanging rock. With considerable relief, I did eventually make it and quickly tied a series of hand and foot loops in one end of the rope before lowering it down for the others and belayed them up using the other end. It was tough for them but we all made it to the top and out into fresh air, very relieved at our escape.

This classic schoolboy error is certainly nothing to be proud of and taught us a sobering lesson. However, it was with some relief and amusement that I later heard that we weren't the only group to make the same mistake. I told Alan Steele about our near miss and, with great hilarity, he relayed the tale of a similar

I'd been persuaded by Nick to go on a simple caving trip with a couple of others from work. I hadn't been in a cave since I was at school, and it'd been very straightforward back then. I didn't really understand what was going on. I was just along for the ride.

It seemed to be going well. We'd descended down a steep drop into a large chamber and Nick appeared confident that the entrance to the next passage was somewhere in the dark recesses of the lower cave. He pointed his directions and confidently collected the rope we'd used for our descent. We searched in vain, and it slowly dawned on me that something wasn't right. It appeared that the only way out was the way we'd come in. Our headtorch lights glistened off the steep, wet wall of rock we'd recently abseiled down. Craning my neck to look up that wall I knew this was not now the fun, easy exploration I'd signed up for. We had a serious problem.

Three things went through my mind: probably should've told someone where we were going; how did two expert pot-holers and three so-called Health & Safety experts get into such a mess; and, thirdly, if I don't die in the cave my wife will kill me anyway. Thankfully while I had been thinking of ways to survive a night in a cold, wet cavern Nick had been eyeing-up a route up the vertical wall. I've done a little bit of rock climbing and know when to be impressed. We stood below, looking nervously at each other waiting to break his fall if he slipped but we didn't need to. He inched his way up, complete with wellingtons, baggy caving suit and a rope round his waist, to the high ledge above. It was with a huge a sense of both relief and awe that we watched him get to the top and start organising how the rest of us were to follow him up.

Scott Burns

escapade. Some time after our misadventure, another group were planning the same through trip of Swinsto and found themselves, like us, at the bottom of the Turbary Pot pitch with abseil ropes pulled and ready for the rest of the trip. The main difference for this team was that one of their number had decided against participating and had remained at the top of the first pitch, planning to see them out of sight before heading back down the hillside to the road.

When the mistake was discovered, the team were able to shout up to their friend above. He was dispatched off to nearby Ingleton to procure a caving ladder that could be fixed in place for a simple retreat. He duly high-tailed it down to the village and into Inglesport, Alan and Deanne's caving and climbing emporium. "Please, can you help! My mates are stuck down a pot-hole," he blustered in the shop to the ever-attentive shopkeeper Alan. "They went down the wrong hole and pulled their ropes. I need a ladder to help get them out." "Well son, we have a fine array of ladders available for purchase," replied Alan. "You can have this one here at £57 or you might prefer that longer one at £76. Which would you prefer?" The young lad seemed a bit lost for words. Perhaps he was expecting some degree of charity, given the circumstances. He obviously didn't know the wily Mr Steele, who quickly followed up with, "My mate has free-climbed out of that pot, so if you don't want to buy a ladder, perhaps your mates could do the same." Out came the credit card. The deal was done and the rescue accomplished.

Nick had told me all about their potential epic down Turbary Pot and how he'd recovered the situation by climbing out. We'd had a good laugh about it at the time so when this lad appeared in the shop – somewhat flustered and out of breath with his tales of woe – I didn't have quite as much sympathy as he might have expected. In fact, I think he was expecting me to hand over a ladder out of the goodness of my heart! I told him a mate had climbed out of that same pot a few weeks earlier and I also told him, in no uncertain terms, that the cost of mounting a Cave Rescue would be far greater than him buying a ladder. If your mates are in a hole and not in any danger, you must do what you can by yourself if it can be easily fixed. Climbing and caving are often called adventure days, even if they're not especially hard or dangerous outings. I bet they'll remember the day better for getting out by their own efforts and it certainly gave me and Nick something to chuckle about.

Alan Steele

I've often found myself being persuaded to embark on new adventures and activities by well-meaning friends. It was Dom Donnini who got me into kayaking for a spell in 2001. It commenced with a casual suggestion to "give it a go with a few mates". How hard could it be? It was one of those sitting-down sports that us Brits have proved to be so good at in recent years. I'd previously splashed around in a boat and had some basic idea, but certainly never mastered any technique.

My maiden voyage on the Riven Leven, which drains out of the south end of Windermere, started well enough. I got into the kayak and managed to remain upright, propelling myself with adequate strokes of the paddle. I was given some basic pointers and even had the concept of moving out into the stream from an eddy and vice versa. So far so good. Then we hit the white water.

It was January, it'd been quite wet and there was a lot of wild water. Over I went and out I popped, resurfacing next to my upturned boat as the others came over to assist. This was pretty much the pattern for the day, with a lot of time spent swimming but no harm done. Finally, we'd progressed down the river, me in my own fashion, to the small village of Backbarrow. We all pulled over to the riverbank and got out to scout the next section. "You'll want to walk round this section," I was told. "Why, what is so special about this bit?" I bridled. "It's quite tough," was the simple explanation. All I could see was another waterfall and jumble of white water as it powered beneath the stone bridge. "What's the worst that could happen?" I wondered – another swim? "I'll give it a go!" I declared to the rest of the group.

After my companions had gracefully glided down the appropriate line in the fall, I took my turn, remembering the simple advice "Keep paddling!" I did what I could as I hurtled towards the watery abyss ahead, the water thundering all around. I imagine that riding on a very bumpy roller-coaster that finally comes off its runners is akin to what I experienced next. Thankfully, there was a soft landing, albeit upside down in the subsequent pool. Just another swim.

Later that year I met someone who'd been paddling for many years who told me that it was several years before he finally attempted to run Backbarrow Bridge. I wasn't deterred by my watery christening and as the year progressed, I got more and more hooked into the sport. 2001 was the year of the foot and mouth outbreak that had such a massive impact on the Lake District which meant access to the fells and hence the crags was severely restricted, while the rivers were still accessible. If we weren't paddling the Lakeland rivers, we'd regularly make the trek over to the white-water course at the Tees barrage. This clever construction uses the flow of the tide to provide man-made rapids, a bit like going to the climbing wall.

It was during one of these visits that we bumped into Tim Whiteley. I'd met Tim out climbing a few times but it wasn't until then that we really became acquainted. Living in Preston at the time, Tim would come and join us on our forays down local rivers. Tim had a bit more paddling behind him, but I was quickly catching up. If the Tees was like climbing on the lead wall, then our weekly trips to the local swimming pool to practise specific techniques was like the bouldering wall. It was here that I soon mastered my rolling technique which prevented quite as many swims. I was hungry for as much knowledge as possible. I watched videos and read books, trying to pick up hints and tips. Dom had a good library of information and I pored over as many as I could trying to soak up knowledge. One book explained all manner of techniques in comic-strip form. I'm not sure I was taking it all in but it couldn't do any harm.

During one dry period and for a change from the Tees, we made a few trips to the Tryweryn river in Wales. Unlike the tidal Tees, this course relies on dam-release and provides a more natural experience. I was there with Tim on one occasion and, as we were both still prone to do, he capsized at a point just outside the canoe centre. As he rolled back up, I could see blood pouring down his face. He was blissfully unaware of why I was shouting at him with a look of horror on my face. It turned out that he had caught his forehead on a rock on the bed of the river as he went over but the cold of the water meant he felt nothing. We got him out and to the first aider on duty in the centre. There he was patched up but with the recommendation that the cut should be stitched, which meant a trip to the local doctor. It was Sunday lunchtime and the nearest doctor, on duty or not, was not impressed to have his Sunday roast disturbed. I'm sure this had some impact on the resulting treatment that consisted of the worst example of stitching I've ever seen, apparently done with baler twine. For many years Tim had a significant scar running vertically down the centre of his forehead to remind him of that day and looked rather like a Klingon from *Star Trek*!

As the year progressed, we ticked a lot of rivers and our technique improved. The most memorable were trips to the River Swale near Keld in Yorkshire and Glen Etive, both with many big waterfalls to be run. By the end of the year our confidence and, to some degree, our competence had reached a significant level, so when a trip to Ecuador – with Dom, Tim and Steve Edmundson – was proposed, I was all for it. Steve was really quite proficient, Dom was handy enough

Steve Edmondson in Upper Swaledale

but Tim and I were still surviving one trip at a time. We managed to get hold of a very basic paddling guidebook to Ecuador and it sounded great: a combination of high Andean creeks and larger, big water Amazonian tributaries. In the run-up to the trip, one of our big concerns was the threat of anacondas. These huge snakes often reach five metres and eat all manner of large prey. It was said that one of their regular favourites is catfish, about the size (and shape) of a kayak. We took a large knife, attached to our buoyancy aids, in case we needed to cut our way out!

On arrival in Quito, a bustling city with a sense of faded Spanish colonialism, we picked up our boats and paddles and headed off for Tena, approximately 200km east of Quito, in the Amazon rainforest, to try out the Misahualli River. Getting around the country by local buses and taxis was easy, even with kayaks sticking out of windows or strapped on top of the vehicles. The Upper Mis flows south towards Tena and in this section it provides fairly fast-flowing creek kayaking, not that dissimilar to what we're used to in Scotland and the Lakes – just a bit bigger. It's steep and technical. The conditions were hot and sticky and the walk-ins were often through deep mud and primary jungle along narrow paths but it was absolutely worth the effort.

Beyond Tena, the Lower Mis takes on a completely different character. Here, it is classic big water. It transforms into a wider, slower-moving river that regularly accelerates through narrow sections and choke points creating some big rapids. For much of this stretch, the river flows through a steep-sided gorge preventing escape from the river and, in many cases, there is no way to portage (carry your kayak) round the difficult sections. Surrounded by thick rainforest with no habitation from put-in to take-out, it was fully committing. On the chosen day for our trip down the Lower Mis, Tim had a sudden, inspired moment of common sense and decided that he would give this particular trip a miss. Sadly I had no such second thoughts.

We put in at the end of the trail a few miles outside Tena, watched by a handful of scruffy, smiling children who were always keen to carry boats and paddles. It soon became apparent that this river was very different to the one a few miles upstream. It was big and, although slower moving, the sense of its power was quite unnerving to someone as new as I was to this game. Where possible we'd pull in before the many, large obstacles and more challenging sections. I remember one such occasion quite clearly. We were able to get onto a small, sandy beach just before a significant drop that had a large tree creating a major hazard in the middle of the stream. "You really must avoid that tree; you absolutely have to get to that point over there." Warned Steve Ed with a genuinely concerned look on his face. By now we were in the steep-sided gorge, which meant that just beyond our little beach, there was nothing but a steep rock wall. "Are you happy with running this?" he asked. I looked again. "I haven't any choice, have I?" I replied. "No!" came back the emphatic response.

It was an action-packed and exhausting day. On another section, lower down the river, I capsized as I went over a fall. I hadn't given myself enough power to launch off the drop. I rolled back up simply enough, only to be whipped back over almost immediately. I was in a fairly powerful 'stopper', where the surface flow of the water is being recirculated back upstream. This can be seen at any weir on your local river, where debris will be held, bobbing about just below the fall. I kept rolling up, snatching a quick breath, and going over again. What happened next probably happened very quickly but felt to be in slow motion. I was considering my options. Should I pull my spray deck, bail out and try to swim? Then what? What if the boat was still held in the stopper? I then recalled a clear image from the cartoon-based instruction book I'd borrowed from Dom months before, back home. It showed someone in my current predicament. The instruction was clearly illustrated: while you're upside-down you stretch your arms and paddle above your head to go deeper into the water. Here the water is flowing downstream and that flow will pull you out of the stopper. I grabbed another deep breath, went over, and stretched out my arms. I held that position for ten seconds or so then rolled up. I was indeed downstream of the stopper; I'd released myself from its clutches. I had no idea that I knew that was what I needed to do. If I'd been asked beforehand, I wouldn't have been able to say.

But it wasn't over yet! Somewhere up ahead was a legendary rapid with the ominous-sounding name Land of the Giants – the previous ones hadn't exactly been midgets! We were aware that the initial Class 6 waterfall could be avoided by a portage on the right. When we reached a large pool with a forbidding horizon line and a constant sound of thunder, we pulled over to find the way round. It wasn't obvious. There was no way round at or just above water level and the alternative was a steep muddy slope up into the thick jungle. This must be it then, unlikely as it seemed. It's funny how you can convince yourself, a bit like when you stand at the bottom of an unknown crag and manage to make the route descriptions from the guidebook fit what you can see, only to find that you are looking at the wrong buttress! We made our way up the steep slope, battling with mud and undergrowth. It soon became apparent that there was no route to be had in that direction. We were now well above the waterline with a significant crag below us.

The only option was to lower ourselves and boats down the steep slope, using our throw-lines, to a small ledge on top of the crag and brace ourselves for a significant seal launch into the water below. I had practised a successful seal launch before – off a flat riverbank, from a height of a couple of feet, into calm water. Currently, I was looking at a 20ft drop into swirling, white water from a cramped ledge, less than 3ft square. Dom went first with some trepidation, which didn't fill me with the greatest confidence, but landed it well and went straight into a neat manoeuvre to get himself on the correct line and out of danger. "Make sure you make that turn, as soon as you hit the water – okay?" stressed Steve. "I'll try my best!" I had no option but to go, it was the moment of truth. It all went in something of a blur but it must have gone right. I stayed upright and, as it turned out, that was the last of our major travails of this testing day. We discovered later that the water level had risen overnight, thus obscuring the simple traverse round the initial fall. By the time we reached the take-out at Puerto Misahualli, the river was wide and slow although our river paled into insignificance in comparison to the mighty Napo that it joined. It was very apparent that we had reached one of the great tributaries of the Amazon. From this point it is over 1200 miles of slowly meandering river to the Atlantic Ocean, and Puerto Misahualli is approximately 1300 feet above sea level – a drop of just over one foot a mile for 1200 miles. Not much more white water then! What a great take-out, though, with a bar right next to the river, frequented by friendly monkeys eager to take snacks from your hand.

Back in Tena we were staying in a nice hotel with bedrooms in separate lodges in the grounds of the main building. The four of us were split between two twin rooms – me and Dom upstairs, Tim and Steve downstairs. Except we weren't the only occupants. Dom found a very attractive, slender snake with colourful banding along the length of its body, exploring his holdall. Not wanting to keep his find to himself, Dom picked it up with a long stick and took it downstairs to wave it in Tim's face with a flourish. At this point Steve and I arrived back in the room along with the hotel owner, a friendly and garrulous character. Seeing the snake, our friendly host let out a concerned shriek along with a lot of babbling and gestures that clearly meant only one thing: "get that thing out of here – now!" Respecting his local knowledge, we duly dispatched it out of the window and into the river below. Subsequent research suggested that Dom had found a coral snake – the most venomous breed in Ecuador.

Our next base was the town of Banos, in the high mountains, several hours' drive away by kayak-laden pick-up truck. Our arrival coincided with a remarkable spectacle – the annual go-kart race in which dozens of reckless youths ride self-propelled go-karts in pairs, starting in a neighbouring town and finishing down the precipitous streets of Banos to the town centre. Many streets cross the fall-line, each junction providing a hair-raising flat launch pad for the home-made buggies – not all of which survive. To add to the chaos, the streets are packed with spectators, Tour de France-like, all converging in the centre of the road to get the best view of the approaching competitors. It was mayhem with many spectacular crashes, which all got the greatest cheers.

After a couple of days in this mountain retreat, it was back to Quito and eventually homeward. On the way back, our plane was delayed in Bogota for several hours by fog, which meant that we missed our connection in New York and were bumped to a flight the following day – a bit of a bonus, in the end, because we were upgraded to Business Class for the trans-Atlantic leg of our journey and had a day to spend in New York. Having been put up in the worst hotel imaginable near the airport in Newark, with some very unsavoury detritus left under the bed from the previous, amorous occupants, we got the train into Manhattan for a look-around. This involved a trip down to Lower Manhattan to see the still-smouldering remnants of the Twin Towers – a very poignant and sobering moment. At one point Dom peeled off to visit a shop somewhere else in the city. We arranged to rendezvous at the entrance to a well-known hotel before heading back to the airport but when Tim and I got there, no Dom! "Bloody typical, always cutting it fine." We gave him a bit longer – still no show. "Where the hell is he?" Eventually, we had to set off at a run for Grand Central Station. "Serve him

Mad-cap scenes on the streets of Banos for the annual go-kart race

right if he misses the flight!" although, in truth, we were a bit concerned for him. We got on the train out to the airport just as the doors were closing. What had become of Dom? Was he alright? Was he lost? Was he in trouble? But as we got to the check-in desk, there he was, sat on his bag, without a care in the world. "Hi, lads, where've you been?" "Where the hell were you?" "I turned up, you weren't there so I left." His explanation was that there must have been two entrances to the hotel and we were on opposite sides of the building. We still weren't entirely convinced and suspect he left it too late to come and find us so just headed for the airport. If nothing else, it added one last shot of adrenaline to an already high-octane trip.

Back at home we had a few more paddling trips that winter. Most exciting was a descent of the Duddon in high water. After Ecuador it felt relatively straightforward but it was still a good challenge. Towards the bottom there was a sizeable fall to be run with the strict instruction: "As you go over, you must go right." First man over, all went well – nice drop and he went right. My turn, over I went – all successful, I went right. Tim's turn – over he went and he went left! He hit some very messy water between a small crag on the bank and a large boulder, was flipped over in an instant and his boat half-disappeared beneath one of the rock walls. And there it stayed – with no sign of Tim. All that we could see was the bottom of his kayak. The initial moment stretched with still no sign of him. We were helpless. We couldn't get to him. Where was he? Eventually, after what felt like an age, he re-emerged gasping for breath. He'd been under for a very long time. His boat was still wedged solid, upside down, firmly jammed in an underwater gap. The rock had trapped his spray deck, preventing him from releasing it. Eventually he'd managed to squeeze his slender hips through the tight aperture and so release himself, but only after a great deal of effort. We had genuinely thought he was a goner.

After 20 years, the incident on the Duddon remains the defining moment of a brief period of reckless enthusiasm for white-water kayaking. In the space of a few months, I'd escaped from a flooded river in Scotland by means of grabbing an overhanging branch and swinging hand-over-hand to dry land, quickly having to drag free my kayaking partner, who had become pinned upside down against a tree. I got that scar on the Tryweryn and shortly after the Duddon we had the ten days or so somehow surviving in Ecuador. By the time we'd made it to Banos I seem to remember finally being conscious of a deep level of fear I'd only experienced climbing once or twice – and then only after the event.

The nuances of what went wrong prior to being pinned have long since merged into the multitude of other kayaking incidents. However, there are some crystal clear memories: a sense of relief at making it over the last drop still upright; someone shouting to paddle right; hitting a submerged rock and the force of the water causing the front of the boat to rise; breathing in, instinctively, really deeply just before being submerged; and finding myself pinned under a rock.

The large boulder formed a sharp triangle with the river bed into which the front of the kayak was wedged with myself and the deck of the kayak stuck flat to the underside of a large smooth boulder. I couldn't get a hand between rock and spraydeck to pull it free. I was wedged in. The spraydeck is a neoprene skirt that fits very snugly round your waist and is then stretched tightly round the kayak entrance. It's tight enough to prevent most water ingress. To keep warm and as feasibly dry as possible I also had a semi-dry nylon cag with the waistband pulled tightly against the spraydeck.

Pushing with all the might I could muster, somehow I suddenly popped out of the boat leaving the spraydeck still firmly attached to the kayak. I'm fairly convinced I couldn't have done that on dry land. How long I'd been under I'm not sure – a few seconds can feel like a long time when you're fighting to right yourself – and the consensus was somewhere between one and two minutes. However long it was, it was way too long to be something to repeat and certainly the cause of my hands involuntarily shaking at the thought of getting back into white water.

Tim Whiteley

After too many near-death experiences, kayaking taught me one thing – just how safe climbing is. It's also different to climbing in that you can be gently floating down one stretch of river without a care in the world and moments later you are thrown into full-on action before once again settling back down. It oscillates very rapidly from very safe to very dangerous. While climbing, even though there are harder and easier sections, you are always operating at height and therefore there is always some base level of hazard. In climbing we can protect ourselves with good use of equipment. In paddling you have to rely entirely on your own ability to survive.

One aspect of the Lakes that is frustrating and disappointing is the inconsistency of the winter climbing conditions. There are some cracking winter lines all around the Lakes and surrounding areas, but they so rarely come into good condition these days. Maybe I have a rosy view of past winters or maybe it is something to do with climate change but we certainly don't seem to get decent winter conditions very often. A few years back when we had a run of half-decent winters, I teamed up with ageing rock hot-shot Mick Lovatt (known to many in the climbing world as 'The Perfect Man'). Together we ticked many great routes including: *Inaccessible Gully* on Dove Crag and *Botterill's Slab* on Scafell. The main pitch of the latter was superb climbing up the corner just right of the summer route, using hooks and torques with ice axe picks in the crack along with thin ice smears on the steep slab. Above, there is a steep continuation slab that forms a body-width chimney with another wall, thickly coated in perfect ice.

I also got out with Dom Donnini, Steve Scott, Tim Whiteley and others, ticking all the Lakeland routes in the fabulous, winter version of the *Classic/Hard/Extreme* Rock series *Cold Climbs* along with many others. One of these is *Great Gully Right Hand* on the Screes in Wasdale, which we went to climb one Boxing Day. It was perfect conditions for me, Dom and Paul O'Reilly, another good friend from Kendal. The climbing was brilliant, but the most hilarious part of the day was watching Dom throw up the remains of his Christmas lunch on the steep approach walk. Another festive ascent was one glorious sunny Christmas Eve at a well-frozen *Cautley Spout* on the east side of the Howgills with physiotherapist friend, Iain Cole, with the added pressure of getting finished in time to pick up our turkey from the butcher before they closed.

The most extreme winter climbing days out have all been with Brian Davison. I've been dragged to many esoteric venues with Brian and marvelled at

Dom Donnini running the big fall on the River Swale

his ability to get up seemingly impenetrable lines. At the time, Brian was probably one of the best winter climbers in the country, constantly forging ahead with new routes at ever-increasing standards. All this achieved with the most ancient and outdated gear. I always wondered what he could've achieved with more modern equipment.

Because of the limited conditions, it was inevitable that we'd make trips further afield, to Scotland most often but also abroad. I like to think of Rjukan in Norway as the ice-climbing equivalent of the Costa Blanca or other 'Sun Rock' destinations. The climbing is superb, easily accessible and as-good-as guaranteed. There are a whole series of waterfalls that cascade into the main valley which, when frozen, provide a winter playground. This is also home to the famous wartime story of the German heavy water factory, essential for the Nazi efforts to create an atomic bomb, made famous by the 1965 film *The Heroes of Telemark* starring Kirk Douglas and Richard Harris as the brave saboteurs. The

Dom and Woody beneath the mighty *Rjukanfossen*

rebuilt factory still sits there and indeed some of the routes finish by belaying to its boundary fence.

I had a trip there one winter with Woody, Dom and Richard Baker. Other teams were there at the same time and we had a very sociable time as well as getting up a lot of fabulous ice routes. In the evenings we'd head to the sports centre and swimming pool complex in the town, a great way to relax after a hard day in the cold you might think, except it was anything but relaxing. Twisting its way down into the pool was a long, enclosed waterslide equipped with a precision timer that measured each person's descent. We soon discovered that by arching your back you could fly down the chute on your heels and shoulder blades for maximum speed. The competition was on. Time after time we'd shave tenths or hundredths of a second off our times to set a new record. I think Woody was the ultimate winner, but it was a close-run thing.

It's not only the ice climbing that suffers from the variable conditions in the Lakes. The topography of the area would lend itself to fantastic ski-touring, if only we got more, better snow. Occasionally we are still blessed with good snow cover and many of the passes and some of the summits make for great tours. I had one such day with Shelley Barlow, a great friend from Staveley, near Kendal. Shelley is a keen biker, climber and an excellent yoga teacher. One glorious, sunny day the two of us headed round to the head of Haweswater on the eastern side of the Lakes. We set off up Gatesgarth Pass, initially carrying our skis but very quickly being able to put them on and skin up the line of the popular path. Nearing the pass, we could see that the west-facing slope of Branstree, a relatively small Wainwright summit to our left, had a full covering of beautiful, smooth snow, with a peculiar, wind-blown cornice part way down the slope. We headed up left to the top of the slope for a fantastic descent, taking in the jump that the cornice provided and back to the col. From here, the snow-plastered path led us up onto the higher point of Harter Fell for a fabulous view down the flooded valley of Mardale and east to the Pennines. Our route that day took us in the opposite direction, down into Kentmere, picking our way down the best lines before once again heading back up to our high point via Nan Bield Pass. Once we were back on top of Harter Fell again, we made our final descent of the day, this time heading north towards Small Water, down a tremendous line that we'd eyed-up on the previous ascent. It was a magnificent day out in fabulous conditions to match any day of ski-touring in the Alps.

Rjukan thin ice *Lipton*, WI7

Approaching the belay at top of *Botterill's Slab* main pitch

The Helvellyn range is another great area for ski-touring. I've had many great days there, usually with a pleasant walk up Raise Beck from Dunmail Raise followed by skinning up onto Dollywagon Pike and all along the ridge to the summit of Helvellyn. From here, the East Face headwall overlooking Red Tarn provides an excellent, steep descent. I was on the summit one glorious February day a few years ago on a classic cold, blue-sky day with a great snowpack and apparently perfect conditions on the headwall. As I stood on the edge, surveying the best line for a descent, a noisy bunch of likely-looking lads from Liverpool, out for a day on the hill, came wandering over. "Alright mate, where are you going to ski?" they asked in broad Scouse. "I'm going down here," I explained, pointing over the cornice, down the steep face. "No, seriously, where are you going?" they persisted. "You can't go down there." "I'm going down here, down this steep face here," I insisted. "Nobody could go down there, mate. That's death down there!" It went on like this for some time. "Blimey mate, you must have balls the size of a horse!" was their final pronouncement on the matter.

Local ski-touring on Harter Fell overlooking Mardale 📷 Shelley Barlow

By now I'd planned my line and readied myself for the descent. I leapt off the cornice to wild cheers from my new fans. That might have been the end of the story but, as chance would have it, we met again. A year later I found myself on Helvellyn once more in similar conditions. Just as I was approaching the summit, among hordes of walkers, I heard a loud Scouse shout: "Hey lads, look. It's Big Balls!"

QUESTION

Q. *You mention Brian's ability to get up seemingly impenetrable lines. What is it that makes a line seemingly impenetrable for one person and not for another? What did he spot that you hadn't? Is this an extra layer of talent? Insight? Imagination?*

A. First of all, spotting a new line is something of a talent in itself, particularly in a well-established area like the Lakes. Most routes that can be done have been done. It requires a certain kind of imagination to see a possibility that others have overlooked and to visualise how the difficulties might be overcome. Brian is excellent at this and is definitely driven towards finding new lines. Secondly, having seen the line of a new route, you then have to actually get up it. When it comes to mixed winter routes (climbing a combination of rock and ice), I would frequently be amazed at just how little Brian needed, by way of holds, to make upward progress. I learned a great deal from going out with him.

Shelley Barlow by Small Water, Mardale after descent of Harter Fell North Face

14 - The Long Run

E5 6A NORTH STACK WALL, GOGARTH

The Classic Rock Challenge

I'd always enjoyed running – in the cross-country team at school, at university and in the army and I'd managed a good time in the Great North Run half marathon road race in Newcastle. But being in the Lakes meant fell running. I started by going out on my own and getting used to running over the trails, footpaths and rough fell of the Cumbrian countryside and soon discovered there was a regular schedule of fell races I could test myself in.

The first one I went along to was the popular Kentmere Horseshoe. A big field set off from the tiny hamlet of Kentmere. Among the crowd I bumped into Tim Lofthouse, an experienced fell runner. As we raced up the initial stretch of tarmac, I felt someone grabbing the back of my vest. It was Lofty. "Slow down, you've got a long way to go." He meant to be helpful but I couldn't help myself. I've always been a bit over-enthusiastic and on this occasion I found myself right up at the front of several hundred runners with only one or two whippets ahead of me. Luckily, I'd walked the Kentmere Horseshoe, so I knew the way – up the track of Garburn Pass then turn right and follow the broad ridge to Yoke – or so I thought! When the guy in front of me left the track and started veering rightwards up the fellside, I actually tried to put him right. "Here, mate, you're going the wrong way." I carried on, all the way up the track, undeterred by having nobody behind me. It was only after I'd turned right at the top of the pass and was part way towards the first summit that I could see a long stream of runners coming in from the right. By now I was halfway down the field, having just added an extra kilometre by running two sides of the triangle. Doh! I never made that mistake again.

Something I noticed, as I started to notch up a few of these events, was how cautious many runners were running downhill. I'd struggle going up the hills, getting regularly overtaken, only to catch up and race past them on the way back down. On some of the higher routes the terrain can get quite rocky and many runners end up picking their way slowly and carefully from one rock to the next. Perhaps it was the result of years of walking to and from crags, over scree slopes, that gave me the advantage, but I could cover this ground much more quickly, sub-consciously judging which boulders to stand on and which to avoid. On one occasion during the Borrowdale race, which goes to the summit of Scafell Pike, I was tearing down a shortcut from the summit to the Corridor Route when several of my fellow competitors started shouting at me in alarm: "Slow down, be careful, you'll hurt yourself!" Slow down? It's supposed to be a race!

The best known fell running challenge in the country is the Bob Graham Round (BG). This feat of athletic endurance was established in 1932 when the eponymous Bob Graham made his 'long walk', traversing 42 summits in the Lake District within 24 hours. The BG starts and finishes at the Moot Hall in the centre of Keswick; the rules are simple: visit all 42 summits and be back at the start point within 24 hours. People go either clockwise or anti-clockwise – down to personal preference. The route is typically broken down into 5 Legs as there are 4 points where it crosses a road - at Threlkeld, Dunmail Raise, Wasdale and Honister Pass. It would be another 30 years before the original record was broken by Alan Heaton who ran over the same 42 summits in 22 hours 18 mins. Since then, the BG has grown in popularity and renown and is the ultimate 'tick' for many fell runners. Up to the end of 2020, the list of those who have successfully completed a round, recorded by the Bob Graham Club, still sits at under 2500 – testament to just how challenging it is when you consider that 30,000 people complete the London Marathon each year. My own round in 2003 is listed as number 1201 with a respectable time of 21 hours and 4 mins. After completing the BG myself, I helped pace many other contenders over one or more of the 5 legs in the same way that many of my friends and running partners assisted me.

The record for the fastest round stands at a staggering 12 hours 52 minutes set in July 2018 by Kilian Jornet, the Catalan mega-star of the ultra-running world.

Nick running up Keswick Main St on the final metres of the BG with Flora, supported by many great friends including Matt Beresford (R) 📷 Dom Donnini

The longest and toughest section is from Dunmail Raise to Wasdale. This stretch takes in the highest peaks including the tough, rocky terrain of the Scafell massif and, for me, the most interesting section between Scafell Pike and its neighbour Scafell. There are several route options with the most direct being up straight up Broad Stand, a short rocky scramble/climb from the col at Mickledore up to the summit of Scafell. This is the same place that Coleridge had found himself in a spot of bother in 1802. It can feel quite challenging by that stage of the round!

I've always felt that there wasn't enough rock climbing in fell running and Brian Davison and I went some way to redressing that balance in 2005.

Both fell running and climbing have a long tradition of linking individual summits or routes to create a memorable challenge and it became apparent to us that there were more and more people in the Lakes doing both activities. What better place to design a fun-filled day out for the climber that also runs, or the runner that also climbs? So Brian and I decided to do just that, by climbing all 15 routes in Ken Wilson's *Classic Rock*, and running between them, in under 24 hours. It was to become known as the Classic Rock Challenge.

Route Name	Grade	Crag
Murray's Route	S	Dow Crag, Coniston
Ash Tree Slabs	VD	Gimmer Crag, Langdale
C Route	S	Gimmer Crag, Langdale
Bracket and Slab	S	Gimmer Crag, Langdale
Bowfell Buttress	VD	Bowfell, Langdale
Jones' Route Direct	HS	Scafell, Wasdale
Moss Ghyll Grooves	MVS	Scafell, Wasdale
Tophet Wall	HS	Great Gable, Wasdale
Needle Ridge	VD	Napes
Napes Needle	HS	Napes
Rib and Slab	HS	Pillar Rock, Ennerdale
New West Climb	VD	Pillar Rock, Ennerdale
Gillercombe Buttress	S	Gillercombe, Borrowdale
Troutdale Pinnacle	S	Black Crag, Borrowdale
Little Chamonix	VD	Shepherds Crag, Borrowdale

The plan wasn't entirely new. All the routes had been climbed in under 24 hours in 1994 by Dave Willis, Tim Gould and Mike van Gullick, but with the use of a car for two sections. Our aim was to get round entirely on foot, unsupported, shifting the emphasis further in the direction of running. We planned a route of approximately 40 miles from south to north. It would involve around 16,000ft of ascent and 4000ft on the rock. In addition to running kit, we took rock shoes, a 20m length of 9mm rope (cut off the end of a previously discarded half-rope), 5 wires, 4 slings and 4 karabiners – a normal Wharton/Davison rack, some might say! We also took a supply of flapjack from Wilf's (the famous Staveley café) and some chocolate biscuits. With hindsight, and we'd have known it if we'd done a more thorough recce, the rope and wires were probably not necessary, but I would still take what we did – just in case. We didn't want to fail for want of a little reassurance if we came across a patch of damp rock. Another question we posed ourselves was whether or not to down-climb some of the routes. In the end

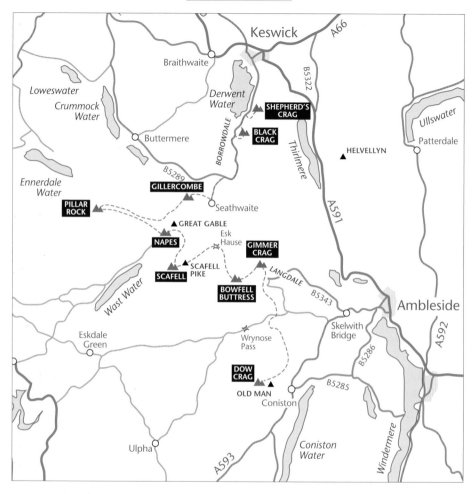

we considered it fair game – down-climbing is still climbing. Just because most of the first ascensionists were blinkered into starting at the bottom didn't mean we should be. After all, Haskett Smith first did Needle Ridge, one of our routes, from top to bottom.

Our chosen date was 9 July 2005, a day that turned out to be very hot indeed. We left a car in Borrowdale overnight and the fun started near Coniston at the southern end of the Lakes. We walked up the Walna Scar Road towards our start point on Dow Crag and at 4am in the emerging daylight we had the crag all to ourselves. We stood at the foot of *Murray's Route*, a Severe route with an iconic first section that makes its way across a short, steep slab with one good foothold in the centre. The clock started. Because of the dim light, and because we are both very careful, sensible chaps, we tied the 9mm rope round our waists and started climbing together, trying to keep at least one piece of protection between us.

That route finishes part way up B Buttress and so, rather than make the usual descent, we scrambled the rest of the way to the summit before running down to Goat's Hause, the col between Dow Crag and Coniston Old Man. From here the path leads up to Brim Fell and the ridge that runs north from the Old Man to Swirl How.

Coniston Old Man used to be the highest point in Lancashire until it was annexed in the land-grab of 1974 which resulted in this area of Lancashire-over-the-Sands becoming part of Cumbria. That's why the annual Old County Tops fell race takes in Helvellyn (Westmorland), Scafell Pike (Cumberland) and Coniston Old Man (Lancashire). The three counties met at the top of Wrynose Pass, a point that is still marked by the Three Shires Stone.

On that early summer's morning, our descent down Wet Side Edge was spectacular as the sun rose over the Eastern Fells and illuminated pools of mist sitting over Little Langdale. We jogged past a deserted Blea Tarn with the Langdale Pikes looking glorious ahead of us. The climb up to Gimmer was remarkably easy in the cool of the early morning and without the burden of a normal climbing rucksack – a welcome change from the other times we've slogged up there with a full rack of gear and ropes. We linked *Ash Tree Slabs* (V Diff) with *C Route* (Severe) before a lengthy descent down the South East Gully to return to the top via *Bracket and Slab* (Severe). In retrospect, a reverse solo of the latter would have saved a considerable amount time.

Next on the agenda was Bowfell. This is tantalisingly close as the crow flies – right there, just across the valley – but, not being crows, there was a major route choice to be made. Should we choose to stay high and traverse round the head of the valley beneath Rossett Pike, or take the much shorter direct line? We chose the latter so had to face the long but quick drop into the valley and a slog up the other side – and it was getting warmer. *Bowfell Buttress* (V Diff), once we were there, passed without incident, bathed in morning sunshine. It's an easy route in summer, much more interesting and very popular under iced-up winter conditions, which accounts for the scratched rock all the way up and particularly on the short steep wall in the middle of the route. A traverse underneath Esk Pike to Esk Hause, reversing the Langdale race route, lined us up for the approach to

Scafell. It must've been getting hot because I remember thinking (for the first and possibly last time in my life) how good it was to see Scafell Crag in the shade. In fact, we'd chosen the day of the Wasdale fell race, a Championship race that year, and it turned out to be so hot that day that an unprecedented number of runners dropped out or were timed-out at checkpoints. As we approached Mickledore, the col between the two sides of the mighty crag, we could see a single party on the East Buttress, down to our left. We couldn't help but be interested in who was climbing there and what route they were doing. To our delight it was Dave and Mary Birkett. We didn't stop to chat but shouted our greetings before dropping down to the right, beneath Scafell Crag.

Jones' Route Direct (Hard Severe) has one tricky move for its grade, an exposed and precarious mantleshelf, but this soon yielded and after a quick descent of *Steep Ghyll* with the assistance of our bit of rope we were soon racing other climbers to the foot of *Moss Ghyll Grooves* (Mild VS). It would have been very frustrating to find ourselves behind another team, unable to climb past without seeming inconsiderate, but the situation never arose. On paper, this route was supposed to be the hardest one of the day – the guide certainly says so. I hadn't done it before, and Brian only in full winter conditions 20 years before! For the first time that day feeling some degree of trepidation, we tied on for the main pitch with the move out to the arête, although I'm not sure how much benefit that would've provided in the event of an actual fall. It just shows how easy it is to be taken in by a guidebook description, which led us to expect it to be much harder than it really is. In reality, it's only mild VS which was well within our capability and we needn't have bothered with the rope after all. It's magnificent climbing with great exposure, overlooking the vast sweep of Scafell Crag's north-facing Central Buttress. In fact, it's an impressive and audacious line, surrounded by harder routes, first climbed in 1926 by Harry Kelly, a leading Lakeland climber of the early inter-war years. It wasn't as hard as the earlier *Botterill's Slab* or *Central Buttress* but was considered a more serious undertaking at the time for lack of resting ledges, limited opportunity for protection and less escape options.

Cloud suddenly came in over Scafell at that point but we escaped it by running down the Corridor Route to Styhead and on past Kern Knotts to the Napes for the finest route of the day – *Tophet Wall* (Hard Severe), another route first climbed by HM Kelly the year before *Moss Ghyll Grooves*. (He was on a roll!) The exposure and Big Wall-feel of the route combined with great climbing makes this one of the best outings in the Lakes, especially at a grade that anyone can manage. The hand-traverse right on the third pitch is easy but spectacular and is the highlight of the route. Having reached the summit without any trouble, we located the top of *Needle Ridge* (V Diff), which we reversed down – just as WP Haskett Smith had done over 120 years before.

This landed us nicely next to one of the most striking of all rock structures in the Lakes and symbol of the FRCC – Napes Needle. When Haskett Smith got his first glimpse of the Needle from across the valley at Greta Force, "...emerging seductively though partially drawn curtains of mist..." he described it as "a slender pinnacle of rock, standing out against the background of cloud without a sign of any other rock near it, and appearing to shoot up 200–300 feet". No wonder he was "resolved to take an early opportunity of hunting down the mysterious rock". Sadly, the reality is not quite as impressive but it's nevertheless a fine formation that begs to be climbed. And so we did, via the same route (now graded HS) that our illustrious predecessor had done. When Haskett Smith first climbed it, solo, in 1886 he writes that he threw stones onto the top to see if they would stay as "an indication of a moderately flat top, and would hold out hopes of the edge being found not too much rounded to afford a good grip for the fingers" (even though he'd already climbed *Needle Ridge* two years previously, which would've given him a perfectly clear view of the top of the Needle). We cracked on without the stone throwing. Nor did we need to leave a handkerchief on top to prove we'd been there, as he had – so the story goes. Meanwhile a large family group were having a great time doing what's known as 'Threading the Needle' – scrambling up one side and down the other of the cleft between Napes Needle and the base of the main cliff.

After the fun and games of the Napes came the nightmare section – the long slog out west to Pillar, overlooking remote Ennerdale. Along the way we passed some sorry-looking runners on the Wasdale race. Apart from a few committed devotees, led by Stephen Reid, Pillar doesn't get as many visitors as other, more accessible crags. Those who do make the effort usually get a really early start and cram as much into the day as possible to make the long trek worthwhile. We had to run all the way out there in the middle of the day, do two routes and leave immediately. When we got there, a quick slug of an energy gel did its magic and I was fired up again. We reversed *New West Climb* (V Diff) – very exciting at the start of the chimney pitch. At the bottom we met Stephen Reid and Chris King climbing a new route *Rib and Rib* (E1). We made our apologies as we scrambled over Chris on a common section at the start of our route, *Rib and Slab* (Hard Severe). Once back on top, we had the tedious return of the outward trip. We chose the obvious route past Black Sail Pass and along the north side of Kirk Fell and Gable to traverse underneath Green Gable and so on up to eventually reach the top of Gillercombe. The route *Gillercombe Buttress* (Severe) is, in my opinion, the least attractive of all the Classic Rock routes. It is somewhat rambling and suffers from a lot of heathery ledges but there are some good bits in between. A recce beforehand could've saved us a lot of time. If we'd known where the route went, we could easily and quickly have down-climbed it. As it was, neither of us had even been to the crag before and so were forced into using the long descent route in order to climb it bottom-up.

From the hamlet of Seathwaite, down in the valley, it's just along the road, heading north down Borrowdale. Let me say that again: "it's just along the road". You cannot imagine how far along that road it is, especially at the end of a very long day, wearing fell shoes, with swollen feet in agony from having been re-peatedly squashed into hot, sweaty rock shoes. I felt completely wasted on the approach up through the woods to Black Crag and *Troutdale Pinnacle* (Severe). But a remarkable thing happened on arrival at the crag, which might give some indication of the balance of the challenge between the running and climbing, for me at least. Having once more squeezed sore feet into rock shoes, as soon

Brian Davison soloing *Rib and Slab*, Pillar

as I gingerly stepped onto the rock and started climbing, I felt fresh again as if it were the first route of the day. The climbing was easy, even in the gathering gloom of dusk. The traverse down and left across the slabs may be intimidating but the holds are good. Similarly, the climbing up the pinnacle itself, although spectacular, has an ample supply of perfect jugs.

By the time we'd made the last, short dash along the valley and reached *Little Chamonix* (V Diff) at Shepherd's Crag it was completely dark and so the last route of the day was done by head torch. Caff's dad had famously done this in boxing gloves and roller skates – how hard could it be? We'd both also done this classic, easy route many times and knew that it was a simple route on which to finish. We topped-out at 11.38pm – having taken 19 hours and 38 minutes. Maybe it was the time of day or the dehydration, or maybe it was the lack of any supporters around, but at the end I felt considerably more exhausted than when I'd done the Bob Graham Round. In fact, Brian did an unsupported Bob Graham three weeks later and reported that he felt fresher at the end of that than at the end of that first Classic Rock Challenge. We just needed some relief from the still warm evening so we headed down to the lake shore and waded out into Derwentwater, which was disappointingly shallow and not as cold as I'd hoped.

It'd been a tremendous day out with a great combination of the things I like doing best. The weather was always going to be challenging. If you want a clear day with maximum light it has to be the middle of summer and so it is likely to be hot. The alternative is an overcast, claggy day with risk of damp greasy rock – and anyway it's never like that in the Lakes.

The satisfying postscript to our adventure is the growing interest that now surrounds it. Many more people have repeated the round aiming to beat our time. It has even been the subject of a short film. Most recently there's been fierce competition between Tom Randall and Will Birkett to set a new record with the top spot yo-yoing between them. Will first broke the 12-hour barrier and has gone on to beat Tom's response to that with an astounding 10 hours and 41 minutes. Who knows what might happen in the future? Certainly, their outings appear to have captured people's imagination, which should encourage plenty of others to take up the challenge.

The Partner's Perspective

I put the magazine down and sat back contemplating what I'd read. The three chaps in the article had run 26 miles around the 15 *Classic Rock* routes. It sounded like a good challenge. I got out my map and started looking at routes but whatever line I plotted between the crags, it always came out at around 40 miles. Still, if I could keep up four miles an hour which I knew would be optimistic and allow 30 minutes for each climb it should be possible in about 18 hours so was doable in daylight hours during the summer. I'd started setting myself daft endurance challenges, which I usually did on my own. That way I could just take off when I had the time and the conditions were right, and it meant I didn't have to drag anyone else into my hair-brain schemes. With the potential of falling off a climb, this challenge had more than the average degree of danger involved. It would only need a few feet of wet rock to scupper the whole day. A partner and a light rack would increase the safety and chances of success but would anyone be interested? Nick Wharton had been on one of those mad-cap schemes when we mountain-biked around all of the FRCC Lake District huts one weekend. I knew he was enjoying both his climbing and his fell running at the time.

Not only was Nick keen, he also knew one of the people who'd tried it before and was able to discover that they'd used a car on various sections, so that solved my mystery over distances. Now all we had to do was find a suitable day when we were both available.

It turned out to be a very hot summer's day. You could feel the heat coming off the rocks as we walked, in the dark, past the Old Man to start our first route on Dow Crag. Neither of us had done all the routes before nor covered all of the ground between the crags so it was nice to cover some new ground. I enjoyed the run along to Gimmer in the early morning. As I pushed my feet into my rock slippers they felt uncomfortable after the run and it was hot even this early in the day. This was going to be painful later on. Most of the time we soloed with or without changing into rock boots. By midday we were at Scafell. Part way up *Jones' Route* on the Scafell Pinnacle Nick shouted down for a rope due to damp rock. I threw it up and took a belay as he tied himself in with a bowline.

Soon we were scurrying across ledges to *Moss Ghyll Grooves*. Two parties below asked each other where the start of the route was. I felt somewhat mean not mentioning where it was until we were on the route, but we didn't have time to get stuck behind other groups. Running down the Corridor Route to Gable, Nick was leaving me behind and I could feel a blister developing. I had thoughts of maybe doing a Bob Graham Round later in the summer so was reluctant to damage my feet too much. If I stopped he'd be well away. I needed to focus on today and accept the pain. Thankfully Nick met a friend and stopped for a chat allowing me a chance to catch up and stick a plaster on. He talked long enough for me to fill up my water in the stream and recover a bit.

Tophet Wall felt very exposed as I pulled up and out following Nick – this was one of the routes I didn't know and one of my favourites of the day. Then it was down to the *Needle* and onto Pillar. The Wasdale racers coming in the opposite direction were confused by us heading the wrong way. A quick scrabble up and down routes and over a climbing Stephen Reid and partner and we were soon heading away from Pillar. This big crag is a long way from anywhere and the distance was telling as we headed to Gillercombe. Nick was tiring this time – a stop for an energy gel helped.

Once in Borrowdale we were both feeling the efforts of the day. We agreed to walk up the hills and run the downhills and along the flat. Even though we were heading towards Keswick, it still felt as though there was a lot of uphill from the head of the valley.

A descent from Troutdale Pinnacle in the twilight led to a final headlight ascent of *Little Chamonix*. We'd dropped a car at the finish so we had time for a clean-up in a very warm Derwentwater before I drove us sleepily back to Nick's in Kendal.

These two sports were opposites. Running raises your heart rate but climbing needs calm and control. The closest combination I can think of would be the Winter Olympic discipline of Biathlon, the combination of cross-country skiing and rifle shooting where you have to relax again to focus on hitting the target. With running and climbing if you fail you don't miss the target, you fall off.

Brian Davison

The Challenger's Perspective

I first heard about the CRC when Chris Fisher did it. He set a new record of 15 hours and 25 minutes in April 2019. I thought it sounded mega. It was so far and with so much climbing, it seemed impossible. Early in 2020 I was back from America and was going well when lockdown hit. Because of it, I ended up doing a lot of running, which was fantastic. It was great to be out on the fells with nobody else out there. As a challenge it's like a low-end ultra-marathon. It isn't just the miles to be covered but the climbing as well; you have to be right on your game. I did it first with Callum Coldwell-Storry in May. We set a new record of 12 hours and 54 minutes, which was pretty good then Tom Randall came along in August and did it in just over 12 hours. Could I do it in under 12? It was hard – psychologically as well as physically – trying to maintain the motivation and the concentration, focussing on the climbing when you're really tired. When you're doing it faster, there's also a real danger of your muscles cramping up, which adds a whole new dimension of risk.

In the end, I went on my own at the end of August as Callum was away. I got round in 11 hrs 50 mins. I'd beaten Tom and I'd broken the 12 hours. Awesome!

When Callum and I did it, we worked out what we could achieve – we refined the route between the crags and worked out just what we needed to do on each section. As a result, we had a schedule and tried to stick to it and we could see we were up on our schedule times. Now it was getting more and more competitive. When Tom went back again and beat my time, getting down to 11 hours and 10 minutes I had to get straight out. The very next day I smashed it – 10 hours and 41 minutes. A new record and I reckon it can go below 10 hours.

Why did I keep doing it? It's probably a bit of an ego thing but I just love being out on the fells. The route takes a fabulous line through the Lakes. I'd go as far as to say it's one of the best days out that I've ever had.

Most people seem to agree that *Tophet Wall* is the best route of them all. The section on *Rib and Slab* where you traverse across the slab to the arete is the most frightening – it's so exposed and by then you're truly knackered.

In some respects, I hope it doesn't get too big. I wouldn't try and persuade others to do it unless I knew they were good enough, especially if they're soloing and pushing the time. There's such a potential to get it wrong. I'd hate to see someone get hurt. But for all that, it's brilliant to see that the CRC has had so much attention.

Will Birkett

Accompanying me on many of my fell running adventures was Milly, our second Yellow Labrador. Hannah, the beautiful young girl who'd won my heart and introduced me to Karen, had eventually died and shortly afterwards along came Milly. The two of them couldn't have been more different. If the warm-hearted, lovable Hannah was put on this Earth to please everyone, then the strong-minded and focussed Milly was here to please herself. After Flora, she was my other 'leggy blonde'. She was from field trials stock, her mother having been a champion. She was extremely fit and agile, easily jumping a 5-bar gate from a standing start and competing with all the collies who ran with us during

Milly, a great companion on the fells

Kendal Athletic Club training runs. She accompanied me on many occasions when I was supporting fellow runners on legs of the Bob Graham Round.

On one occasion, Milly and I were supporting Kendal-based runner and ex-Lancaster Royal Grammar School acquaintance Simon Theobald over the middle leg from Dunmail Raise to Wasdale. As we descended from Pike o' Stickle in Langdale, heading for Rossett Pike across the featureless Mart Crag Moor, we were suddenly engulfed in low cloud. Our visibility was reduced to next to nothing. At this point on the route there was no distinct path to follow and we hadn't, up until that point, seen the need to take a bearing. Milly to the rescue! She confidently ran off in what we could see was vaguely the right direction. With no other option, we followed. After some time and several hundred metres, her route took us straight past a small cairn that had been left by a previous party showing that we were on exactly the right line.

On another occasion, I was running in the Howgills with Tim Whiteley. There was snow on the ground and the weather was not great. We set off from the road at Carlingill on the west of the range, heading up over Knowles until turning left and up the ridge to Fell Head. On the descent, the light was very flat and visibility rather poor. Milly, running in front as always, suddenly stopped and I nearly tripped over her. I told her off and continued down the hill. Meanwhile she looked somewhat put-out but eventually continued after us. We got lower and lower until we dropped below the cloud level and could see that we'd descended way too far. We should've turned right where Milly had stopped. When Milly eventually died at the age of 14, Karen, Flora and I scattered her ashes on Mart Crag Moor and erected a cairn that will hopefully act to guide others, just as she did on that day.

15 - Risk Business
E5 6A TUNNEL WALL, GLENCOE
Reflections on the nature of risk

"But climbing is really dangerous, isn't it?" No, climbing is *hazardous*, which means there are dangers associated with it but that is not the same thing as saying it is *dangerous*. Just to get technical for a second, a hazard is something with a potential to cause harm while risk is a product of the likelihood and severity of that harm.

None of us want to get hurt so we employ control measures to reduce the likelihood of that potential harm being realised. Boulderers stay close to the ground and protect themselves with crash mats. Sport climbers rely on regularly-placed, secure bolts to minimise the distance fallen while Trad climbers utilise a wide range of protective devices including nuts, slings and cams, hand-placed on the lead, to achieve the same end with varying degrees of certainty. We also occasionally wear protective equipment – most notably a helmet, to reduce the severity of the harm. These are only the controls that we rely on once failure has occurred. The most significant protective measures prevent us from falling in the first place. In no particular order, these include route selection, fitness, technique, good communication, footwear, chalk, appropriate use of gear.

Getting your head round the concept of risk is vitally important in all aspects of our lives – at work, at home and at play. In my career in Health & Safety,

I used my climbing experiences to help people understand what risk was really all about. To counteract most people's workplace experience of H&S – that of someone erecting all manner of barriers in the way of getting a job done – I started most of my sessions with a picture or two of me climbing. I wanted to make the point that focussing on safety doesn't have to stop you doing something. In fact it allows you to push the boundaries and still be around to talk about it afterwards.

By definition, military activities carry a significant level of danger. In the world of industrial safety we often use the phrase 'it isn't worth getting hurt for'. In the armed forces – at times – it is. Although one individual's ineptitude landed me in hospital with heat exhaustion, on the whole the army was pretty good with keeping us safe. At times the approach could seem over-protective – often, such as in weapons training – for very good reason. But training has to feel realistic to some degree and that increases the risk.

The best example of this I can recall was during very specialised firearms training. On a normal range there would be very strict controls, with carefully monitored arcs of fire making it nigh on impossible to shoot someone accidentally. But we had gone way beyond that.

One exercise involved four of us driving a regular saloon car into a fully-enclosed firing range. Targets would then suddenly appear in front of us. The driver slammed on the brakes while the front seat passenger was shooting at the targets through the windscreen (we got through a lot of windscreens!) Meanwhile the two rear passengers dived out of their doors and started to engage the 'terrorists' in front of us. While they were giving covering fire, the driver and front seat passenger would also throw themselves out onto the road and start to make their way to better cover. We were firing pistols within feet of our team members.

The ultimate example of such weapons training was a scenario of a hostage situation in a specially-designed house. As I crashed into the room, there in front of me was one of my colleagues stood shoulder-to-shoulder with a man-size target. I shot the target with a double-tap of the 9mm before spotting another potential threat on the other side of the room and dealing with that equally efficiently. It took some bottle to be the hostage! This example of extreme hazard could only be sanctioned because the high level of skill we had all acquired over weeks and months of training kept the level of actual risk in check. Clearly, we were also prepared to accept a considerably higher level of risk than most.

The job of safety culture consultant took me to many different clients all around the world: the US, Russia, Middle East, many parts of Europe, Africa and, on numerous occasions, India. The jet-setting lifestyle – lots of sitting around in airports, too many nights in soulless hotels and altogether too much time away from home – was in fact pretty tedious. What made up for it was getting to work with so many different people in such a wide range of industries, businesses and roles. Seeing them gain some real, tangible benefit from my input was very satisfying. The explicit attitudes towards safety in the workplace varied considerably in all these diverse locations but what was very clear to me was that, all around the world, whatever our background or culture, at the heart of it we are all pretty much the same. We want to do a job, provide for our families, and go home without being injured or made unwell.

The highlight of my wide-ranging international career was, without question, working at the Royal Opera House in Covent Garden. For me this is one of the most iconic buildings in London, housing undeniably the best opera and ballet companies in the world. The privilege of being able to walk through the stage door, pick up my staff pass, wander around this hallowed place and work with

Taj Mahal at sunrise – a rare opportunity for sightseeing on a work trip

such talented people was second to none. The opportunity came to me when I showed a photo of myself climbing at the start of an introductory workshop that I was presenting in London. In the audience that day was the Opera House's lovely Health & Safety Manager Dominique Perrissin-Fabert. Originally from near Chamonix with many years' experience of climbing in the Aravis, when she saw the climbing photo she piped up, in her French accent, "I do that also". Thanks to that connection I was invited to work with her and her colleagues.

I am the Health & Safety Manager at the Royal Opera House in Covent Garden and I've been an occupational safety professional for over 15 years. I will always remember the first time that I went to a H&S workshop to find it being delivered by a fellow climber and someone with a similar attitude to risk as me – and that was Nick, of course.

I'd signed up for a session to learn about safety culture and behaviours – something I thought we needed to work on at the Opera House. During the initial introductions, up popped a photo of our tutor clinging on to a Lakeland rock face, way above his last protection. Nick made the point: "Safety shouldn't stop you doing things… in fact it allows you to push at the boundaries and not get hurt, to stand right at the edge but not fall over". This was exactly what I needed to hear.

My experience as a climber has had a significant impact on the way I approach my work in the live entertainment sector. As a climber it was easy to demonstrate that I'm not risk averse. In the live entertainment sector, I believe that to produce great shows we need to push boundaries, and work at the edge of what is considered to be dangerous. I recall a Wagner opera rehearsal in which I had to set part of the stage alight just above the heads of the performers. Or, in the ballet *Frankenstein*, when I had to hang a ballerina from a tree in order to simulate her execution.

The directors wanted to express their artistic visions by bringing those scenes onto a live stage and it was not the role of the H&S Manager to limit their creative process but to help them realise those visions in the safest way. If I'd had a risk-averse mindset, my life would have been a misery. I would have lost countless nights of sleep worrying about one scene or another. I would not have survived in that environment. Climbing has taught me to take risks but also to fail-safe! It would be mad to plan for scenes and only imagine things going perfectly well. The planning of potential failure will keep the performers safe even if the scene 'fails'. A fail-safe is what our rope does when we take a fall. Knowing that I have a fail-safe system allows me to climb better and to push boundaries.

The other major correlation between climbing effectively and successfully putting on a live show on our Covent Garden stage is the ability to make a dynamic risk assessment, to understand what it takes to make that safe decision in the heat of the moment. A traditional risk assessment requires planning the potential risks in advance and putting in place control measures but the reality of many live scenes is that you can't plan for everything that could go wrong. So, the question is, how can I equip the team to make that judgment about safety quickly in the moment? One answer is to empower every single member to feel they can stop the scene at any point without blame – that failure is okay. In rehearsals I have often used the climbing acronym for FAIL – First Attempt In Learning – to ensure there is an acceptance of failure and that the team moves away from a culture of acrimony and finger-pointing. It's also about assessing an individual's capacity to focus and concentrate while experiencing the adrenaline rush of live performance. These are all elements that need to be integrated in order to make safe decisions and they are not so different to those made when we climb.

Dominique Perrissin-Fabert

Over the following months I visited Covent Garden on numerous occasions, carrying out an assessment and working with the senior team to help them build an even better safety culture. During every visit I would also get the chance to see behind the scenes, watch rehearsals and understand the workings of the vast array of departments that all go together to produce their amazing performances.

One situation that particularly tickled me was on an occasion when I was stood in the sumptuous main auditorium with its opulent gold and rich, deep red décor. We were passing through and had stopped to listen to a rehearsal of La Traviata. During a short break, the Italian tenor playing Alfredo approached our group and speaking directly to me he asked, "How was it? Are you pleased with how it sounds?" "It sounds fabulous, you were marvellous," I assured him. I have no idea who he thought I was, but he'd clearly mistaken me for someone else. Or maybe, he was a keen climber and recognised me from photos in the Lake District guidebooks!

Over the years, many people have asked with incredulity, "How can you reconcile your approach to climbing with the job you do as a H&S advisor?" I see no contradiction here at all. It's all about understanding risk and I feel l know what I'm talking about here. The last 25 years of my professional life were spent studying, assessing, controlling and mitigating hazards and risks in the workplace. My MSc thesis looked into health and safety at outdoor activity centres just a year after the Lyme Bay kayaking tragedy in which four teenagers lost their lives. I did my master's placement in South Lakeland where the industry was naturally big business. After that I was involved in the formation of the Adventure Activity Licencing Regulations. I was a Local Authority representative on the Adventure Activity Industry Advisory Committee, set up at the time by the Health & Safety Executive.

Most people have a very poor grasp of the concept of risk as highlighted by the time when Dom, Steve, Tim and I travelled to Ecuador for that paddling trip in November 2001. It was just over two months since the 9/11 attacks on the World Trade Centre and many of our friends, colleagues and family members thought we were mad to be flying through New York – never mind the massive rivers we were going to be facing, with no chance of rescue if anything went wrong. It was, in fact, probably the safest time ever to fly with all the brand new checks and restrictions in place. If there was a 9/11-related risk it might have been the National Guardsmen patrolling JFK Airport, armed with high-powered rifles and primed to take out potential terrorists.

Similarly, the most dangerous part of a day out climbing will be the drive from home to the crag, yet nobody gives that a moment's consideration. In reality, very few people get hurt when out climbing. When 'climbing' accidents do arise, they're most likely to occur after the climb has been completed, on the descent. This is perhaps not entirely surprising. We focus all our efforts on what we perceive to be the dangerous bit – climbing up and potentially falling off. It can be all-absorbing, but we allow ourselves to be engrossed in the process, using all our skills and talents to get to the top unscathed. Once we're here there's a huge sense of release. Success! We've done it! We relax, we take our eyes off the ball and we allow our focus to soften just at the point when we're most tired, unable to think straight and unlikely to make the best choices.

A prime example of this came, for me, during a rock climbing trip to Chamonix in the French Alps with my old friend John Vlasto. Part of that trip was spent on the large granite cliffs above the Mer de Glace. We were staying at the Refuge de l'Envers des Aiguilles and climbing each day on the fantastic multi-pitch routes that tower over the north side of this stunning valley. With this type of climbing, the level of risk is potentially a couple of notches higher due to additional hazards introduced by the mountain environment and greater commitment once the route is started. In response to this there is a need for a corresponding increase in personal awareness as well as greater teamwork.

On one of these days, we chose a hard-ish route of 8 pitches or rope-lengths amounting to approximately 300 metres of ascent. The climbing was absorbing with difficult moves, sometimes with a significant fall potential. Those steep granite slabs are characterised by an apparent lack of any grips at all! We reached the top without incident but the return to the glacier by abseil was also quite involved. It meant repeatedly pulling the ropes through and reattaching them for the next section, sometimes just onto a single bolt. When I regained the glacier at the foot of the route (not quite *terra firma*), it was a pleasure to remove my tight rock shoes and cool my hot, swollen feet in the snow prior to putting on my heavier, more solid mountain boots and crampons for the return across the glacier to the refuge.

After the hard, taxing climb and the technical, tricky descent, maybe it was inevitable that we would relax. It was at this moment that, without thinking, I carelessly stepped down and caught my exposed ankle on one of the super-sharp points on my crampons. The deep gash in the fleshy part below the ankle bone started bleeding profusely, no doubt leaving a grim sight for future teams. After applying copious amounts of snow to reduce the bleeding and strapping it up, I was able to walk back ok – and, more importantly, it didn't stop us doing any of the climbs we'd planned to do in the next few days. But it could have been much worse.

Climbing on the blank granite above L'Envers, Chamonix

I used this story in my safety training, the lesson being that often it is not the big items that hurt you, but the minor, supplementary things after the main task is over. We are so careful with assessing the risks, taking precautions and looking out for each other during significant tasks, but as soon as the perceived danger is gone, we drop our guard. This is one manifestation of the Theory of Risk Homeostasis which suggests that we compensate for lower risks in one aspect of a task by taking greater risks in another (when we have more protective measures in place, we take less care) or, conversely, when the risk is higher, we compensate by taking more precautions. So, when we plan an activity, we have to be sure to consider the supplementary activities too and, once the main task is over, take a few moments to consider what could still go wrong.

Going back to my initial definition, risk is the product of the likelihood and severity of a particular harm. So we've looked a little at the likelihood – you are more likely to come to harm after your climb, for example, than on way up – so what about severity? For example, non-climbers considering the hazards of climbing often seem to be fixated with falling. But what is the real danger in falling? In most Trad (or even more so Sport) climbing, the answer is: not significant.

As it happens, I've fallen off my bike and done more damage in my six years as a serious cyclist than in more than 40 years of climbing. In fact, I know many cyclists who've done the same as I did when I broke my femur on that black ice a few years back – the bike has gone from under them on icy, wet or muddy roads or, in one case, on the slippery white segment of a zebra crossing on a bend and they've ended up with serious injuries.

Which is not to say that any climber wants to fall. I've often been asked: "Aren't you afraid of falling off, when you're climbing?" And the answer is a resounding, "Yes!". In fact, that fear has sometimes stopped me from really committing to a difficult sequence – or even trying a route in the first place. But the fear doesn't always come from the physical act of losing contact with the rock and flying through the air; more often than not, what I'm really afraid of is *failure*. You only ever have one chance to on-sight a route; fall off and that chance is lost forever. This debilitating feeling can prevent you from committing to a sequence of moves on a route. I've known many climbers not try a route for fear of not being able to get up it; in their mind it's better not to try it at all, so as to avoid failing, rather than try it and have the possibility of success. Maybe we're all hardwired to try and avoid falling when at height – it's some kind of evolved self-preservation, even when logically we know we have a means of protecting ourselves from harm.

If you want to progress in your climbing, you absolutely must overcome any fear of falling you might have. I don't think I've ever, really had a problem with the act of falling. I had enough early experiences to teach me that you can fall off and get away with it. Others may need to practise this important side of the game. One way to start is by doing simple 'drop-falls' on an indoor climbing wall, and slowly increasing the height above the last bolt as the process begins to feel natural. Just as important is the behaviour of your belayer, who needs to know how to provide you with a comfortable landing. Keeping the rope too tight when you're only a short way above the protection will result in a hard and uncomfortable fall, slamming you into the rock and giving you a more severe jarring. However, falling on a climbing wall or outside on a well-protected Sport route is one thing; extending that to a Trad route is a whole new game. Trad – or 'traditional' – climbing is where the leader places their own protection as they progress up the route, which is removed by the 'second' as they follow. The leader-placed protection is clearly critical; it is this that stops you plummeting to the ground. Getting it right

Keith Phizacklea takes a big fall from *Woodhouse's Arete*, Dow Crag
Rob Matheson

is quite important.

The nature of Sport climbing, which unlike the aforementioned Trad approach relies on pre-placed, permanent protection, almost demands that you fall off because you're often trying much harder climbs. With the safe protection in place, it's possible to climb at or beyond your limit, comfortable in the knowledge that a fall will not result in any harm. If you don't ever fall off when Sport climbing, you're clearly restricting yourself to routes that are too easy. The other big difference with Trad climbing is that every route is different: unlike on a Sport route, which is just another line of bolts, the Trad route will have different protection at greatly varying distances. Having confidence in the gear, or item of protection you've placed in the rock, is paramount, which is why most climbers who've taken one fall on a Trad route will be okay taking more falls in the same place as the gear is now tested and has proven itself capable of holding a fall. Knowing you can fall off will often mean – strange as it may sound – that you won't fall! There are many routes where it will usually be possible to take a fall safely, but on plenty of others it's not really much of an option, and it can vary throughout the length of a route or even at various points on a single pitch.

The other aspect of falling is the landing zone. A fall on an overhanging face that leaves you dangling in space is of no concern at all, whereas an off-vertical wall with ledges and protrusions is far more dangerous and requires a lot more calculation of where you're likely to end up.

So, what does it feel like when all strength ebbs away and the fingers finally uncurl, or when you commit yourself to that next hold only to discover it's an unusable sloper? There's a horrible, hollow feeling in the guts – presumably a fear reaction caused by a quick release of hormones or the firing of neurones – and often there's a yelp or whimper, of fear or surprise. The fall itself is quick, generally over before you have time to think about it. Provided the landing is okay, then comes the release, an exhalation, maybe a nervous laugh and a sense of relief, possibly depending on the circumstances … followed by frustration, annoyance and self-recrimination.

So the real question is not, 'what's the danger here?' but, 'what level of risk am I prepared to accept?' The answer depends on your individual risk *appetite*, but is also determined by the risk-benefit analysis – in other words, how important is this to you? How much do you want to succeed on this route, and I mean *really* want it? We face these questions every day in many other situations. If we want to cross a road, we weigh up the danger by looking at the traffic: how fast is it going, how frequently are vehicles passing? We then consider our own ability at that moment: are we fit? How quickly can we move? What are we wearing – trainers or high-heels? Are we encumbered with heavy shopping bags? All these questions will tell us about the risk involved in crossing the road and we will make a decision. But then, how urgent is it? Are we in a hurry or do we have all day? This will determine our choice of behaviour.

Another very important aspect is what others around us are doing. If you're at a pedestrian crossing in Germany and the little man on the sign is red, everyone else will wait for him to turn green. What do we do? Probably also wait for the change because we like to fit in with the behaviour of others. In the UK, people tend to ignore the colour of the little man and make up their own mind and cross when they see fit – and maybe even a German visitor to the UK will cross with the light on red along with the crowd. This is the power of *culture* – the collective mindset and its subsequent behaviours.

I have to be honest and recognise that there have been times when I have over-stepped the mark on risk-taking, choices that might be regarded as reckless. Soloing routes that weren't all that far within my limits – especially those located somewhere like off the Terrace at Malham Cove. I put this down to youthful foolhardiness and a belief that is prevalent in many teenagers and young adults that we are immortal. Far worse, probably were my behaviours while driving at times back then. So much of that behaviour is about hormones and the macho tendencies. I remember vividly one occasion when John Wilson had picked me up from the Clachaig Inn in Glencoe. He was driving down the valley – probably too fast with me in the passenger seat. I briefly considered putting on my seat belt but checked myself with the thought, "what will he think if I put my seat belt on? Will he think I don't trust him?"

There have also been times when the risk assessment wasn't really what it should have been – like the paddling trip to Ecuador, at least two of us really weren't good enough to be tackling those rivers; or when we went down the wrong cave – it is a basic control measure to check the guidebook in order to ensure you're in the right place rather than boldly rely on memory.

Somewhat tongue-in-cheek, right at the start I said that this affliction had "put me at great risk, even made me selfishly push others into danger". I don't believe I have ever actually put others in real danger by my choices or actions, but I may well have pushed them way beyond their own comfort zones due to the difference in our perceptions of risk and our relative risk appetites – and that is just as bad. On one memorable occasion, my best mate John thumped me on the jaw – hard – when I got back to the ground after leading a very runout route. He was so worried/frightened by my apparent blasé attitude while climbing so far above my gear that the emotion erupted. While I was comfortable with my situation, I clearly had no consideration for how it might look and feel for him holding my ropes down on the ground. Sorry!

Climbing a route (particularly a Trad route) is one of the best examples of a dynamic risk assessment I know. Every move above a piece of gear sees the risk go up slightly until another piece is placed and the risk reduces, providing the placement is secure. Along the way we're considering the nature of the rock – might a hold break, might that last piece of gear fail? The weather conditions, the difficulty of the ground we are climbing, our deteriorating strength, who's holding the rope? All of us have to decide the level of risk that we're prepared to accept.

Take a very easy route, say *Devil's Slide,* graded HS, on Lundy, a clean 400 foot sweep of steepening slab on the beautiful granite island in the Bristol Channel. There is very little protection so a fall would result in a very long and uncomfortable fall-come-tumble down the slab. But for most people, the likelihood of falling is very slim indeed, so the risk posed by this route is minimal; I and many others have been more than happy to solo this route. Were it to start raining however, the likelihood of slipping is greatly increased and so is the risk. At the other end of the scale, anyone could throw themselves at a very hard route on a climbing wall and merrily fall off to their heart's content with no ill effects. Remember: *it's not the falling, it's the hitting the ground*!

The recent, Oscar-winning film *Free Solo* with Alex Honnold soloing El Capitan in Yosemite provokes a wide range of responses. One of these is: *"He's mad, he has no control measures in place"*. This is patently untrue. Firstly, he isn't mad and secondly, he does have control measures in place, it's just that those responsible for such comments do not recognise the controls. Sure, he has no rope to arrest a fall, but he has spent many, many hours on a rope practising the moves until he is absolutely sure of success. On top of this is his finely-honed ability to not be fazed by the situation along with his significant ability achieved through years of training on top of his natural talent.

Alex Honnold's achievement on El Cap and his other solo ascents have been outstanding and so different to many of the other examples of climbers soloing routes. I remember many years ago, non-climbing friends and relatives asking:

"Did you see that French girl climbing on the telly? She doesn't use ropes; she must be very good". Yes, whoever you are referring to probably is very good, but as a climber you can recognise that in most cases when people are being filmed soloing a route they are climbing well within their ability. It may look very impressive to the uninitiated, but the reality is that they could climb much harder. Alex Honnold was climbing at the limit and that was what made *Free Solo* truly impressive.

Ski mountaineering also involves a great deal of risk assessment. The big variable factor here is the snow and the hazards presented by avalanche or, if on a glacier, the presence of crevasses. When you're rock climbing, the risk can change from move to move, minute to minute. On a ski tour, the risk posed by the changing snow conditions is more likely to change day to day and on some occasions, hour to hour.

I have enjoyed many ski mountaineering trips to the Alps over the years. On

French Team on summit of Castor above Zermatt

one of the first I was heading out to Chamonix in the car on my own. To make the journey more bearable, I posted a message on the appropriate UK Climbing forum offering a lift to anyone interested. I got a reply from another skier, Caroline Wilson from North Wales. We arranged to meet up near Birmingham. By remarkable coincidence, within a few minutes of setting off on our long journey, it turned out that she did the same job for Snowdonia National Park as my long-time friend Judy Clavey did for the Lake District National Park and they were well-acquainted with each other. Caroline was a friendly, easy-going companion who was great to have along as a travel partner. Our skiing abilities were very similar: what she gained in technique, I made up for in fitness. Having arrived in the Alps, we actually spent several days skiing together – it made sense as we were both there on our own. After some excellent day tours around Chamonix, we headed over to Switzerland and Zermatt.

Having parked the car in Tasch, we got the train to Zermatt and spent a night in the dormitory accommodation of the well-placed Hotel Bahnhof. Next morning it was an early start up the cable car to the Klein Matterhorn top station at 3,820m making it the highest point in Europe accessible by lift. It also

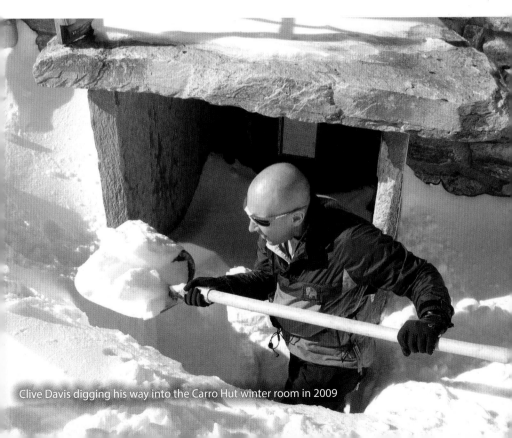

Clive Davis digging his way into the Carro Hut winter room in 2009

makes for easy access to the nearby Breithorn, a 4000m peak. We ascended the Breithorn and were heading for the Rifugio Guide della Val d'Ayas on the Italian side of the border. We descended a lovely snow slope but soon realised it was the wrong direction, which meant having to climb back up to regain the altitude required to get back on the right track. This was fine, but it was all adding to the effort required.

By the time we were on the final run down to our destination, it was mid-afternoon and the sun was shining. This is a dangerous time and perhaps we should've been more cautious. By this time of the day, the snow has been softened by the warm, spring sunshine and the legs are typically tired after a lot of climbing up and skiing down. Because of the tiredness, it's easy to momentarily lose concentration, which is exactly what happened to Caroline: she caught a ski tip in some soft snow and took a tumble, breaking her leg in the process. I went into emergency mode: making her comfortable, removing her skis carefully and planting them in the snow to ease identification, and giving her additional layers of clothing to keep her warm. Once she was stabilised, the best option was for me to ski down the last kilometre or so to the hut and get assistance.

Clive Davis (L) and Nick Hewitt enjoying the delights of 'Plat du Jour' round the stove in a very cold Evettes Hut winter room

On arrival I spoke to the guardian who called the rescue helicopter. Having done that, I said I'd put my skis back on and skin back up to her location to keep her company and await her recovery. He looked at me, asked again how far back up the hill it was before pointing out that the helicopter would be there long before I got anywhere close. "Do you want me to ask the helicopter to stop here to pick you up? That way you can travel with your friend to the hospital," asked the helpful hut guardian. At that point, reality dawned. If I travelled with her in the helicopter to the hospital in Aosta – what would I do? Caroline would be whisked off for treatment and I'd be left, like a spare part, my car many miles away on the other side of the mountain range. How would I get back there? It's not as if I'd known her for long. She was just a travelling companion, nothing more. "No thank you, there's no need for that. I shall stay here," I replied, after my deliberations. And that was that – I might never have seen her again, except that she did call in to see us at home a year or so later.

Now the dilemma I faced was that I was alone and in the high mountains. It's not best practice to go ski touring alone, especially at around 4000m and on glaciers. However, the weather was very good and the snowpack was stable. The following morning, I set out alone, taking in the twin summits of Castor and Pollux before dropping down the Schwarzgletscher and on up to the Monte Rosa Hutte, where I'd already made a loose arrangement to meet another ski tourer from America.

That afternoon, which ended so badly for Caroline, was an example of not reading the conditions as well as we might. I've had many examples where the opposite is true. On another ski trip, this time to the Bernese Oberland with old school friend Clive Davis and Steve Cox, we turned back from the summit of the Gross Fiescherhorn with only 50m or so to go. We'd set out from the Monch Hut early that morning in good conditions but as the day progressed the conditions slowly deteriorated. We climbed up to the Fieschersattel, the col between the two summits and turned left to scramble along the ridge to our objective. As we did, the conditions were getting worse by the minute; visibility was down to just a couple of metres and the wind was howling across the ridge. It was very tempting to press on, we were so close. However, we chose to turn round. The mountain was not going anywhere, it would still be there next time. Not getting to that particular summit did not detract from the fun and sense of adventure we had that day. On a larger scale, we have changed our objectives mid-tour, even when that has meant that we didn't achieve the main objective of the trip. This is all about having enough insight to know when to carry on and when to desist. That has to be based on risk.

Ski Touring above Argentiere Glacier with (L-R) Les Courtes, Les Droites and Aiguille Verte Mont Blanc in the distance

Sadly, I see a growing risk aversion in many aspects of contemporary culture: not letting the kids 'play out' as we used to, wrapping them in cotton wool. How will the next generation ever learn to make a sensible assessment of the risks that they will inevitably face at some point in their lives?

When it comes to the world of climbing, this may be one of the reasons that Trad climbing has fallen out of favour by comparison with Sport climbing. Like most of my contemporaries, I was introduced to climbing on small, local crags with the ever-present risk of injury and learned how to control it from an early age. Nowadays, most people's introduction to climbing is through the safe environment of a climbing wall. Making the transition from climbing on an indoor wall to a crag, particularly one where you are required to find and place your own protection, is a huge step.

Schools have become more risk averse and at the same time budgets for outdoor activities have been cut and so fewer children are being introduced to the delights and benefits that these types of pastimes can deliver. This short-sighted emphasis on saving money at all costs has a detrimental effect, not only on those individual pupils but on society in general. That opportunity to learn how to work closely with, and rely upon, someone else in a challenging situation is hard to replicate.

Recognising and dealing with hazards, at work and at play, and truly understanding how to assess and manage risk on our own or as part of a team, are life skills that we cannot afford to lose. I'd call *that* dangerous.

16 - Conclusion
E1 5B SHEPHERDS CRAG, BORROWDALE
Lessons learned

So, what have I learnt from 40 years of adventure?

About myself? About climbing? About how to get the most of my short time on this earth?

First of all, I *really* like climbing. I have tried lots of other activities, many of which have been terrific, but they don't give me what climbing does. So what might that be? What have I achieved in return for investing all that time, effort and expense on climbing rocky outcrops? What have I achieved in return for all that investment? For me, the benefits are many and varied.

What I've Got From Climbing
Exploring the World

Many, although not all, climbing venues are in attractive locations. They're often in National Parks or Areas of Outstanding Natural Beauty at home and similarly special and protected landscapes abroad. Climbing has given me reason to visit these attractive destinations when I might not otherwise have bothered.

Skill and Strategy

There is something about being in a beautiful location, surrounded by nature in all its forms. Yet I have been just as happy to climb in a scruffy quarry where that argument doesn't hold much water. Equally, just the fluid, efficient movement over the rock is a pleasure. Working out the intricacies of a sequence, thinking several moves ahead, like a snooker player who thinks about potting the black before he has even lined up the red ball, I have often found myself thinking: "If I am to reach that good pocket over there with my right hand, I will need to use that side-pull there, which will allow that undercut to be reached, providing I can smear with my left foot up here…" That ability to read the rock and how the sequence will play out is something that can only really come with time and practice.

A Sense of History

I'm not someone who gets too engrossed in the history of climbing. I have an interest in the development of the sport over the years and I have a huge respect for those who went before us and what they achieved, in just the same way as I respect those who are pushing their limits now. But history is built in to climb-

Photographer Henry Iddon preparing the Abrahams' camera   Ron Kenyon

ing, we record and celebrate who did the first ascent and often seek out routes by certain individuals. The first time I climbed *Central Buttress* on Scafell Crag was on the exact date of the 100th anniversary of the original ascent by Siegfried Herford and George Sansom in April 1914. These and other names stand out from every generation. A profound thought, on climbing that route that day, was that I was using the exact same holds as these pioneers had used 100 years earlier. The appearance of these early forerunners of ours in old photos, many taken by the Abraham brothers of Keswick, suggest that they were much older than they were. Herford was only 23 when he and Sansom finally overcame the puzzle of the Great Flake and so complete *Central Buttress*. They were just young lads, pushing the limits and showing the old guard how it's done. Tragically, Herford, like so many others of his generation, was killed two years later during the Great War.

A further historical connection was made on that day of the 100th anniversary. An old acquaintance of mine, renowned photographer Henry Iddon, captured some images of our ascent that day using the same camera used by the

Image of Scafell on *Central Buttress* anniversary　Henry Iddon using Abrahams' camera

Abrahams all those years ago.

Climbing Central Buttress on Scafell that day, one of the most famous routes in Britain also provides an opportunity to reflect on all the other people over the past 100 years that had similarly ascended the same route using those the same holds. When looking at an old, original oil painting by one of the Grand Masters, it is worth contemplating all the other real people from history who have feasted their eyes on that exact same masterpiece over the centuries. If we think of climbs in the same way, we can all draw something extra from the experience. As you grasp that crucial hold, take a moment to recognise that the exact same pocket was used by Haskett Smith, Herford, Arthur Dolphin, Joe Brown, Chris Bonington, Pete Livesey, Ron Fawcett, Pete Whillance, Ben Moon, Dave Birkett … the list goes on, and will continue to go on, long into the future. That is really something special to be a part of.

Perfect Partnerships

The people with whom we climb, our partners, can make a difference too. I know I've often been inspired to succeed on a route because of who I was climbing with and equally I've backed off a route or failed to climb it cleanly because of who was at the other end of the rope when, if I'm honest, I didn't entirely trust them. On those few occasions, it wasn't that I didn't think they were capable of belaying and holding a fall, but I didn't feel that they had sufficient insight into what I was actually trying to do, running it out a long way above some sketchy gear on tenuous holds. A truly great climbing partner inspires confidence, provides just the right level of encouragement, knows when to say something and when to shut up. When out with that perfect partner, you are truly operating as a single unit. Communication is precise, ropework is slick. It adds to the overall experience.

In the early years, I had exactly that relationship with John Wilson. Each of us knew exactly what the other was going to do before they did it. Communication at the beginning and end of each pitch was minimal. If anything at all, it would consist of a short whistle that would say everything that needed to be said, none of this bellowing out across the crag that we were "SAFE!" or "CLIMBING NOW!" "I know you are". Since then, I have been fortunate to climb with many other people and in many cases have come close to achieving a similar rapport with them. I remember one of the interviews I attended during the Army selection process; the interviewer highlighted the sports that I was involved in: "Karate, cross-country running, rock climbing – not much of a team-player, are you?" This annoyed me, here was someone with a clear lack of understanding, and because of their ignorance, I was being criticised! Having highlighted that the placing in the field of every runner in the team counts to the final result of a cross-country race, I then went on, with some vexation, to defend the teamwork that is required in a successful climbing partnership: *"It isn't just about passing a ball to someone, it's about saving someone's life!"*

What I've Learned About Climbing
Training is Important

I only wish that thirty years ago I'd had more understanding about training for climbing, as well as having access to the kind of facilities that are available today. I remember one time when out in Germany with the Army, an enthusiastic PTI (physical training instructor) who knew I was a keen climber, offered to help me with a training regime. At the time I replied that the only real training for climbing was to climb! Several years later I'd been climbing at Malham one day and was walking back towards the village with my climbing partner of the day. Walking with us was Mark Leach, one of the superstars of the day.

Graham Iles making use of the Sedgwick Bridge training facility while climbing walls are shut

We'd done numerous routes and were pleased with our performance for the day. Mark, however, mentioned that he was heading home to finish off the day doing some training on his home-made wall. I was confused. "Why?" I asked. "Well, I need to make sure I get the most out of the day," was the reply. "Why not just climb another route?" was my naive retort. "It isn't enough," he explained. I just couldn't get my head around the concept. I still couldn't see the difference between specific, focussed training on the one hand and climbing on the other. Now, I understand what he was talking about, I only wish the penny had dropped a lot sooner; I might have had the chance to benefit from it.

There may be some disadvantage that comes from too much training too early on, which I've seen often enough. With climbing, I believe it is possible to become too strong too soon. Good climbing performance comes from a combination of strength and technique and each of these two can, to some degree, compensate for a deficit in the other. But strength, generally arm and finger strength, often negates the need to use the feet quite so efficiently, which is all well and good on an indoor climbing wall route, but that doesn't cut the mustard when it comes to climbing on real rock, out on the crag. Having gained a lot of strength, it's more difficult to then focus on improving technique, while it is always possible to add more strength on top of existing technique.

For me, my foray into cycling helped me to understand the principles of training and to truly recognise the benefits to be gained. Not that the training is the same, but the discipline required, the sticking to a programme and being prepared to take advice from someone who knew what they were doing was a completely new experience. I used a coach for the first time to help me prepare for the Tour du Mont Blanc. I had initially gone for a bike-fit and assessment to Mike Wilson at Better Cycling but that soon progressed on to a full training programme both indoors on the turbo trainer or rollers and out on the roads. Everything was focussed on the numbers – predominantly the power output readings from a power meter embedded in the crank; sometimes trying to push the numbers higher, but just as importantly, on other occasions ensuring I didn't exceed the required figure. I went back for a reassessment at one point and was shown the changes in my lactate production that demonstrated improvement. However, I commented that I didn't appear to be going any faster! "But you aren't training to go faster," Mike pointed out. "You are training to get you round the 330km and 8000m of the Tour du Mont Blanc. If you want to go faster, we can change the programme". It was then that I really understood two things: firstly, Mike, as a trained coach, knew what he was doing; and secondly, that we have to train for what we want to achieve. The following year we did change the programme to suit the time trials that I was racing in and indeed, I did get much faster. Even at that point, transferring the concept of using a coach into my world of climbing was a challenge. I am prepared to admit that I was under the sad illusion that after 35 years of climbing, I knew what I was doing; what could someone else teach me? Simple answer – a huge amount!

The Training Paradox

"Train harder so you can do your project!" Or so the false prophecy goes. These days we hear from all angles that if you want it badly enough then you've got to spend endless hours leaping around on multi-coloured plastic blobs or dangling from hangboards. To break that next grade then you need to log your benchmark scores in a spreadsheet so that you can keep track of your half-crimp deadhang times. It's a language that would scarcely have been recognised by the early pioneers of climbing but of course, we now have a better understanding of this unique and complex sport. Or do we?

Strangely, as some things advance in climbing, others seem to be going backwards in equal measure. We are now cloning a generation of 'front-wheel-drive' climbers who seem to wheel-spin into the crash barriers as soon as they reach the first runner. When it comes to strength they are grotesquely over-qualified, yet when it comes to the stuff that will actually get you to the top of a mountain crag or sea cliff, it's a different story. Of course, everyone climbs for their own reasons, but let's be clear: there's a disconnect between training and Trad climbing. Otherwise many may be lured into a false sense of security. These days we see the YouTube generation beating their chests and power-screaming mantras such as 'CRUSH IT!', as if the goal is to unleash their pent-up strength on the rock and beat it into submission. This approach might work on a boulder but on a loose, vegetated mountain crag it will bounce back and hit you in the face.

The 'weaker' climber is forced to open their senses to their environment. Rather than trying to stamp their supremacy on the climb, they ask themselves how they can adapt to it. The aim isn't so much to reach the top but to understand what the rock is trying to say. When pulling harder isn't on the menu, we must blend into the rock like a chameleon. Climbers who are weaker in body are invariably stronger in mind. They ask not what they can get from the climb, but what they can give to it, and the reward for their humility is that they are granted the right of passage. Meanwhile, the stronger climber retreats to the gym, scratching his battered head and telling himself that he must train even harder so he will be better prepared next time.

Of course, the truth lies somewhere in the middle and we can aim for the best of both worlds. It's easy to wonder what climbers like Rob Matheson, Nick Wharton or even the mighty Leo Houlding would have achieved if they had 'trained'; yet these guys are amongst the most accomplished climbers I know! Did they really need to climb any harder? Similarly we could ponder what some of today's honed gym specimens might have done if they'd written some rock climbing into their macrocycles, but then we'd be judging them with prejudice and by a different set of rules. You'd think it would be obvious to both groups what they should do but it isn't, it probably never will be and that's the joy of it. There's something deeply engrained in the psyche of climbers like Nick Wharton – when pondering the possibility of a training session, a switch trips in their heads that says "F**k it! I just want to go climbing!" They don't over-think it, they just go and they certainly don't look back. You won't get far if you try to dissect them as they're made from rock! If you attempt to explain to them that they should sacrifice half the time they spend living by the sword, they'll look at you sideways as if to say: 'What would be the point in that then?!' And what can you possibly say in retort. If the end goal is pure enjoyment then it really is that simple.

Ben Grubb

Neil Gresham

The More Climbers the Merrier

Some climbers appear to be horrified at the thought of a massive influx of new exponents of the sport. Indeed, I have often heard people saying how pleased they are when they can have the crags to themselves. I do not agree with this for a number of reasons. Fewer people climbing means less traffic on routes, which in turn results in them becoming dirty, overgrown and less enjoyable. This in turn means that these routes fall out of favour and so are less attractive to others and so they become less popular, which means even less traffic … and so the decline continues. Furthermore, I think back to the earlier days of my climbing, such as when Neil and I were on Scafell for the *Shere Khan* photos; it was a highly sociable experience – as long as you're not with someone who wants to spend all day talking!

The reality is that there are many times more people who would call themselves climbers now than ever before. The reason we don't see them on the high crags of the Lakes or similar is because they have many more options open to them. Some are clustered around small boulders, others are hanging from bolts on sports routes or even, some climbers have confined themselves to an indoor climbing wall and are yet to venture outside onto real rock. Each to their own. Who am I to pass judgement or criticise, let alone try to understand their motivation? I'm sure they would find it just as hard to understand why I would slog uphill over boggy terrain, carrying a heavy rucksack to climb a rather dirty route with the potential for getting hurt; faff around with twin ropes and lots of complex gear and all for the sake of making relatively easy and unchallenging moves over the rock. Someone who can perfect their strength and technique for climbing on an indoor wall to the extent that they can take their skills to represent their country at the Olympic Games has my utmost respect. The fact that climbing is to become an Olympic Sport is anathema to many traditional climbers. I have absolutely no idea why they might want to deny young athletes the opportunity to perform on the world stage as it'll have no negative impact on them. If anything, it can be positive by raising the profile of the overall sport and hence gaining greater bargaining power when it comes to lobbying issues like funding or access.

Star-ratings are Subjective

So, I am back into full-time climbing mode, I have finally grasped the need to apply focussed training techniques and am even prepared to seek advice and guidance from others. What might I do with this new-found enthusiasm? I'm someone who likes an objective, something to aim for. For many years I'd start off the new climbing season by compiling a list – what routes do I want to try and achieve this year? There'd be a mixture of grades: some easy, some more challenging, many that would push my previous limits. As the year went on,

Nick on Tumbleweed Connection, a three-star route on Goat Crag Borrowdale

I'd tick-off the routes on the list and now and again sneak a couple of new ones in as I reviewed my progress. Just occasionally a route might get deferred to the following year's list if the opportunity didn't arise or if it became clear that I'd overstretched my ambition.

By chance, just as I was resuming my climbing after having given up my full-time job, Al Phizacklea sent out an email to his wide network of climbing contacts in the Lakes. With it he included a spreadsheet of all the three-star extremes that appear in Lake District Rock. This is an FRCC selected guide, produced under the Wired collective. It turns out there are 250 extremes that are given three stars in this publication and Al wanted to use these as a basis for whittling them down to the Top 100 and hence recreate the list first published by Rob Matheson in Mountain magazine in 1977. Of course, as soon as this list appeared, the competitive urge was there, I had to check how many I'd done. To my dismay, I'd only completed 140 of them – time to pull my finger out and crack on. This was just what I needed, a ready-made list of routes to target my efforts upon. Some were glaring omissions: *Gormenghast* on Heron Crag in Eskdale, *Side Walk* on Dow Crag, *The Philistine* on High Crag, Buttermere. Others were more esoteric and indeed, in my opinion, many on the list don't deserve to be there in the first place. But the pursuit of the routes on the list has given me reason to visit some crags for the first time: Raven Crag, High Stile, Upper Heron in Borrowdale, Round How on the Corridor Route to Scafell and Shelter Crag, Langdale to name but a few. I'm currently approaching the two hundred mark on the list. I recognise that I'm unlikely to tick some of the listed routes: John Dunne's incredible *Breathless* on Tophet Wall at E9 7a is maybe a step too far; Dave Pegg's *First and Last and Always* E7 6b on Esk Buttress might be pushing it as might some of the other E7s. But who knows? Maybe with some of that focussed training? There are some old ghosts that need putting to rest. In the past I've failed on some of the routes on the list. I pulled a hold off *Incantations* on Tophet Wall and after a significant fall I didn't fancy getting back on at the time and haven't been back since. I failed when trying to on-sight *Western Union* on Iron Crag and as was the typical way at the time, I walked away from it rather disappointed. Now is the time to fix the return match for both of these classics and others.

Climbing so many 'three-star' routes has certainly thrown a spotlight on what is considered to be worthy of this grand accolade. To my mind, these should be comparable to each other, even if they are of a different style and nature. This list should represent all the truly great Trad climbs that the Lakes has to offer. Sadly, many do not meet that standard – but that is only my opinion. The star-rating

Steve Scott before our ascent of The Old Man of Hoy

of routes is a very subjective concept. I have said that *Skinhead Moonstomp* at Gogarth is the best route that I have ever climbed. Yet, if the weather had been a bit rubbish that day, if our ropes had got tangled at the start or if I had dropped a piece of gear in the sea, would I have enjoyed the climbing experience as much?

I have recently been to the North of Scotland with Steve Scott in search of the classic sea stacks. I have wanted to climb the *Old Man of Hoy* in Orkney for many years but more recently since going to a lecture by Leo Houlding. At the start of his presentation, by way of introduction, he showed himself climbing the *Old Man* as a young boy of 11 and asked those in the audience who had done it to put their hands up. He looked at me and said: "You must have done it". With some shame I could only shake my head.

Of the five pitches on the *Original Route*, only two can really be described as truly great climbing, yet the whole experience, the epic journey to get there and the remoteness, the remarkable location and unlikely structure of the stack all add up to one of the best climbing experiences I have had. Indeed, the climbing was much better than I had been led to expect. I was anticipating dusty, sandy surfaces, copious amounts of guano and indeed I thought we might need to be navigating around many angry fulmars, threatening to project their fishy-smelling, oily vomit over us. There was none of this. The route was clean, dry and barring one gull that was easily skirted, we had the stack to ourselves in beautiful conditions. And to think that Jesse Dufton, blind climber, led it, is truly humbling. *Climbing Blind*, the film of Jesse's ascent made by Alastair Lee should be made compulsory viewing for all climbers.

On the same trip to the far north, we also climbed *Am Buchaille* and this emphasises the point even more so. The actual climbing on the two pitches of this smaller stack is probably only Severe in grade but the 5-mile walk-in to the beautiful and remote Sandwood Bay then out to the headland, followed by the swim across to the base of the climb make for an amazing adventure. Despite the easy nature of the climbing, if something were to go wrong, it would be very serious indeed. The swim across the short channel was probably the highlight. It isn't far but with a choppy swell and a cold wind it wasn't exactly inviting. It is the North Atlantic! As we were preparing for the approach from the rocky outcrop to the base of the stack, with kit in dry bags and me stripped down to my underpants, Steve, like a magician pulling a rabbit from a hat, produced a wet suit from his rucksack. "Whoa! What the hell is that?" I demanded, somewhat taken aback. "You could have brought yours," was his slightly sheepish response, albeit with a sneaky grin lurking somewhere not far beneath the surface. "At no point was a wet suit ever mentioned on the packing-list!" He graciously offered to go first so, while I might be stood around on the landward side in my shreddies, at least I was still dry. And for anyone planning on doing this in future, my top tip would be don't bother with a wetsuit, it isn't worth the effort and only detracts from the full experience.

Gradings are Contextual

Grading comparisons also throw up some challenges. These are also subjective to some degree. I have generally found that climbing in a new area, where there is a particular style of climbing required, often due to the nature of the rock, can be disheartening. Climbing on French granite around Chamonix can be a shocker for the newcomer. "But there aren't any holds!" is often the cry. "How can it possibly be that grade?" Of course, the answer is simple: the routes are graded by the locals who are familiar with the style required and have been brought up on a diet of friction and balance. The same goes for other areas. We just need time to adjust to the new conditions.

With Trad climbing it is often a matter of what we are used to; how much protection is adequate will vary from one person to the next. You can certainly have too much protection. One of the clearest examples of this is *Left Wall* on Dinas Cromlech. I have seen too many aspiring leaders run out of strength and fall off as they near the top. And why did they run out of strength? Because they spent far too long placing too much gear lower down. It is as if they feel obliged to place a piece of protection in every placement that offers itself up, even though they already have a perfectly adequate, bomb-proof piece just a couple of feet below. I know that sometimes I have gone too far in the other direction but as the saying goes: "It's not the falling off that is the problem, it's the hitting the ground" and as long as you can be sure that isn't going to happen, why waste the time and effort?

If I reflect on what I have found to be the hardest route for its grade, I am immediately reminded of *Long Kesh* on Cyrn Las, high up on the south side of Llanberis Pass. Graded at E5 6b, it is well below what I should have been capable of getting up successfully at the time. However, the exposed position, along with a combination of technical and strenuous climbing with some less-than-ideal protection had me literally retching with effort and gasping for breath as I pulled over the top roof. I remember it being a cold, grey day and Cyrn Las can be pretty foreboding at the best of times. Once again, there is a lot of subjectivity, driven by conditions, personal fitness and it being early in the year.

At the other end of the scale, the easiest routes for their grade are perhaps not so easy to recall as they don't etch themselves quite so indelibly in the mind.

I have always found the routes at Lower Sharpnose in North Devon to be very generous. Likewise, some of the slate routes I have done over the years have felt to be easy wins, but then that is because the style of climbing suits me well. When it comes to climbing at Gogarth, I have learned that there is a simple trick to make the climbing easier. On many of the routes, the quartzite holds, particularly the small flaky ones, often feel a bit creaky when first grasped. This can be a bit alarming, with the thought that the hold is about to break. This concern about your first choice of hold often leads to sketching around for something that feels more secure, but then that alternative one either it isn't as good or, it too, feels similarly creaky and we search again. Eventually after a lot of dithering you inevitably end up back on the original hold and, heart in mouth, you pull on it hoping it doesn't break. Top Tip: they never break! Just accept the creakiness and use the first hold you chose. It saves loads of time and effort and makes the whole route feel a lot easier.

Not only are there differences between the various approaches to climbing but also within the different styles. These have evolved over time and each generation will determine what it wants to do and the informal rules it will adhere to. As my climbing was developing, the on-sight was everything. It was what we all aspired to. It would rarely, if ever cross my mind to inspect or even practise the moves before tying-on and leading up from the ground. I know there was all sorts of skulduggery going on in the shadows – of course there was, sometimes openly admitted but more often than not, it was kept quiet and just the odd rumour or gossip would occasionally leak out. These days this approach has been legitimised by giving it the title of *head point*. Clearly, this term has been coined as a derivation of the sport climbing equivalent – *red point*, and is effectively the same: practise the moves, eye up all the protection, get it wired then lead it clean in one go. Fantastic! This allows people to push the grades at which they can perform – but I still can't help but think it's not quite as impressive as an on-sight. Recently, my attention was drawn to a fabulous photo of a young hotshot climbing one of the E5s on the Aberdeen sea cliffs that was part of my big day out climbing the six E5s. In fact, this particular route has subsequently been upgraded to E6. It was a great photo showing off both climber and route, but the caption pointed out that he was on-sighting the said route. I was left wondering why that needed saying. Why wouldn't he be climbing it on-sight? Was it genuinely considered to be something worthy of comment? Of course this climber was capable of climbing this and many other routes of equal difficulty without prior knowledge or practice, he is well known as an amazingly talented guy.

Standards are still being pushed at the top end of climbing. Harder and bold-er routes are being created by the elite within the sport, as has always been the case, ever since the days of Herford and Sansom pushing the boundaries when they climbed *Central Buttress* on Scafell in 1914. What I find puzzling and a little disappointing is what's happening below these lofty heights. We've recognised that more people than ever will identify as climbers. They have climbing walls and training facilities that were unimaginable 30 or 40 years ago along with the knowledge and wherewithal to get the most out of them. As a result, this vast army of climbers are stronger than ever before. But here's the mystery – the average Trad climber is still operating at more or less the same level as back in those days of rudimentary ideas around training, non-sticky boots and limited protection. Why aren't they using that new-found strength to keep going on the energy-sapping stamina sections or power through the cruxes of harder routes? This comes back to the earlier point that strength isn't everything. Technique is required along with an ability to read the moves, but perhaps more important is the ability to push it out above a piece of gear, to trust in yourself and give it a go. What could possibly go wrong?

Trad Climbing Just Needs a Bit of PR

One reason for the apparent reduction in Trad climbing may be the kit – it's expensive, complex and heavy, compared to a rack of quickdraws or a bouldering mat – or maybe it's an image problem. "Trad climbers are boring old farts with beards" might be the perception of many younger climbers.

Perhaps Trad climbing needs to do some better marketing. Personally, what sets Trad climbing apart is the greater degree of personal responsibility for route finding and self-protection. From this comes more adventure and a greater sense of achievement. When I think back over the routes I've climbed, very few sport routes stick in my mind, whereas I have vivid memories of many great Trad routes. This is what we need to explain to more climbers of today. We are trying to capture this feeling when publishing the guidebooks to the Lakes. Photos in particular are so important when putting a guidebook together. They are the marketing material that will attract climbers to the area. The best photos manage to inspire people to seek out and do the route as well as providing some insight into what to expect. The image presented in photos along with crag and route descriptions have to sell the idea of making the effort of walking to the crag to climb a specific route. At the same time, they do have to be realistic and honest – despite the image that most guides project, the sun is not always shining on the crags! There is also something about projecting an image of who is involved in the sport. We include as many pictures of female climbers as possible as well as the young, old and families. Some of our climbing walls have successfully recognised the value of running courses to transition their customers from the relative safety of an indoor wall environment to the world of climbing on crags, teaching gear placement and belay set-ups. There is a role for the British Mountaineering Council (BMC) in pushing all disciplines of the sport they represent.

There are some truly brilliant young role models in the world of Trad climbing and I believe we should make more use of these talented people to promote this style of climbing. In the Lakes, Craig Matheson has taken over the mantle from his dad, Rob. He's just as talented and twice as strong. Craig is producing some amazing new routes of his own as well as repeating many of Dave Birkett's hard testpieces. Dave himself is still climbing well and is as strong as ever, working hard at passing on his skills to his younger cousin Will Birkett, Bill's son and thus continuing the historical bloodline that's been at the heart of Lake District climbing for many generations. Up in the north of the county, Adam Hocking, stable mate of James McHaffie, is setting high standards along with Al Wilson and others. There is also a small group of younger talent making their presence known. On a bigger stage, Leo Houlding, originally from Appleby and now resident in Staveley near Kendal, is the epitome of the modern-day adventurer and explorer with awe-inspiring expeditions, often captured in mind-blowing films to be enjoyed by a wide audience.

It's not just the home-grown talent; the Lakes has attracted many others to take up residence in the area. All-round climbing super-star and training guru Neil Gresham has made his home here and is pushing the limits on the higher crags with some very bold and very powerful new routes. These individuals along with the rest of our amazing young talent can help to reverse the apparent downward trend in Trad climbing.

This country has an amazing history of Trad climbing, it's one of the main reasons why visitors come climbing here from overseas. Plenty of other countries do it, but this is where it started. If climbing were ice cream, I would describe sport climbing as vanilla. Don't get me wrong, I love vanilla ice cream, but there are so many exciting, exotic flavours out there waiting to be sampled. Some look good but taste unremarkable. Some are a little too out-there for most people's taste. We will all make our personal choices but if you've only ever tasted one variety, you're missing out.

It's important to respect our heritage and maintaining those lines in the sand that say: "No bolts to protect routes on mountain crags," is essential and should be defended strongly. Thankfully, at present, most people recognise and understand where the line is to be drawn.

Climbing is a broad church with many disciplines, enjoyed by a wide range of enthusiasts with all manner of purposes and motivations. It's a fabulous way to spend time in the natural environment; it's a way to stay fit and healthy, to push yourself to your limits; to spend time with friends or to represent your country.

Life Lessons

Of course, you don't *have* to climb when you visit the stunning Yosemite Valley. Indeed, the vast majority of visitors don't. But the act of climbing holds some fascination for most of these people, otherwise they wouldn't stand in the Meadow, craning their necks upwards to gawp, open-mouthed at the players on the vertical stage of El Capitan. But when someone is adamant that, "I could *never* do that," I find it rather sad. It's sad that so many people are prepared to limit their own horizons with such finality. It is like sitting in a restaurant and declaring, "I couldn't eat *that*," without at least having a taste – I did try goat brain curry on one visit to Delhi!

There are many things that I'll probably not fit into my allocated time – learning to fly, show jumping, rowing – or more cerebral pursuits like speaking Mandarin Chinese, understanding Quantum Theory or learning about Fine Art. But after 40 years of testing my limits and trying things out, I now know that it isn't that I *can't* do these things. If I decided to put in the time, effort and money, and if I wanted to prioritise them, I believe that I could – and, if I ever really want to, I expect I'll give myself a chance at least to try them out. Given the opportunity, why wouldn't you?

To call it a 'philosophy' would be a bit pretentious, but the approach expressed in the title of this book has served me well over the years – in work, in my climbing and in all the other crazy activities that I've been drawn into. But it goes way beyond that.

A few years ago, after a gap of around 45 years, I finally decided to get in touch with my father, David. At the time, aged 80, he was living in Buxton with his wife Kathleen. I'd written to him and got a response, which was friendly but not exactly gushing. I decided that if we were to build any kind of relationship, it would be up to me to make the first moves. I could see it from his point of view, it had been a very long time, he now had two grown up daughters – my half-sisters. After such a long period, it could naturally be awkward. The situation facing me

Nick enjoying steep, pocketed limestone on *Kleiner Wahnsinn*, Donautal, Germany

Flora at Humphrey Head, South Lakes

felt like standing at the foot of a crag below a tough route that I really wanted to climb but knowing that it had a big reputation with a potential for failure, and who knows, maybe even getting hurt if it didn't go well. "What could possibly go wrong?" I was working in Staffordshire one day, filming a work video. At the end of the shoot, I decided to launch myself at this new challenge. Taking the same approach as my attitude towards climbing, I realised this was no time for a fear of failure. I drove back via the Peak District and, with as large a dose of self-confidence that I could muster, located the house (identified the line of the route); thought about what I was going to say (surveyed the line of the route, looking for the holds, protection and potential rest points); took a deep breath (tightened my rock shoes and dipped my hands in my chalk bag) and did it. I walked up to the front door and knocked.

"Hello, is it David?"

"Yes."

"Hi, I'm Nick, your son."

"You'd better come in then."

I was through the crux moves, the rest of it should be plain sailing. Kathleen made tea and we had a very affable chat. The ice was broken. It would've been very easy to have never faced up to the challenge. But then if you aren't prepared to give it a go, you'll never succeed.

To maintain the climbing analogy for just a moment, let's imagine this was a multi-pitch route and that visit was the first pitch. The initial success on that first visit would normally lead on to other, similar pitches above, hopefully meeting the standard first encountered, if not getting better and better as we continued to the summit. After all, I'd made the effort to overcome the crux at the start. Despite a few highlights along the way – taking Karen and Flora to meet David, Kathleen and Sarah (one of my half-sisters) – the rest of this particular climb is something that still needs more work.

Let's make sure we embrace whatever challenges we have thrust in our way or those we set ourselves, enjoy the ride and encourage others to do likewise, after all – how hard can it be?

The bold *Merzuga*, Dragon Rock, Morocco

Epilogue

2020 promised to be quite a year. I had good early-season fitness having spent the winter months climbing at the wall and Leo's Fly Cave at least three times a week. In February I had my first trip to Morocco with Joe Gittins. We began by taking a group up Mount Toubkal – North Africa's highest peak at just over 4000m – with Joe's business, All Terrain Adventures. Then we moved south to the Anti-Atlas region for some rock climbing. This has to be one of the most fantastic climbing holiday destinations. The crags are endless, everywhere you look, and the rock is made for climbing – a reddish quartzite with perfect edges and cracks up slabs and walls of every angle. And it's all Trad. Add to that the welcoming locals with their fabulous cuisine and all at a bargain price. Steve Scott and Pete Sterling joined us for the climbing, too, which made a great trip even better.

After the heat of North Africa, the next stop was going to be the snowy expanse of the high Swiss Alps – two weeks ski-touring with Flora who'd been working in Switzerland since the previous summer.

And then it hit! The new coronavirus started its unrelenting assault on the world which started to shut down. I was due to fly to Geneva on the Saturday but instead Flora came home as France, Switzerland and other European countries went into lockdown. We were disappointed and frustrated. No one yet grasped the significance of what was unfolding. Then a few weeks later Britain followed suit. Now what?

We made the most of it by going for bike rides around narrow Lake District roads usually busy with tourist traffic but now eerily quiet. With all the climbing walls closed, the only training available to me was to be found on the bridge at Sedgwick, south of Kendal, for some finger traversing. As a result, when we were finally allowed back out onto the crags, I found I had the strongest fingers I'd had for years. The weather, for once, was generous and I was in for a pretty successful summer.

I had no work – all training and consultancy had dried up – and, like many other self-employed workers, I fell through the cracks of the Chancellor's otherwise generous grants and furlough scheme. Luckily, I was able to work with Joe, once that was permitted, taking groups gill scrambling, abseiling and caving. It still left me with time on my hands so I finally got round to writing down all these stories from the past 40 years.

Towards the end of the year, as the result of a chance conversation related to this book, I ended up back in my old job as an Environmental Health Officer. My

Emma Twyford on the beautiful *Hiddenite*, Iron Crag one of the best single pitch E2s in the Lakes

time was spent exclusively following up on all the positive Covid-19 cases in the South Lakes in an attempt to trace the source of infection and hence the patterns of local outbreaks. It gave me a fascinating insight into the pandemic from the inside and a very rich picture of how it was affecting its victims. 2020 had turned out to be 'quite a year' after all – just not in the way we'd all imagined.

As I write this, in early spring 2021, we are still in lockdown in the UK, but one day this will all be over. No doubt we'll look back on this period with a wide range of emotions: relief that it's all over, sadness at the loss of loved ones, no doubt some frustration at the restrictions imposed and the disruption although I'm sure this will fade from the memory as things get back to normal. We will return to normality and, thank goodness, the mountains, crags and rivers will still be here, in the Lake District and in the UK. Whatever the future of international travel turns out to be, at some point we'll be off on plenty of quests to foreign parts. In the meantime, let's look forward to many more adventures and cope with the challenges of the moment. After all, how hard can it be?

Glossary of Climbing Terms

Abseil	Sliding down a rope, usually by means of an abseil device, which is often the same as a belay device. Comes from the German – literally 'down rope'
Aid climbing	To climb up a route by pulling on gear rather than just using your own hand and footholds. This is a style of climbing of its own with many proponents, particularly on Big Walls. It can be very hard and very scary. See 'Free climbing' for the opposite
Arete	A rock edge. These make for great climbing as there are often holds on the walls on both sides of the edge, or on the edge itself. Climbing on an arete can, however, be quite precarious with added exposure.
Belay	(noun) A point on a route where a climber attaches themselves to the rock. (verb) Holding another climber's rope to protect them in the event of a fall.
Belay device	A device to help control the rope while belaying. There are a huge range of devices available that all do the same thing –add friction to the rope so that it can be paid out as needed but also hold a fall.
Beta	Prior knowledge about a route – derived from the Betamax video
Big Wall climbing	Climbing multi-pitch routes generally requiring more than a day to complete and often involving aid.
Bolt	Permanent steel anchors drilled into the rock providing a very secure attachment point. These are either expansion bolts or are held in place with resin. They are regarded as the most reliable protection. They can be placed where no other natural protection is available. In the UK their use is restricted to certain locations and rock types.

Bouldering	A type of climbing without ropes that consists of a limited number of moves, usually on small rocks or at the bottom of larger outcrops. This can be the hardest, most powerful and technical climbing. Protection is often provided by thick foam mats placed on the ground beneath the boulder problem.
Bowline	A type of knot often used for attaching a rope to a harness
Camming device	A type of mechanical protection that expands to the size of the crack or pocket that it is placed into. There are many types. The original cams were sold under the brand name 'Friends' – a term still used, whatever the make.
Chalk	Magnesium carbonate powder used by climbers to keep hands dry and sweat-free, kept in a chalk bag tied around the waist
Chockstone	A rock, firmly wedged in a crack, that will allow a sling to be threaded round it for protection
Crag	An outcrop of rock
Cragging	A term often used for climbing on smaller outcrops
Crimp	A finger-edge hold
Crux	The hardest section of a climb or the hardest pitch on a longer route
Dynamic rope	Rope used for climbing that has a natural stretch which will absorb much of the force in the event of a fall
Dyno	A dynamic move, a jump for the next hold
EBs	One of the earliest rock-climbing boots. They looked a bit like baseball boots with a canvas upper and smooth rubber sole

Figure 8	A metal device in the shape of a figure 8 with a large and a small hole used predominantly for abseiling and rarely for belaying
Figure 8 knot	A common knot used for attaching a rope to a harness or another fixing point
Fingery (or Thin)	Climbing that has small holds that only allow the use of the finger ends
First ascent	The first time that a specific route is climbed. The person who does this will give the route a name and suggest a grade
Flash	Climb a route on the first attempt without falling
Free climbing	Climbing with only the use of hand and footholds and without getting any mechanical advantage from gear. The term Free climbing is often mistakenly thought to mean climbing without ropes - this is Soloing. In the US the term Free Solo is often used because they would also use the term Aid Solo - climbing an Aid route on your own.
Gear	The collective term for all climbing equipment
Grigri	A type of belay device produced by Petzl – the original active assisted braking device
Groove	The opposite of an arete – a long indentation between two rock faces
Gully	A deep vertical recess in a cliff. Often used as a route for descent in summer or for climbing in winter when frozen
Head point	Climbing a Trad route after practising the moves

Jamming	Wedging part or all of the hand (or foot) in a crack. A finger jam is one only wide enough to allow fingers to be inserted – a hand jam or fist jam is wider. Once the part of the hand is inserted, it is held in place by twisting the fingers or expanding the hand. A toe or foot jam is achieved by inserting the toe/foot and twisting. It can be as painful as it sounds but can also be very secure
Jug	A large handhold, from the idea of a jug handle (easy to hold on to)
Jumar	An item of equipment that clamps onto a rope – it will slide up but not down allowing a rope to be climbed. Used in aid climbing
Karabiner/Krab	A metal clip with a spring-loaded gate used as a link between gear and rope. Some have a locking gate for added security
Layback	Move that involves pulling horizontally with the hands while usually pushing away with the feet. To layback up a vertical crack, you would pull on the closer side of the crack while your feet push out on the opposite side
Lead	Go up a route first, placing the equipment while the rope trails below, clipped through the gear, belayed by a second
Nut (or Chock, Wire)	A simple form of protection. A metal wedge threaded with rope or wire placed into a crack and clipped to the rope with a karabiner. The name comes from the very earliest pioneers who used simple engineering nuts threaded on cord.
Off-width	Crack too wide for a hand or fist but too narrow to get the body into
On-sight	(verb) To climb a route with little or no prior knowledge and no practice. A climber only ever has one chance at an on-sight ascent of a route

Overhang (or Roof)	Horizontal section of rock that sticks out from the rock below
Pinch grip	Hold with the fingers on one side and the thumb on the other side
Pitch	Single rope length of a climb. Some routes are single-pitch (one rope length), others are multi-pitch (several rope lengths with a 'belay' between each pitch)
Piton/Peg	Metal spike hammered into a crack for protection. There are many sizes and designs to fit a wide range of placements. Pegs are not used so much these days as other, more easily placed and removed equipment is available. Pegs are most often left in place after their use
Pocket	Natural indentation in the rock of varying sizes, from one finger size ('mono') upwards
Prusik	Loop of thin cord that can be looped around a rope to enable it to be climbed. It will slide up the rope but not slide down under load
Pumpy	Very tiring on the arms. Arms get 'pumped' – the muscles run out of energy and fill with lactic acid giving a burning sensation which often precedes falling off
Quickdraw	Two snap-gate karabiners linked by a short sling used to attach the rope to a piece of gear. In Sport climbing where all the protection is provided by bolts, the climber will take just a rack of quickdraws with them. The name comes from a gunslinger quickly pulling out his revolver
Rack	A collection of gear taken on a climb by a leader. Usually the gear is 'racked' on the gear loops of a leader's harness

Red point	Ascent of a sport route from bottom to top after practising or 'working' it. The name comes from Germany in the 70s when a red dot (rot punkt) would be painted on the rock at the bottom of a route once it had been climbed cleanly without any falls or rests
Rock-over	Move that involves a high step-up with the foot, at or above waist height, then pulling the body up to get the centre of gravity over the high foot
Runners	Short for 'running belays' – the cams, nuts or other protection placed on a climb to protect the leader
Runout	(noun) Long section of climb without any protection (adjective) Without protection
Scree	Loose stones covering the hillside beneath a crag
Second	(noun) Second person on the rope who comes up once the leader is at a belay and secure. They belay the leader while climbing (verb) To follow the leader up a climb
Sequence	A series of moves on a climb. If a climb is described as 'sequency' it means there's a specific way of climbing it
Slab	Rock at an angle significantly less than vertical
Sling	Loop of tape or rope used for placing over a spike or around chockstones for protection.
Sloper	Flat, sloping 'hold' without any positive edges to grip, relying purely on friction to enable the hand or fingers to get some purchase
Smear	(noun) Foot equivalent of a sloper (verb) Using your foot on a completely blank wall
Soloing	Climbing on your own without the protection of ropes

Sport climbing	Climbing on routes that are protected by pre-existing bolts – safer than Trad climbing with the emphasis on physical and technical difficulty
SRT	(Single Rope Technique) Method of caving involving abseiling down ropes then climbing back up them using mechanical devices avoiding the use of wire, caving ladders
Static rope	Rope that does not stretch, regularly used in caving for abseiling and climbing back up by SRT and rarely used by climbers except as a separate abseil rope. See Dynamic rope
Tat	Old bits of rope and tape left on a route, often at belays, abseil points or attached to pegs
Thrutch	To climb awkwardly, often involving wide cracks or chimneys
Top rope	To climb with a rope above you
Topo	(Topographical guide) Illustrations or photographs of a crag with routes marked on, sometimes showing specific features
Trad climbing	(Traditional climbing) Climbing where the leader places their own protection as they progress up the route, removed by the second as they follow, requiring skill to find and place adequate protection.
Turbo trainer	A static device on which a bicycle can be mounted so that the cyclist can pedal but stay in the same place and the effort required to turn the pedals can be altered. Used for training indoors
Undercut	An upside-down hand hold used by pulling upwards
Wall	An expanse of rock, more or less vertical. A slabby wall is steeper than a slab but less than vertical, a steep wall is vertical, an overhanging wall is steeper than vertical

An Explanation of Climbing Grades

On the one hand these are absolutely essential to ensure the appropriate route is selected for the sake of challenge, enjoyment and safety – yet on the other hand they are totally baffling to anyone not in the know. Grades and grading generate more debate and disagreement than anything else in the sport. Different grading systems are used in different countries and for different styles of climbing.

Trad Grades

In the UK we use a two-part system of grading (giving twice as much scope for argument). First is the adjectival grade. This is the first part of the grade and attempts to give an overall assessment of how hard the route is and takes into account how much effort is required, how long the hard section goes on for and – most significant – what the potential dangers are. For really easy routes this is all you get. These adjectives have evolved and expanded over many years and go as follows: Easy (barely climbing), Moderate (M) (still not really rock climbing) and Difficult (D) (very easy climbing!) Next comes Severe (S), but before that we like to add a few sub-divisions: Hard Diff (HD), Very Difficult (VD) and Hard Very Difficult (HVD). Keep up! Back to Severe, we sometimes get a Mild Severe (MS) and Hard Severe (HS) either side of the original but the next significant jump is Very Severe (VS). Whilst Mild VS is a relatively little-used grade, Hard VS is the next big jump. Beyond that we get into Extremely Severe and these then become the open-ended system: E1, E2, E3 … all the way up to somewhere around E10 – for now.

Hopefully that was all clear and simple because we're only half-way there. Next, we add on the technical grade. These are used to indicate the hardest single move on any route or pitch. They tend to start around 4a and progress as follows: 4a, 4b, 4c, 5a, 5b, 5c, 6a … get the picture? This system is also, supposedly, open-ended but in truth probably runs out at around 7a or 7b but in reality, true 7a is pretty rare.

When the two are combined it actually provides a really good impression of what to expect on a route. But that's before you add in all the other subjective factors like preference and specific competencies. One climber might grade a technically desperate, holdless and runnerless slab climb E4 6a only for some other *Smart Alec* who likes that kind of thing to suggest it only deserves HVS 5b.

You might think - Why not just have a hierarchy of numbers or letters, Roman numerals or even the Greek alphabet? The Europeans, Americans and Australians have systems built like this, but they all lack that extra dimension created by the British system.

Sport Grades

Don't worry, these are much easier to understand. They don't have to concern themselves with how terrified someone might be as they are used on routes with fixed protection that are perfectly safe. They focus purely on how hard the route is – a combination of strength, endurance and technique. Here in the UK we have adopted the French system so they're often preceded by F. Strictly speaking they start at 1 but it's rare to see anything below 3. They progress as so: 3, 4, 4+, 5, 5+, (sometimes you also get 5a, 5b, 5c) 6a, 6a+, 6b, 6b+, 6c, 6c+ …. until somewhere in the upper stratosphere around 9c. Once again this is an open-ended system that will run and run.

And now to try and explain the rules of cricket to some American friends …

Other Voices

John Wilson – School days and Aberdeen sea cliffs extravaganza
Pete Robinson – Tour du Mont Blanc
Phil Baines – University, Footless Crow and Creation
John Vlasto – Sandhurst
Bernie Catterall – Army Youth Team
James McHaffie – Climbing trips to Scotland and Pembroke
Stuart Wood – Climbing at Tre Cime
Steve Scott – Climbing in the Lakes and ever since
Alan Steele – High performance climbing and caving shopkeeper
David Birkett – Climbing on Scafell
Scott Burns – Caving trip
Tim Whiteley – Kayaking
Brian Davison – Classic Rock Challenge
Will Birkett – Classic Rock Challenge
Dominique Perrissin-Fabert – Health & Safety at work
Neil Gresham – The Training Paradox

Nick's 3-Star Routes

This list is copied directly from my trusty old notebooks, in which I kept a record of all the extreme grade routes that I led. This record runs from 1981 to 2001 when, sadly, I stopped writing them down. I make no apologies for the repetition of superlatives – these comments were written for each individual route at the time. Grades may have been subsequently changed and some of the routes may have changed in character. At the time, I felt they deserved my own 3-star rating.

Route	Grade	Cliff	Partner	Comments
Wombat	E2 5c	Malham	Mike Hoff	Excellent. Good all the way from a technical start to an airy finish (since soloed)
Vector	E2 5c	Tremadog	Neil Craig	Excellent route, harder than expected
Darius	E1 5b	High Tor	Mark Jackson	Really excellent route, one of the best! Long and sustained pitch – probably E2 5c
Silly Arete	E3 5c	Tremadog	Leo Hermacinski	A brilliant route ranking with the very best. Very delicate climbing with negligible protection in a brilliant position
Pleasure Dome	E3 6a	Pembroke	Neil Foster	Very probably the best route I have done so far. Perfect position, atmosphere, rock and climbing
Left Wall	E3 5c	Cromlech	Rick Cooper	Absolute classic. Very good route – fairly easy, marvellous position (since soloed)

Route	Grade	Crag	First Ascent	Description
Stiff Little Fingers	E3 5c	Hodge Close	Phil Baines	Excellent route on brilliant jams. Hard top section (now fallen down!)
Capital Punishment	E4 6a	Suicide Wall	John Whittock	Fantastic route. Good climbing, negligible protection, fairly easy
Great Wall	E3 5c	Craig y Forwyn	Leo Hermacinski	An excellent route on very good rock. Technical and very strenuous
Nagasaki Grooves	E4 6b	Great End	Phil Baines	This route is the technically hardest route I have ever done. It is also probably the best.
Void	E3 6a	Tremadog	Graham Harrison	A marvellous route, one of the best. More sustained than Cream. Well worth waiting for.
Right Wall	E5 6a	Cromlech	Iwan Jones	A stunning route. Finally done after much waiting. It is as good as it looks, not too hard but sustained and well-spaced gear
Sultans of Swing	E4 6a	Tremadog	Tom Thomas	An excellent route. Marvellous 2nd pitch across head-wall, even having done Cream and Void it is a very good route. Sustained and quite strenuous
Poetry Pink	E5 6a	Rainbow Slab	John Wilson	A tremendous slate route. Very technical above good bolts it still feels pushy as the 2 bolts are well-spaced
R n S Special	E5 6a	Raven, Langdale	Mark McGowan, John Wilson	A long-awaited route. Really good, thin, and delicate climbing. Necky!!

Route	Grade	Crag	First Ascent	Description
GTX	E3 5c	Raven, Threshthwaite	John Wilson	A fantastic route. Different climbing throughout. Good gear. Particularly good top.
Crimson Cruiser	E5 6a	Craig y Clipiau	John Wilson, Iwan Jones	A stunning route on a good crag. An excellent line up very good rock. Much easier than expected
First Night Nerves	E5 6b	Hodge Close	John Wilson	A fantastic route. Hard lower section followed by long, delicate slab with a big run-out. Excellent!
Deliverance	E5 6b	Gordale	Mick Lovatt	A magnificent route. Hard, thin and a bit scary. Both technical and strenuous
Obsession	7b+	Malham	John Burrell	Stunning. Brilliant climbing in a most fantastic position. Hard moves at start and right at the top
Herbie	7c+	Malham	Stuart Wood	A magnificent route with tremendous climbing up the wall and tufa. Technical and strenuous with brilliant moves
Dominatrix	7c	Kilnsey	John Burrell	Utterly brilliant. Tremendous climbing up outrageous rock in an amazing position. Wild finish.
Internal Combustion	E6 6b	Raven, Threshthwaite	Stuart Wood	One of the best pieces of rock in the Lake District. A stunning route. Easier than expected
Fear & Fascination	E5 6a	Dove	Mark Lardener	Fantastic route. Very good, sustained climbing. Not too hard but excellent holds and solid rock. A real classic

Route	Grade	Crag	First Ascensionist	Description
Hells Wall	E6 6c	Bowderstone	John Fletcher	Technically hard and sustained. A very good route all the way. Good finishing position
Barbarella	E5 6a	Pembroke	Cliff Fanshawe	Brilliant climbing up the thin crack. Couple of hard sections. Very enjoyable
Lord of the Flies	E6 6a	Cromlech	Alan Steele	An outstanding route. Very imposing line with scant protection. Excellent climbing on pockets and edges. Harder at top than expected. Brilliant!
Dream/Liberator	E4 6a	Bosigran	Alan Steele	Tremendous route, from wild approach to two excellent pitches. Crux not too bad but difficult before and after. Made more difficult by damp rock and mad seagull
Darkinbad the Brightdayler	E5 6a	Pentire Head	Alan Steele	An excellent route on a stunning crag. Fairly straightforward but sustained. Many lovely moves
Chasing the Dragon	E5 6b	Malham	Cliff Fanshawe	Two hard pitches with excellent, different climbing. Powerful first and delicate second
The Cad	E6 6a	Gogarth	Brian Davison	A brilliant route climbed without assistance of the bot. This gives an extreme exercise in willpower and commitment to say nothing of considerable technical ability and finger strength. Technically harder than expected
Positron	E5 6a	Gogarth	Brian Davison	Very enjoyable climbing on all pitches, particularly 3rd. Quite easy but great position

Route	Grade	Crag	Climber(s)	Description
Stage Fright	E6 6b	Hodge Close	Paul Clavey	An excellent route with hard. Thin moves in the groove then long beautiful top slab with long run-out
Skinhead Moonstomp	E6 6b	Gogarth	Dom Donnini	Probably the best route I have ever climbed. Both pitches give excellent moves on good rock in tremendous positions. The second pitch up the 'blind flake' is absolutely stunning!!! (4-stars)
Cave Route LH	E6 6c	Gordale	Dom Donnini	Immaculate climbing with one hard section. Really enjoyable, a marvellous route
Road Rage	E7 6c	Raven, Threshthwaite	Dom Donnini, Paul Clavey, Helen Davies	First ascent. Very good climbing in committed position. Reasonable but spaced gear. A worthwhile addition to an excellent crag.
Fast & Furious FFF	E5 6b	Dove	Martin Berzins	Great, easy climbing. Very steep but on huge holds. Better finish
Barbarossa	E6 6b	Gogarth	Liam Grant	A magnificent route. A very hard crux but then continuously good to the top
Widespread Ocean of Fear	E5 6a	Lundy	Alan Steele	Tremendous climbing on superb rock. Quite steady and reasonable gear
Wild Heart	E5 6a	Lundy	Andy Rowell	A magnificent route. Stunning climbing on perfect rock in great conditions
Culinan/Flying the Colours	E5 6a	Lundy	Andy Rowell	Superb, sensational climbing in a fantastic position. Good but very spaced gear

Route	Grade	Crag	Climber	Description
The Cow	E5 6a	Gogarth	Liam Grant	Stunning climbing in amazing positions. Not too hard just excellent
The Long Run	E5 6a	Gogarth	Liam Grant	Easier and better gear than The Cad but just as good climbing – wonderful
Woodhouse's Arete	E6 6b	Dow	Helen Davies	Second ascent of marvellous route. Great climbing in an excellent position
Heart of the Sun Direct	E6 6a	Gogarth	Brian Davison	Excellent climbing on a brilliant wall. Great positions and good moves
Supernatural	E5 6a	Napes	James McHaffie	Excellent, varied climbing. Technical, run-out and strenuous in parts. A great wall
Orange Robe Burning	E6 6b	Pembroke	Brian Davison	Excellent route on good rock. Lower section easier than expected but hard crux at top
Grey English Morning	E5 6a	Pembroke	Brian Davison	Absolutely fantastic. The elusive 4-stars are well deserved for this magnificent route with excellent moves on perfect rock in a stunning position. Add to that a glorious day during a great weekend made this a truly memorable experience. Brilliant (4-stars)

Thanks and Acknowledgements

Time for me to say a big thank you to a lot of people. Firstly, all the long-suffering climbing partners, belayers, fellow runners, cyclists, skiers and others with whom I have shared these many and varied adventures. Thanks for helping to create all the stories and memories with which I have filled these pages.

I am grateful to all those who have gone before me in producing their own, similar books from which I have drawn ideas and which created the notion for this endeavour – in particular Mark Radtke, whose fabulous book 'A Canvas of Rock' was the real inspiration for me to finally get on with writing this.

I am indebted to all who have helped along the way with reading early drafts, giving me feedback and making suggestions. And to those who went a step further and yielded to my requests to write their own contributions that I hope add some variety and colour to the text, along with Leo for writing the foreword.

Initially Matthew Connolly and then Lois Sparling have done a great job of improving the structure of the book and providing essential advice on the content – some of which I even took heed of! Al Davis did a great job of proof reading. Pete Sterling has taken the words and photos and with them created this beautifully presented book, printed to the highest standard by Simon Hodson at Latitude Press.

Finally, a longer term thanks to my family - in particular Karen, who has encouraged and enabled me to keep pursuing the activities that make me who I am.